GCSE PE

For AQA

2nd Edition
Julie Walmsley

OXFORD
UNIVERSITY PRESS

OXFORD
UNIVERSITY PRESS

Great Clarendon Street, Oxford OX2 6DP

Oxford University Press is a department of the University of Oxford.
It furthers the University's objective of excellence in research,
scholarship,and education by publishing worldwide in

Oxford   New York

Auckland   Cape Town   Dar es Salaam   Hong Kong   Karachi
Kuala Lumpur   Madrid   Melbourne   Mexico City   Nairobi
New Delhi   Shanghai   Taipei   Toronto

With offices in

Argentina   Austria   Brazil   Chile   Czech Republic   France   Greece
Guatemala   Hungary   Italy   Japan   Poland   Portugal   Singapore
South Korea   Switzerland   Thailand   Turkey   Ukraine   Vietnam

Oxford is a registered trade mark of Oxford University Press
in the UK and in certain other countries

© Julie Walmsley 2009

The moral rights of the authors have been asserted

Database right Oxford University Press (maker)

First published 2009

British Library Cataloguing in Publication Data

Data available

ISBN 978-1-85008-401-3

FD4013

10 9 8 7 6 5 4 3 2

Printed in Spain by Cayfosa-Impresia Ibérica

Paper used in the production of this book is a natural, recyclable product
made from wood grown in sustainable forests. The manufacturing process
conforms to the environmental regulations of the country of origin.

Editor: Rosie Parrish
Text design: Design by Form (www.form.uk.com)
Layout: Planman
Picture researcher: Thelma Gilbert
Illustrations: Planman
Cover design: Design by Form (www.form.uk.com)

Acknowledgements

p.9 © PA/Empics; p.15 (top) © Brian Keavency/WMA; p.15 (middle) © PA/Empics; p.15 (bottom) © PA/Empics; p.16 (top, bottom) © PA/Empics; p.18 © Action Plus; p.20 (top left, top right) © PA/Empics; p.20 (bottom left) © Action Plus; p.20 (bottom right) © PA/Empics; p.21 © Action Plus; p.22 © PA/Empics; p.23 © Action Plus; p.24 (left, middle, right) © PA/Empics; p.25 © PA/Empics; p.26 © PA/Empics; p.27 (left) © PA/Empics; p.27 (right) © Neil Cannon/Alamy; p.29 © PA/Empics; p.33 (top, bottom) © PA/Empics; p.34 © PA/Empics; p.35 © PA/Empics; p.36 (left) © PA/Empics; p.36 (middle) © Realimage/Alamy; p.36 (right) © Colin Hutchings/Alamy; p.37 (left) © Jeff Greenberg/Alamy; p.37 (right) © Paul Mattock/Alamy; p.39 © Action Plus; p.41 © PA/Empics; p.42 (top left, top middle, top right, bottom) © PA/Empics; p.43 © PA/Empics; p.45 (top, bottom) © PA/Empics; p.46 © PA/Empics; p.49 (top) © Action Plus; p.49 (bottom) © PA/Empics; p.50 © iStockphoto.com/damaianty; p.51 © iStockphoto.com/ChristianAnthony; p.52 © Action Plus; p.54 © PA/Empics; p.55 (top, bottom) © PA/Empics; p.60 © Action Plus; p.61 (top) © PA/Empics; p.61 (bottom) © iStockphoto.com/ROMAOSLO; p.62 © Gabe Palmer/Alamy; p.64 © Action Plus; p.65 © Action Plus; p.67 © Action Plus; p.69 © PA/Empics; p.70 © Action Plus; p.71 © Action Plus; p.72 © PA/Empics; p.74 (left, middle) © PA/Empics; p.74 (right) © iStockphoto.com/WoodenDinosaur; p.75 © PA/Empics; p.76 (top, bottom left, bottom right) © PA/Empics; p.77 (top left, top right, bottom left) © PA/Empics; p.77 (bottom right) © Action Plus; p.78 (top) © Action Plus; p.78 (bottom) © PA/Empics; p.79 (top) © PA/Empics; p.79 (bottom) © Action Plus; p.81 (top left, top right, middle right) © PA/Empics; p.81 (middle left, bottom) © Action Plus; p.83 (top left) © iStockphoto.com/Bliz; p.83 (top right, bottom right) © Action Plus; p.83 (bottom left) © Rex Features; p.84 © iStockphoto.com/Sean Locke; p.85 © Corbis; p.86 (left, right) © Action Plus; p.91 © PA/Empics; p.95 © PA/Empics; p.96 (top) © PA/Empics; p.96 (bottom) © Action Plus; p.98 © Action Plus; p.111 © iStockphoto.com/Lighthousebay; p.113 (top left, bottom) © PA/Empics; p.113 (top middle) © Action Plus; p.113 (top right) © Rex Features; p.115 © iStockphoto.com/dlewis33; p.118 © iStockphoto.com/technotr; p.119 © Action Plus p.122 © Danwar Productions/Alamy; p.123 © PA/Empics; p.126 © PA/Empics; p.127 © PA/Empics; p.128 © PA/Empics; p.130 © PA/Empics; p.132 © PA/Empics; p.137 © PA/Empics; p.140 (top) © iStockphoto.com detchimo; p.140 (bottom) Martyn F Chillmaid/Science Photo Library; p.141 (top, bottom) © PA/Empics; p.142 © Action Plus; p.145 © Action Plus; p.146 © Sally & Richard Greenhill/Alamy; p.147 © Eitan Simamor Alamy; p.148 (top) © Action Plus; p.148 (bottom) © PA/Empics; p.149 Logo courtesy of the National Healthy Schools Programme; p.150 © PA Empics; p.152 © Steven May/Alamy; p.153 (top) © PA/Empics; p.153 (bottom) © Action Plus; p.156 © Roger Scruton; p.157 Logo used with permission of the Youth Sport Trust www.youthsporttrust.org; p.158 (top) Courtesy of Youth Sport Trust; p.158 (bottom) Logo used with permission of the Amateur Swimming Association; p.159 © Ted Foxx/Alamy; Pg 160 Diagram reproduced with kind the permission of Youth Sport Trust. Diagram accurate at time of going to print; p.161 Courtesy of Youth Sport Trust; p.162 Courtesy of Youth Sport Trust; p.165 © PA/Empics; p.168 © PA/Empics; p.169 (top) © Adrian Sherratt/Alamy; p.169 (bottom left) © Action Plus; p.169 (bottom right) © PA/Empics; p.171 © PA/Empics; p.172 (top) © PA/Empics; p.172 (bottom) © Sally & Richard Greenhill/Alamy; p.173 © Stock Connection Blue/Alamy; p.174 © PA/Empics; p.179 © PA/Empics; p.180 © iStockphoto.com/mrloz; p.181 © PA/Empics; p.182 (left) © Linda Gore/British Gymnastics; p.182 (middle, right) © PA/Empics; p.183 © iStockphoto.com/tacojim; p.185 (left, right) © PA/Empics; p.186 © PA/Empics; p.187 © PA/Empics; p.188 © PA/Empics; p.190 © Action Plus; p.194 Courtesy of Blackpool FC; p.195 © PA/Empics; p.196 Courtesy of Hawkeye Innovations; p.197 (top) © IML Image Group/Alamy; p.197 (bottom) © PA/Empics; p.198 © PA/Empics; p.200 Courtesy of Kellogg; p.202 (top, bottom) © PA/Empics; p.203 © PA/Empics; p.204 © PA/Empics; p.206 © Advertising Archives; p.210 © PA/Empics; p.214 © PA/Empics; p.215 © PA/Empics; p.216 © PA/Empics; p.217 (top) © Rex Features; p.217 (bottom) © PA/Empics; p.218 © PA/Empics; p.219 © PA/Empics; p.220 © PA/Empics; p.221 © Advertising Archives; p.223 © Action Plus; p.224 © PA/Empics; p.225 (top left, top right, bottom left, bottom right) © PA/Empics; p.228 © PA/Empics; p.230 © PA/Empics; p.232 © Pictor International; p.234 © PA/Empics; p.236 © PA/Empics; p.237 © PA/Empics; p.238 © PA/Empics; p.239 © PA/Empics; p.240 © PA/Empics; p.244 (left, right) © Action Plus; p.245 (left) © PA/Empics; p.245 (right) © Action Plus; p.246 © PA/Empics; p.248 © PA/Empics; p.249 (top, bottom left, bottom right) © PA/Empics; p.249 (middle) © Action Plus; p.250 (left, right) © PA/Empics; p.251 (top) © Action Plus; p.251 (bottom) © iStockphoto.com/HKPNC; p.253 © Anton Want/Getty Images; p.254 © J. Clarke/Getty Images; p.255 (top, bottom) © Action Plus; p.258 © PA/Empics; p.263 (left) © Action Plus; p.263 (right) © PA/Empics; p.268 © PA/Empics; p.269 © Acton Plus; p.270 © Action Plus; p.271 (left, right) © PA/Empics; p.272 (left, right) © PA/Empics; p.273 (top) © Action Plus; p.273 (bottom) © PA/Empics; p.274 (top, bottom) © PA/Empics; p.283 © PA/Empics; p.284 (left, right) © Action Plus; p.287 © Action Plus; p.289 © Action Plus; p.292 (top, bottom) © PA/Empics; p.293 © PA/Empics

Contents

Introduction

The content of this book covers the theory of the GCSE PE for AQA specification for the Short Course, Full Course and Double Award. This includes:

Units 1 and 3:   **3.1 Knowledge and understanding for the active participant**
(Short Course, Full Course and Double Award)

Units 2, 4 and 6:   **3.3 The active participant**
Key process C: Evaluating and improving
(Short Course, Full Course and Double Award)

Unit 5:   **3.4 Knowledge and understanding for the involved participant**
(Double Award)

Candidates following the Short Course will be asked multiple-choice questions, short answer questions and a scenario-based question on Unit 1. This exam will take 45 minutes and is worth 40 per cent of their total mark. They will also undertake a controlled assessment for Unit 2, worth 60 per cent of their total mark.

Candidates following the Full Course will be asked multiple-choice questions, short answer questions and a scenario-based question on Unit 3. This exam will take 1 hour 30 minutes and is worth 40 per cent of their total mark. They will also undertake a controlled assessment for Unit 4, worth 60 per cent of their total mark.

Candidates following the Double Award will be asked multiple-choice questions, short answer questions and a scenario-based question on Unit 3. This exam will take 1 hour 30 minutes and is worth 20 per cent of their total mark. They will also be asked short-answer questions and a scenario-based question on Unit 5. This exam will take 1 hour 30 minutes and is worth 20 per cent of their total mark. They will also undertake controlled assessments for Unit 4 (worth 30 per cent) and Unit 6 (worth 30 per cent).

The book layout

This book is set out so that it matches the AQA specification for GCSE PE. Topics with a large amount of information are split into separately named sections, a, b, c, and so on. If you work your way carefully through this book you will cover everything that the awarding body requires of you. To help you further, the material is presented in small, easy-to-digest chunks that are broken down using frequent sub-headings.

To help you know which section is relevant to you, the content for the Short Course, Full Course and Double Award are different colours. The Short Course is blue and purple. The Full Course is orange and red. The Double Award is green and turquoise.

- If you are studying the Double Award you will need to learn the Short Course, Full Course and Double Award material.
- If you are studying the Full Course you will need to learn the Short Course and Full Course material.
- If you are studying the Short Course you will only need to learn the Short Course material.

There are many photographs, illustrations and diagrams used to give you a visual way of remembering the work. Each photograph has a caption bringing your attention to the main point so that the link with the information is unmistakable. There are also numerous learning features built into this book.

Topics

At the beginning of each section, you will find a list of all the topics you will learn about in that section. Each topic is numbered, which is especially useful when you are revising, as it will be quicker to find relevant information and to check you know all of the points you are supposed to.

What you will learn about in this topic:

1 — Range of activities
2 — The roles of the active participant
3 — Individual differences
4 — The demands of performance

Tasks

Each section involves completing a series of numbered tasks. Completing tasks involves referring to the work just read or discussed in class. Tasks need to be recorded in your workbook or file.

Task 1

1 – Give three reasons why a warm-up helps a performer.

2 – List three types of exercise that would be included in a warm-up.

3 – Draw a spider diagram of the main points and reasons for a warm-down.

By keeping your workbook up-to-date with completed tasks, the work recorded will build up into your personal revision document. It is important that when you are working, information you write down can be read easily when you refer back to it. Take time to make your words legible.

Active challenges

Active challenges are thought-provoking tasks, which often involve working with a partner. Completing these tasks will open your mind to the section being worked on and give you the chance to verbally engage with the topic.

Active challenge

Think of three reasons why it is important to take part in a wide range of activities. Share your ideas with four other students to expand your list.

Spider diagrams

Spider diagrams are quick and easy to understand. They are an excellent way of recording and remembering the main points of a topic.

Muscular strength (Hand grip dynamometer test)

Speed (30m sprint test)

Power/explosive strength (vertical jump test and standing long jump test)

Reaction-time (ruler drop test)

Testing fitness components that serve the body

Cardiovascular endurance (multi-stage fitness test)

Coordination (alternate hand wall throw)

Muscular endurance (abdominal curl-up test)

Balance (stork stand test)

Agility (Illinois agility test)

Flexibility (sit and reach test)

Key terms

Wherever there are words in **bold** in the book they will be found in the key terms boxes. There boxes indicate important words for you to remember together with their definitions.

Key terms

Leisure – free time to do what a person chooses

Recreation – time to relax and do something active

Summary

At the end of each section there is a summary that rounds up the essential information that you need to remember from the topics covered. It acts as a short collection of the ideas that are the most important in the section. When revising, the summaries can be used as a starting point to remind you of the main ideas. You can then add to them with more detailed information from memory or by re-reading the text.

Summary

Changes in lifestyle over recent years have brought about a rise in leisure pursuits. People now have more control over their leisure time than ever before. Many people set aside time in their day or week for exercise. To help meet this increased demand for sports facilities, both the public and private sector have increased the amount of amenities available. Choosing physical recreation to fill available leisure time can provide a person with an active pursuit for the rest of their life.

Glossary

Many words that you come across in this book are explained in the glossary. When you come across a word and you are unsure of its meaning, look it up in the glossary.

Index

The index at the back of the book helps you to find a particular subject quickly. The index gives you a page reference and should take you to one or more places in the text where the subject occurs.

Exam questions

At the end of each section there are a series of examination-style questions for you to answer. They include multiple-choice, short answer and longer answer questions, matching the types of questions you will meet in the final exam. Depending on the course you are taking, the final examination may include questions on a scenario, which is released

Exam questions

Multiple-choice questions

1. Having access to good facilities can have an influence on participation. Which of the following relate to this?

☐ A Location, funding, access, expected use and demand

☐ C Whether the kit suits the person, suitability for a sport, how the sport meets personal needs, the different roles involved in the sport

☐ D Experience of the sport, suitability for a sport, how the sport meets personal needs, the different roles involved in the sport

(1 mark)

for you to study before the exam. You will be required to answer scenario-based questions in sentences. There are many questions requiring answers in sentences provided in this book, giving you ample experience to respond correctly to the scenario-based questions.

For all questions look carefully at the key words being used and what you are being asked such as how, where, which, when or what. Always think logically through the question before answering.

Multiple-choice questions

Multiple-choice questions are worth one mark per correct answer. There are two types of multiple-choice question:

Questions using maths

1. The correct target zone for an endurance athlete is 120 to 160 bpm, how old is the athlete?

☐ A 15

☐ B 20

☐ C 25

☐ D 40

(1 mark)

This question requires you to:

- Know how to work out the maximum heart rate (220 – age).
- Know what the target zone is (60 to 80 per cent of the maximum heart rate).
- Be able to work out and recognize the target zone in the question.

You can tackle this by trial and error:

Option A:
220 – 15 = 205 divided by 100 x 60 = 123
220 – 15 = 205 divided by 100 x 80 = 164

Option B:
220 – 20 = 200 divided by 100 x 60 = 120
220 – 20 = 200 divided by 100 x 80 = 160

Option B is the correct answer so you may want to stop there, but there should be enough time to double-check by working out the other options to make sure of your choice.

Questions requiring a choice made from knowledge and value judgement

2. Which of the following statements gives the **most** important reason for wearing the correct clothing when taking part in physical activity?

☐ A It gives you the opportunity to look good

☐ B It gives you a psychological advantage over the opposition

☐ C It reduces the chance of injury

☐ D It is in the rules of the practical activity

(1 mark)

This question requires you to:

- Know the reasons for wearing correct clothing.
- Recognize that the word 'most' is in bold because it is important.
- Make a value judgement on what the 'most' important reason is.

Option A is the weakest alternative.
Option B may give an edge competitively and is more important than A.
Option C is more important than A and B.
Option D is more important than A and B but it is not more important than C. So the correct answer is C.

Short answer questions

Short answer questions can be worth one to three marks each in this book. There is usually one mark given per correct idea or response. These questions often give a leading sentence, which require a single word, a list of words or a few sentences on a single idea.

3. (a) Which fitness component does a badminton player depend on when they reach for a shot?
   (b) When voluntary muscles are used for a long period, which fitness component is required?

(2 marks)

This question requires you to understand fitness components.

(a) The key word is 'reach'. This relates to joints and range of movement and so relates to flexibility.

(b) The key words are 'long period' and 'voluntary muscles'. The answer will include endurance, but is it muscular endurance and stamina or cardiovascular endurance and stamina? As the question relates to 'voluntary muscles' then it must be muscular endurance. If the question had been about the entire body then it would have been about the heart and lungs and so the answer would have been cardiovascular endurance.

Longer answer questions

The final exam includes a pre-released scenario based question, which is broken down into short answer questions and longer answer questions. The longer answer questions in this book will help you to prepare for the scenario based question.

Longer answer questions can be worth up to eight marks. The question can be set out with an opening sentence giving the subject and the key ideas to focus on. Instructions will be given to tell you what to do.

4. Jenny plays netball. She is in the school team and wants to improve her skills of the game and general fitness. She is learning about circuit training and thinks this can help her improve her play. She plans a six-station circuit of her own.

   Station 1 – chest passing against a wall
   Station 2 – dribbling a ball between cones
   Station 3 – aiming a tennis ball at a target on the wall
   Station 4 – shooting into a netball post
   Station 5 – serving a shuttle into a target area
   Station 6 – playing bounce passes against a wall

   Evaluate Jenny's circuit, taking into account the circuit's strengths, weaknesses and what could be done to improve it.

   (6 marks)

This question requires you to:

- Apply your knowledge of circuit training.
- Decide what the strengths of the circuit are. For example, as it involves three netball skills activities, three different skills are addressed.
- Decide what the weaknesses of the circuit are. For example, it does not involve any fitness stations or activities not related to netball.
- Decide how you would improve it. For example, by involving fitness stations relating to the skill of the game, such as sprinting between cones to help speed over short distances and change of direction, step ups to strengthen leg muscles and bench lifts to strengthen arms.

There are six marks available so, with three areas to comment on, work on earning two marks for each group of comments.

3.1.1 ~ The range of physical activities and the different roles that the active participant can choose from

3.1.1a Range of activities and the roles of the active participant

What you will learn about in this topic:

1 — Range of activities
2 — The roles of the active participant
3 — Individual differences
4 — The demands of performance

1 — Range of activities

Building up a broad knowledge and understanding of physical activity gives you a strong base on which to make informed choices about your own personal healthy, active lifestyle.

If you have a good knowledge and understanding of physical activity you will be able to:

- make informed choices about your involvement in physical activity
- realize you can make choices based on your suitability for a given activity
- make informed choices about which sports meet your needs
- understandand develop knowledge of the roles that the active participant can get involved in
- understand what an effective performance is in each different role.

For physical activity to be most beneficial to the performer it should be:

- appropriate to the sport or activity
- safe
- enjoyable.

Fulfilling all these criteria will benefit the well-being of a person physically, mentally and socially.

Whatever physical activity a person chooses, it should be suitable, safe and enjoyable.

Taking part in a range of activities provides a wide variety of benefits to the performer. Each type of activity offers a different challenge and requires a particular way in which to succeed. Being able to meet the demands of different activities has lifelong benefits, for example:

• widening your physical, mental and social experiences
• developing your personal and group skills
• training your body in different ways
• increasing your ability to succeed in different situations and environments
• allowing participants to experience different kinds of pressure
• teaching participants to apply different disciplines to succeed
• teaching participants to adapt to changing conditions
• broadening understanding of physical activity
• realizing the different ways success can be achieved.

There are a range of reasons for and benefits of choosing different types of activities:

Games activities exercise the skill of outwitting opponents in competitive situations by working as a team. Success is measured by overcoming opponents by directly affecting each other's performance.

Gymnastic activities require the accurate replication of actions, phrases and sequences as perfectly as possible.

Dance activities aim to explore and communicate ideas, concepts and emotions. Success is measured by how well a performer or choreographer expresses their ideas, feelings, concepts and emotions to communicate artistic or choreographic intentions to an audience.

Benefits of different activities

Fitness and health activities require the skill of exercising safely and effectively to improve health and well-being. Success is measured by the improvement of feelings of health, fitness and well-being.

Life saving, personal survival and outdoor adventurous activities require the skills of identifying and solving problems to overcome challenges of an adventurous nature in an effective and safe way.

Athletics activities require a person to perform at maximum levels in relation to speed, height, distance, strength or accuracy. Success is measured by a person achieving personal best scores or times and in competition with others' scores or times.

Active challenge

Think of three reasons why it is important to take part in a wide range of activities. Share your ideas with four other students to expand your list.

2 — The roles of the active participant

Active participation is often considered to be actively performing individually in a team or individually in an event. However, there are several other important roles that can also be regarded as active participation. Each role has its own challenging and demanding skills, which must be mastered in order to fulfil the role successfully. These roles can be undertaken on a local, national and international level, with structure in place for people to develop and progress in their chosen role.

Player or performer

There are structures in place for a player or performer to go from foundation, participation, regional and elite performances. The pathways a young performer learns and progresses through can include the following:

- School provides the learning of fundamental skills.
- School develops a young person's skills by providing sports clubs and teams.
- Clubs provide training which leads to competitive events at local and district level.
- Regional and local participation status can be gained through clubs.
- Selection for international representation can be gained through clubs.

Active challenge

With a partner, choose a sport and research on the Internet the pathways available for progress through the sport.

The sports participation pyramid shows the structure of progression in sport. It clearly identifies the different groups of performers involved at each level and the pathways for them to progress to a higher level, working from the bottom upwards.

For example:

- Foundation – students at school taking part in sport
- Participation – people taking part in sport in their free time, such as extra-curricular activities
- Performance – performer receiving local and regional coaching and training, and enters local competitions and leagues
- Elite – top-class, elite performers taking part in international competitions.

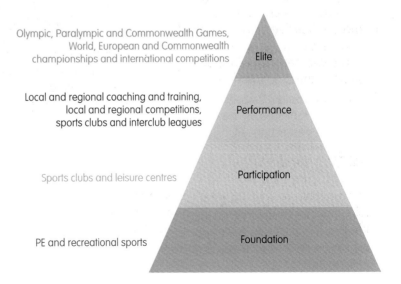

Olympic, Paralympic and Commonwealth Games, World, European and Commonwealth championships and international competitions — **Elite**

Local and regional coaching and training, local and regional competitions, sports clubs and interclub leagues — **Performance**

Sports clubs and leisure centres — **Participation**

PE and recreational sports — **Foundation**

To make sport development succeed so that the performance and elite stages are achieved, the Sports Council for Wales identified the following as areas to be addressed:

- Increasing club and **governing body** membership.
- Increasing numbers of volunteers.
- Increasing numbers and improving standards of coaches.
- Increasing numbers of trained officials (such as referees).
- Increasing numbers of administrators at all levels of sport.
- Better access to better facilities.
- Appropriate competition.
- Talent is identified and developed.
- Better access to support services (such as sports science).

Each sport has its own pathways planned. For example, the Football Association (FA) has created a player pathway using the participation pyramid. They want everyone, whatever their age, background, culture, ability or gender, to have a chance to find a way to play the game. They had data on 38,000 clubs in every area of England, helping people to find a club in which to play. The FA has identified what is needed at the foundation level, the elements needed for participation and performance all the way through to elite at the top of the pyramid pathway. They have put in place links for players to progress in this chosen sport. The FA has also created pathways for different roles within the game: if a person wants to be a volunteer, coach or referee, the Association shows them how.

Task 1

1 – Look on the Football Association website www.thefa.com and find 'Get into Football'.

2 – Find information about your nearest club.

3 – Identify football academies and centres of excellence for boys and girls.

Organizer

An organizer oversees an event from start to finish. All aspects of arranging the event are down to them. This can include booking the venue, arranging equipment, performers and spectators. An organizer may delegate tasks to a team of people that are responsible for specific parts of the event, but even then the organizer still has to continually check the progress and effectiveness of the team to make sure everything is being done properly and the event is running smoothly. An organizer brings together all of the main ingredients of an event at the right time, in the right place, in order to maximize promotion, participation and high quality performances.

Leader or coach

A sports leader or coach is an important influence on individuals or groups with regards a performer's goals or on behaviour in sport. They are specialists in an activity, responsible for preparing a performer in skill acquisition, correct technique, correct physical state or correct mental state.

sports coach UK is a charitable organization concerned with coaching. They have set up the UK Coaching Framework, a structure for planning and implementing a comprehensive system to support children, adults and players and athletes with skilled coaches. Players at all stages will be supported so that by 2016 the framework becomes a world-leading example.

The framework links:

- the governing bodies of each sport
- the four Home Country Sports Councils
- UK Sport
- Skills Active
- Youth Sport Trust.

The objectives are to help sports improve their coaching, see coaches play a key role in increasing sport participation and improving sporting performances, and help build a clear career structure for coaches. This will give a lasting legacy with coaching being recognized as a professional career.

"Implementation will create world class coaching expertise from grassroots to elite … the vital role coaches play in introducing people to sport, helping them to realise their potential, and spotting and nurturing our stars of the future."

(Sport England, UK Coaching Framework)

Sports Leaders UK is a registered charity, which provides the opportunity for people to gain qualifications and develop core skills and competencies in sporting activities. Groups are run in the local area, using schools, community halls or wherever is suitable for running practical and theory sessions. The nationally recognized awards help develop essential personal skills such as confidence, motivation, communication and teamwork. The practical aspect of the awards can equip the candidate with lifelong skills of self-management and leadership.

The qualifications can act as a stepping-stone for employment as well as develop character and personality.

Active challenge

Look on the website www.sportsleaders.org to find out about the organization's core values and the different qualifications available.

Choreographer

A choreographer is the designer or arranger of a staged dance or performace such as a ballet.

Experience through school and dance groups can help build choreographer skills. Courses are available to further study this skill and employment can be found as a member of a dance troupe or as a dance teacher.

Official

An official is someone who controls the activity and interprets the rules, laws or regulations of an activity, including checking the equipment.

In 2007 to 2008 the Youth Sport Trust funded training for young people aged 16 to 19 to officiate at sports such as athletics, volleyball, swimming, judo and sports for disabled athletes.

The aim of this training is to give young people skills to help at local events, national events, such as the UK School Games, and major events alongside top officials.

The following partners are involved:

- National governing bodies of sport
- School Sport Partnerships
- Competition Managers.

The national governing bodies of sport design courses for people interested in becoming officials in their chosen sport. Each pathway is different according to the nature of the sport.

Active challenge

Using the Internet, find the pathway a person needs to follow to become a football referee.

3 — Individual differences

Individual differences are factors outside the control of a performer that influence their performance and level of participation. These factors include age, disability, gender, physique, the environment, risks and challenges, activity levels and training.

Age

The age of a person may influence their chances of participating in certain activities. There may be age limits for participation or joining of some clubs, such as for golf, netball or rugby. For example, the age for competing in international gymnastic meets, such as the Olympic Games, is 16. This rule is set out by the FIG (Federation Internationale de Gymnastique) and allows time for the gymnasts to mature both mentally and physically enough to meet the demands of competition.

Depending on the size of the club, each age group usually has its own section with separate competition and coaching. Guidelines may be set by the sport's governing body to help organization and for clubs to meet the needs of groups of different ages.

The ageing process has varying effects on various body systems. This is why there are different age groups for some events, providing **balanced competition**. The physical development of muscles, bones, joints and cardiovascular capacity takes place at different ages. To make the competition fair and safe, age limits are put in place, especially in activities where physical strength, power and **speed** have a bearing on success.

Active challenge

Choose two competitive physical activities. Using the Internet, find out about any age limits or categories that may be in place for these activities. Share your findings with two other people.

As the trend for a healthier lifestyle continues, older people realize the need to keep exercising. Although they may be carrying an injury or a condition, if they are properly educated about a problem and are sensible about how much they take on, they will continue to benefit from exercising.

Older people have the chance to learn new skills as many public and private centres now cater for older age groups. More people are planning for their retirement, but money may still be a problem for the older generation. In some cases, concessions are made for older participants and off-peak times are set aside for them. For example, swimming and court hire rates may be reduced for people over the age of 60. The World Masters Athletics (WMA) creates opportunities for people to take part in athletics for life. They organize athletic events for people between the ages of 35 and 95. They have a clear age structure so people can compete with other similar aged athletes.

As the age of the population increases there are more older people that want to keep fit; therefore, more opportunity and publicity of activities for this age group is necessary. There has been a slow increase in the television coverage of the seniors' golf tournaments and the occasional veterans' tennis matches, but more coverage, promoting older people and top-class sport, is necessary if there is to be an increase of older, active sportspeople.

Disability

Disability can be physical or mental, temporary or permanent, and can have an effect on participation and performance in physical activity. With disability laws in place, greater provision is being made for disabled people to participate in sport. An increasing number of sports centres and clubs have wheelchair access, adapted facilities and integrated or specialized sports sessions for disabled participants. The media is increasingly covering disabled sporting events, helping to raise awareness. Wheelchair and blind athletes feature strongly in the televised coverage of the London Marathon and The Great North Run. There is also televised coverage of the Paralympic Games. Sport England, the body responsible for delivering the government's sporting objectives, has recognized the needs of disabled people and as a result, has developed a scheme known as the Inclusive Fitness Initiative (IFI). The IFI aims to ensure disabled

The World Masters Athletics provides the opportunity for experienced older participants to compete against others of a similar age.

Demands for sporting opportunities span all generations.

Disabled participants compete in their own right in many sports. Here, Britain and Canada compete in ice sledge hockey at the winter Paralympics.

people can profit from the physical, social and psychological benefits associated with **fitness** based leisure. The overall aim of the IFI is to make it easier for the disabled community to join in sport. The IFI also aims to ensure that disabled people can access inclusive fitness equipment that has features which make it suitable for all users in a targeted number of local authority facilities.

There are now more newspaper articles and radio broadcasts dealing with performances, results and issues of disabled athletes. For example, Dame Tanni Grey-Thompson is championing the cause for disabled athletes. She made a good living in wheelchair athletics and continues to show what is possible by encouraging more people to get involved.

Further progress could be made if there were more specialized coaches for disabled athletes and if sport centres made steps to actively welcome disabled participants. If governing bodies planned new events, providing opportunities for participation and competition, more people could get involved. Although there is still a long way to go to get as many people involved as possible, changes are being made across the country. For example, established facilities are being adapted to accommodate the varied needs of disabled players. Ramps and stair lifts, are installed, changing areas and accessible toilets are modified to make accessibility easier.

Lottery grants for sports facilities have helped usage for the disabled because often, part of the deal for funding is to make sure disabled facilities are in place.

Special groups are formed to help participation, for example, Disability Sport Cymru is focused on sport and recreation opportunities for the disabled in Wales. The Sports Aid Charitable Trust gives financial help to young people developing their talent and sportspeople with disabilities. Able and disabled athletes compete alongside each other where appropriate. For example, wheelchair athletes can achieve as high a standard as standing athletes in archery.

Gender

Both males and females are encouraged to participate in most sports. Ideally everyone who has an interest should be able to participate and compete in their chosen activity. However, sometimes there are constraints: some clubs may only offer single-sex teams due to a lack of facilities and qualified coaches even though popular trends are moving away from gender stereotyping where girls only play netball and boys only play football.

Oscar Pistorius is a role model for all those with disabilities.

Women's football continues to show a high increase in participation.

Although most sports are available to both sexes, each sex generally competes separately. This is due to safety reasons such as the physical differences in physique – size and strength – in order to allow fair play. Some sports such as tennis and golf have their own governing bodies for each **gender**. Two of the few major sporting events to have male and female competitors in the same event are show jumping and mixed-doubles matches in tennis and badminton.

Hormone and metabolism differences

Men and women have hormone and metabolism differences, which affect participation and performance in physical activity as they do not use glycogen in the same way. At different times of the month the female hormone balance changes and this affects the way energy is released. Ovarian hormones affect the way women metabolize carbohydrates and fat: they promote the use of fat as an energy source, so more is burnt off during exercise, and increase the amount of glycogen that is stored, which helps in endurance events. The male hormone testosterone affects participation by influencing a naturally more aggressive approach in competition. During puberty, boys become stronger and their muscles develop due to testosterone, making them quicker and more powerful than girls.

Opportunities for women in sport have steadily increased and have become more financially rewarding whereas traditionally there have always been more opportunities for men in sport. There is now greater representation for women in the national authorities. The Sports Council supports women's participation in sport and has ways in place to raise levels of achievement. More governing bodies are also recognizing the place of women in their sports.

In 1969, the Women's Football Association (WFA) was formed, supporting female talent in the game. The Women's Sport and Fitness Foundation (WSFF), founded in 1984, also pioneers the female cause, working hard to increase media coverage and raising awareness of top-class women's sporting success. Events such as the Women's Rugby World Cup show women playing the game at its highest level of skill, helping it to become more popular. There are increasingly more opportunities for women to have careers linked with sport in the media. This may be a first career or an occupation taken up after competitive life is over. On a local level, many sports centres make time during the day for women's activities. They may also provide crèche facilities to help as many women as possible take part.

Physique

There are many differences in people's physical shape and size. The following are the main factors creating the individual shape of a person:

- height
- weight
- body fat
- muscle girth
- bone size.

Depending on the combination of these different components, a person may be influenced to participate in a certain sport or even to play in a particular position within a team due to the suitability of their shape and size.

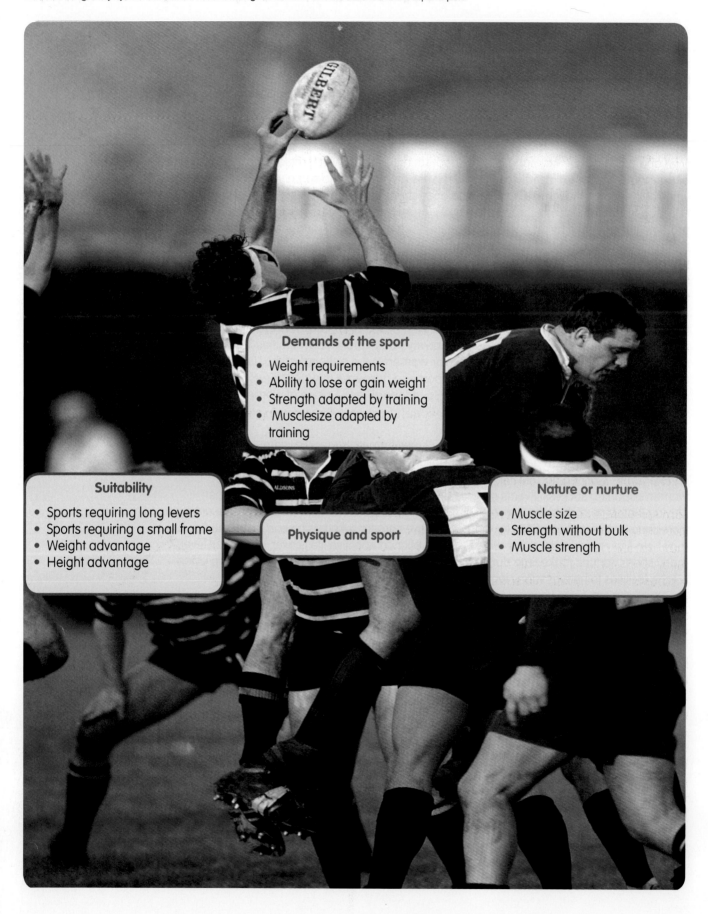

Demands of the sport

- Weight requirements
- Ability to lose or gain weight
- Strength adapted by training
- Musclesize adapted by training

Suitability

- Sports requiring long levers
- Sports requiring a small frame
- Weight advantage
- Height advantage

Physique and sport

Nature or nurture

- Muscle size
- Strength without bulk
- Muscle strength

Task 2

1 – Choose a variety of sports from a variety of categories such as invasion, racket, target and athletic.

2 – Decide if your sporting choices would attract a particular physique.

3 – Write down the reasons why that physique would be advantageous for each of your chosen sports.

Somatotypes

Somatotyping is a method of identifying people by their body shape. WH Sheldon devised this method in 1940 when he originally adapted his findings to criminology. Professor Tanner studied sportspeople from the 1960 Olympics and applied Sheldon's ideas to sport. There are three extreme categories of body type. Each type is determined by the amount of fat, muscle and bone that makes up the body.

The three **somatotypes** are:

- **Endomorph:** tendency to put on fat, soft roundness of shape, short tapering limbs, small bones and wide hips.
- **Mesomorph:** high proportion of muscle, bone, large trunk, heavy chest, broad shoulders and narrow hips.
- **Ectomorph:** lean, fragile, delicate body, small bones, narrow at shoulders and hips.

Each somatotype has a one to seven score; one is low and seven is high. Each person is measured to find their personal mark. Measuring a person to find their somatotype involves measuring their body fat, bone, muscle and weight, with each measurement compared to a score chart. A non-sportsperson may have the following combination: four, three, three (four = medium endomorphy, three = low mesomorphy, three = low ectomorphy).

SPORT ATTRACTS EXTREMES There are very few people with the extreme examples of each somatotype. Most people have a combination of all three. However, sportspeople have more mesomorphic (muscle) and ectomorphic (thinness) than endomorphic (fatness) characteristics and a top-class sport will attract the best extremes of body type suitable to that game. Basketball, for instance, will attract players who are very tall and thin with sinewy muscles, falling into the ectomorph/ mesomorph categories.

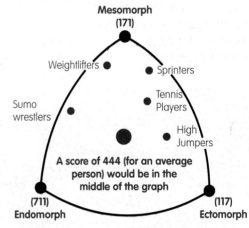

Diagram showing somatotypes for different sportspeople. The numbers show the degrees of that characteristic, for example, endomorph: 7 for tendency to put on fat, 1 for muscle and 1 for thinness.

Each sport is different so each will suit people of a different somatotype.

Task 3

1 – Put the following into the correct somatotype category:

a. basketball player   **c.** rugby prop forward   **e.** swimmer   **g.** shot-putter
b. hockey player   **d.** gymnast   **f.** marathon runner

2 – For each of the above sportspeople write a sentence on how they might describe
themselves.

> You may need to do some research to find out about the sports mentioned. Use your judgement to decide the somatotype by using the photographs on page 20 to help your decisions.

When working out a person's somatotype, their age, gender, height, weight, size of bones, amount of fat on their body and size of muscle are all taken into consideration.

Knowing your somatotype can steer you into a sport to which you are naturally suited or can show areas of the body that need to change in order to reach the maximum success rate in an activity. There are four factors to take into consideration when working out a person's somatotype:

1. **Fat ratio of the body** The fat layer is just below the top layer of skin on the body. Fat is a good insulator and can be of benefit for activities in cold climatic conditions. The amount of fat people have on their body varies with age and gender. Babies and women have thicker layers than men. Both sexes can increase their fat percentage as they get older. Men increase the amount around their middle; women the amount on their thighs and buttocks.

2. **Measuring fat** A skin-fold calliper is an adjustable instrument that measures the amount of fat at different places on the body. The method is to place skin and underlying layers of fat between callipers; a dial gives the reading of the thickness of the flesh. There are four main measurements to take:

   1. Biceps – at the front of the upper arm
   2. Triceps – at the back of the upper arm
   3. Suprailiac – at the front of the body above the hips
   4. Subscapula – at the bottom point of the scapula (shoulder blade).

In all cases, care is taken not to include muscle in the callipers.

A skin-fold calliper measures the amount of fat on the body.

3. **Measuring bones** Measuring bones gives the size of bones in relationship to the muscle and fat levels of the body. The places to measure are the elbow and knee joints.

For the elbow:

- Flex the biceps until the joint is at right angles.
- Use a condyle calliper to measure across the elbow at the widest point. This is a condyle measurement of the humerus.

Active challenge

Using the same method for measuring bones as above, write how you would take the condyle measurement of the femur.

4. Measuring muscles This measurement is taken (in centimetres) of a muscle while it is flexed and at its widest point. The muscles measured are the biceps (upper front arm) and gastrocnemius (back lower leg, commonly known as the calf muscle).

Taking a biceps girth reading:

- Hold the humerus horizontally.
- Flex the biceps so the arm is at right angles.
- Take the measurement around the widest part.

Taking a gastrocnemius girth reading:

- Stand with feet slightly apart.
- Flex gastrocnemius by standing on toes.
- Take the measurement around the widest part.

To function at its best, a rugby team requires players of all heights and weights.

Active challenge

Measure your partner's flexed biceps.

Environment

The environment of an area can affect an athlete's participant and their performance in physical activity. The environment includes many factors such as the climate and its condition, the terrain, facilities and their accessibility.

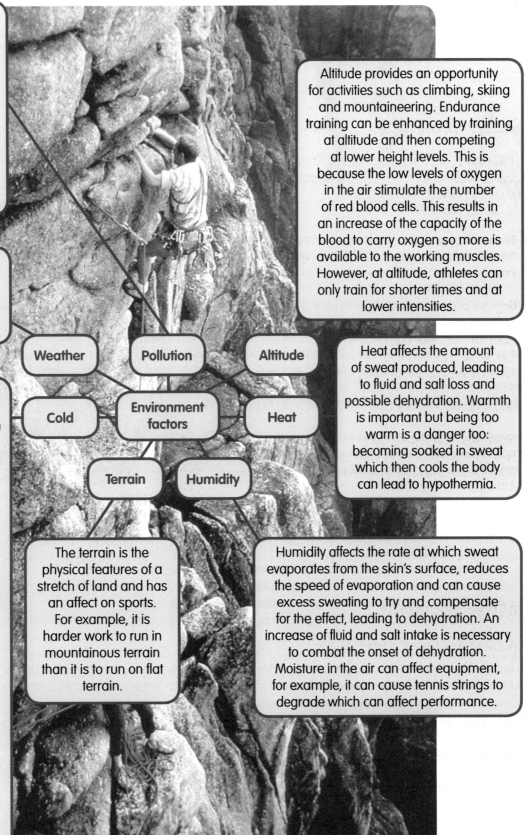

Pollution affects breathing and is dangerous to health. Prior to the Beijing Olympics, Jacques Rogge, (International Olympic Committee president, 2008) conceded that pollution could affect endurance events (any event lasting over an hour).

Altitude provides an opportunity for activities such as climbing, skiing and mountaineering. Endurance training can be enhanced by training at altitude and then competing at lower height levels. This is because the low levels of oxygen in the air stimulate the number of red blood cells. This results in an increase of the capacity of the blood to carry oxygen so more is available to the working muscles. However, at altitude, athletes can only train for shorter times and at lower intensities.

Unsuitable weather can affect particular sports, for example torrential rain could flood a football pitch.

Heat affects the amount of sweat produced, leading to fluid and salt loss and possible dehydration. Warmth is important but being too warm is a danger too: becoming soaked in sweat which then cools the body can lead to hypothermia.

The head, hands and feet need to be protected adequately in cold weather. Wearing layers of clothing is the key as they can be removed as you become warmer. Cooling down in cold temperatures happens at a quick rate so during rest periods be mindful of this and add layers of clothing as a matter of course. Fluid intake is important in cold weather as sweat will still need to be replaced and in colder temperatures urine production increases causing further fluid loss. Always take on fluids regularly before the feeling of thirst arises, as by then dehydration is likely to be affecting the body.

The terrain is the physical features of a stretch of land and has an affect on sports. For example, it is harder work to run in mountainous terrain than it is to run on flat terrain.

Humidity affects the rate at which sweat evaporates from the skin's surface, reduces the speed of evaporation and can cause excess sweating to try and compensate for the effect, leading to dehydration. An increase of fluid and salt intake is necessary to combat the onset of dehydration. Moisture in the air can affect equipment, for example, it can cause tennis strings to degrade which can affect performance.

Weather — Pollution — Altitude

Cold — Environment factors — Heat

Terrain — Humidity

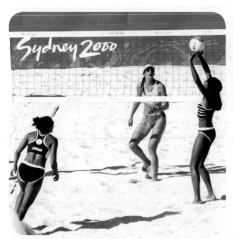

Heat: beach volleyball players in Australia need to keep their fluid levels up and use suncream to protect themselves.

Cold: layers of clothing are needed when skiing to protect the head and hands from the cold.

Heat: Spain's Yngling Skipper Monica Azon takes on water to combat dehydration.

Access to facilites

Where facilities for certain activities are good, there may be more chance that more people will participate. For example, Norfolk Academy of Gymnastics is sited in Besthorpe, a small rural town in Norfolk, which gives access to all ranges of ability, up to and including elite gymnasts. The greater the involvement, the better the possibility of a higher standard of sports play, which then attracts more players and coaches. In small communities, there may be an interest but not enough people living locally to make the facilities viable. Unless transport is available to towns with established clubs, the opportunity to play is lost.

The provision of and access to indoor and outdoor facilities depends on many factors. All areas of the country would like excellent local facilities, but providing these would not be financially or practically workable. There are many issues taken into consideration when deciding on new facilities:

- Location: certain sites naturally lend themselves to various activities. For example, outdoor pursuit centres are situated where there are hills, rivers, lakes and forests suited to the particular activities they offer.
- Funding: money to increase or improve facilities can come from different sources. For example, the government may set aside money in their annual budget, lottery funding may meet part of the cost or an individual may personally finance a team.
- Access: poor road and rail links to facilities may have a direct bearing on the amount of people that are able to use a sports centre.
- Expected use and demand: whether it is private or publicly funded, the aim is to have as many people use the facility for as much of the time as possible. When deciding on a site for a new facility the expected use and demand of the facilities has to be worked out as enough people should be available in the area to make full use of it.

Active challenge

Research into what sports facilities there are in your area. Refine your search to find the facilities that you would like to use, for example, a swimming pool, gym, climbing wall, and so on.

Risk and challenge

Each sporting environment presents different risks to be managed. Assessing and controlling the degree of risk to yourself and others is essential for safe participation in physical activity.

Outdoor and adventurous activities

- Be prepared and confident of your own abilities.
- Make sure training has equipped you with the correct personal and practical skills for an expedition.
- Are individuals experienced and have an understanding of the challenges ahead?
- Take a full range of equipment and clothing to meet all eventualities and make sure the group is familiar with it all.
- Make sure equipment is in good condition, for example, waterproof boots that are waterproof and have a good grip.

- Have an understanding of group dynamics.
- Be prepared with a contingency plan for if things go wrong.
- The group leader should understand the needs and capabilities of the individuals in the group, and should be able to make decisions under pressure.
- The group leader should recognize changes in the weather early and act accordingly.

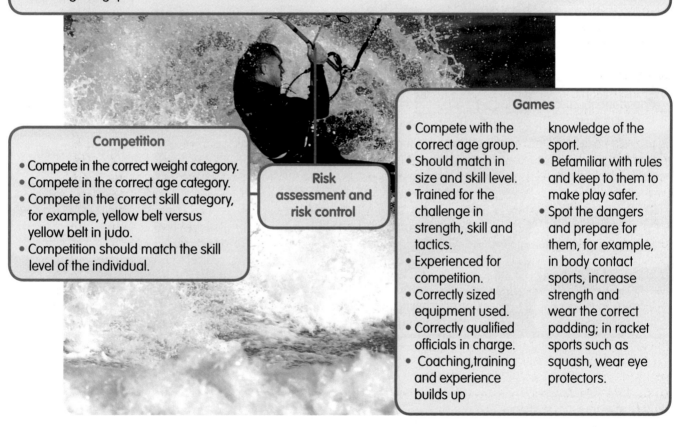

Risk assessment and risk control

Competition

- Compete in the correct weight category.
- Compete in the correct age category.
- Compete in the correct skill category, for example, yellow belt versus yellow belt in judo.
- Competition should match the skill level of the individual.

Games

- Compete with the correct age group.
- Should match in size and skill level.
- Trained for the challenge in strength, skill and tactics.
- Experienced for competition.
- Correctly sized equipment used.
- Correctly qualified officials in charge.
- Coaching, training and experience builds up

- knowledge of the sport.
- Be familiar with rules and keep to them to make play safer.
- Spot the dangers and prepare for them, for example, in body contact sports, increase strength and wear the correct padding; in racket sports such as squash, wear eye protectors.

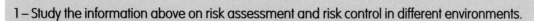

Task 4

1 – Study the information above on risk assessment and risk control in different environments.

2 – Create a table and add any other personal or practical qualities and skills a person needs in order to participate safely or lead others in sporting participation.

Activity levels

Different activities have different effects and make different demands on the body. The activity levels required to complete various activities changes. Personal response to the demands also varies with the individual. People learn at a different pace so take on board new strategies and tactics at a quicker or slower rate when actively becoming involved at a different level. Some sports are easier to learn and perform than others, which again affects the activity levels.

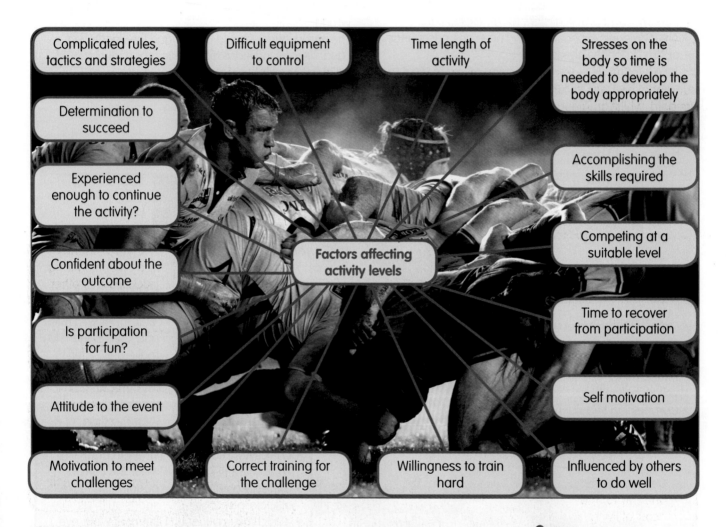

Complicated rules, tactics and strategies

Difficult equipment to control

Time length of activity

Stresses on the body so time is needed to develop the body appropriately

Determination to succeed

Accomplishing the skills required

Experienced enough to continue the activity?

Factors affecting activity levels

Competing at a suitable level

Confident about the outcome

Time to recover from participation

Is participation for fun?

Attitude to the event

Self motivation

Motivation to meet challenges

Correct training for the challenge

Willingness to train hard

Influenced by others to do well

Task 5

1 – Study the information on factors that affect activity levels.

2 – In a table, group the information into personal differences and sporting differences.

Active challenge

With a partner, discuss several different sporting activities and compare how difficult the rules are to learn, the skills are to perform and the tactics are to understand.

For example, you could compare cricket with rounders.

Training

Training is affected by the amount of time and funds that are available. The status of the participant also affects funding. For example, professional performers train as their job and are paid, whilst amateurs have to fit sport around their full-time employment and have to pay to participate and train. Amateurs may be restricted to the amount of time they can spend on their sport and how much disposable income they have available to spend on an activity.

- Buy equipment
- Sport may be a full-time job
- Afford to eat the right diet
- Restricted times may mean sharing facilities with other users
- Pay for entry fees
- Receive sponsorship
- Can only train at certain times of the day
- **Activity levels and funding for amateurs and professionals**
- Have the best coach
- Be able to train and pay for the cost of living
- Fit training and playing around job commitments
- Hiring facilities
- Pay for travel to centre of excellence for better coaching
- Pay for travel to training area
- Less time to develop skills and work on tactics
- Employ training partners

Task 6

1 – Study the information on activity levels and funding for amateurs and professionals.

2 – Create a table with two columns, one with the heading 'Professional', the other with the heading 'Amateur'.

3 – Place the information into the appropriate position in your table.

4 — The demands of performance

The demands of performance have both mental and physical effects and taking part in physical activity of any sort involves being able to respond to the physical and mental demands of performance.

Physical demands of performance

Fatigue occurs when there is a lack of oxygen to the working muscles and affects performance by reducing:

- muscle strength
- speed
- coordination
- reaction time
- control of muscles in agility and balance.

Mental demands of performance

It is important for a performer to recognize the stress levels they are experiencing. A certain amount of stress is needed in order to perform at the optimum level. However, too much stress can have a negative effect on performance and the enjoyment of the activity as it can affect fine motor skills through muscular tension and by taking up mental energy needed to devote to the technique. Excessive stress can inhibit focus on the skill and flow required in a performance.

Stress can occur when a performer is under more pressure than normal, such as before a match or during a competitive event, for example, when facing a penalty. A performer may feel stressed when too much is asked of them in too short a time, such as when team members are injured or sent off, when they think that a task is beyond their performance capabilities or when unnecessary obstacles are put in their way. Performing activities such as climbing and canoeing can also cause stress due to the risks involved.

Active challenge

Discuss with a partner a time when your sporting performance has been affected by stress.

Personality and emotions can affect performance. For example, confidence: "I will succeed"; self-doubt: "can I succeed?"; fear of the challenge: "is it too much for me?". These factors can also affect positive thinking, bring about negative thoughts and damage self-confidence.

Feedback or criticism can spur a performer on to adapt and improve, but they may try too hard, leading to injury. Criticism that is not constructive can demotivate a performer.

Tension and anxiety means the performer may worry that they are incapable of success in a big event which could distract concentration and affect performance; competition can be seen as a threat, not a challenge.

Demands of performance and their effects on skill

Boredom and tedium can lead to a lack of motivation. This might be because activities do not present enough variety or challenge which can lead to a half-hearted performance, leading to the use of incorrect technique and the possibility of injury.

Aggression by being assertive or dominant can help in weightlifting but can be dangerous when tackling in a team game such as rugby, leading to possible injury.

Motivation and arousal: adrenalin causes arousal (a desire to do well), alertness and prepares the body for explosive activity, however, it can cause poor judgement, poor execution of fine motor skills and inhibits correct performance of complex skills, for example, a tennis player may over-hit the ball.

Task 7

Study the spider diagram on the demands of performance on page 29. Where appropriate, link a positive and a negative way each heading can affect performance.

> For example, aggression can be positive when attacking the bar in weightlifting to lift the weight, but can be negative when tackling too hard in football, leading to an injury.

Key terms

Governing body – a group responsible for rules, procedures and fixtures of a particular game or event

Balanced competition – grouping based on size, age or experience for an even match

Speed – the fastest rate at which an individual is able to perform a movement or cover a distance in a period of time

Fitness – ability to meet the demands of the environment

Gender – the sex of a person: male or female

Somatotype – classification of body type

Endomorph – a somatotype, individuals with wide hips and narrow shoulders characterized by fatness

Mesomorph – a somatotype, individuals with wide shoulders and narrow hips, characterized by muscularity

Ectomorph – a somatotype, individuals with narrow shoulders and narrow hips, characterized by thinness

Summary

A person can participate in a range of physical activities in different ways. Each activity and role has its own skills and expertise to master in order to be successful.

The amount of participation in physical activity can vary with each person and can be governed by matters out of the individual's control. There are many different groups who use sporting facilities and in some cases the local authority will provide time and concessions to include these groups in sporting activities, for example, the elderly, disabled, mother and toddler groups and the unemployed. There are also physical and environmental factors that influence the type of activity undertaken, which requires the individual to adapt in order to safely and successfully take part.

Exam questions

Multiple-choice questions

1. Having access to good facilities can have an influence on participation. Which of the following relate to this?

   ☐ **A** Location, funding, access, expected use and demand

   ☐ **B** Expected use and demand, location, funding, balanced competition

   ☐ **C** Access, location, stress factors, expected use and demand

   ☐ **D** Weather conditions, funding, access, expected use and demand

   (1 mark)

2. A reduction in the cost of an activity is called a:

   ☐ **A** Concession

   ☐ **B** Comparison

   ☐ **C** Coordinate

   ☐ **D** Candidate

   (1 mark)

3. Disability can take four forms, they are:

   ☐ **A** Temporary, permanent, immature, physical

   ☐ **B** Physical, mental, temporary, permanent

   ☐ **C** Mental, complicated, temporary, permanent

   ☐ **D** Permanent, physical, mental, environmental

   (1 mark)

4. When choosing a physical activity to take part in a person makes a choice based on knowledge and understanding. Which of the following best reflects the experiences a person can draw from in order to make a good choice?

   ☐ **A** How the sport meets personal needs, the different roles involved in the sport, suitability for a sport, if their current diet suits the sport

   ☐ **B** Suitability for a sport, how the sport meets personal needs, if the sport is trendy, the different roles involved in the sport

   ☐ **C** Whether the kit suits the person, suitability for a sport, how the sport meets personal needs, the different roles involved in the sport

   ☐ **D** Experience of the sport, suitability for a sport, how the sport meets personal needs, the different roles involved in the sport

   (1 mark)

Short answer questions

5. Some individual differences affect participation in physical activity. List **three** of these.

   (3 marks)

6. A person's physique can often influence the type of activity that they pursue.

   (a) List the **three** somatotypes.

   (3 marks)

   (b) For each somatotype choose a sport that would suit that physique.

   (3 marks)

7. When undertaking physical activity in an area with extreme weather conditions, the performer has to adapt their behaviour.

   (a) List **three** types of extreme weather conditions a person would have to adapt to.

   (3 marks)

   (b) Give examples of what effects your examples would have on the participant.

   (3 marks)

Longer answer questions

8. What considerations should be made to reduce risks and ensure competitions are safe?

   (4 marks)

9. List **eight** points that can affect activity levels.

   (8 marks)

10. What are the differences in funding between amateur and professional sportspeople?

   (6 marks)

3.1.1 ~ The range of physical activities and the different roles that the active participant can choose from

3.1.1b The demands of performance: injury

What you will learn about in this topic:

1 — Precautions: how to prevent injury
2 — Correct techniques and safe practice
3 — Clothing and equipment
4 — Rules and codes of conduct

1 — Precautions: how to prevent injury

With any competition, physical activity or adventurous pursuit, there are potential dangers. There are many safety precautions a player, coach, teacher, student or any officiator can take to safeguard against injury and mishap. There are common procedures for all and some specific to the individual or the event. Those common to all should be adapted to suit the sport and be applied appropriately.

Injury to yourself and others can be reduced by:

- Understanding and keeping to the rules of the activity.
- Following appropriate training.
- Using the correct equipment.
- Performing skills correctly.
- Maintaining equipment.
- Checking areas of play are free from dangerous objects and other hazards.
- Individuals understanding their role in a situation.
- Training correctly to the highest level.
- Gaining experience in the activity and applying it where necessary.

Appropriate level of competition: performers should be in the correct weight, age and skill grouping for the competition.

Fitness: the body systems should be prepared for the stresses of the activity.

Technique: after learning the skill, performers should be able to apply the correct action in competition.

Skill levels: be able to perform the appropriate skills for the level of competition.

Environment: individuals should understanding how the environment can change and prepare and adapt to these changes. For example, by doing an extra warm-up in cold weather or making contingency plans for outdoor and adventurous activities.

Training: prepare the body, develop the skills and build the knowledge for performance.

Physical development: develop the body in the correct way to perform the activity successfully.

Common safety precautions

Rules of the game: performers should have a sound knowledge of the application and implementation of the rules.

Preparation: mentally and physically prepare to perform successfully as soon as the competition starts.

Footwear: should be correct for the activity and in good order. For example, studs should be smooth to the touch.

Warm-up and warm-down: gradually prepare the body before the activity to perform, during and after the activity, to lessen the risk of discomfort (Delayed Onset Muscular Soreness – DOMS).

Specialized equipment: individuals should have an understanding of and be trained to use specialized equipment, such as a map and compass for mountaineering.

Correct equipment: choose the correct size and weight of equipment for the best results.

Correct clothing: wear clothing that will not hinder or reduce the safety of performance, for instance, remove jewellery before a game.

To guard against injury there should be three parts to an **exercise** session: the **warm-up**, the main activity and the **warm-down**.

Warm-up

A warm-up should precede any physical activity, whether training or competing. Although there are definite phases to all warm-ups, they should be relevant and appropriate to the sport in question. Sport-specific warm-ups are essential as each sport has its own skills, **techniques** and actions so appropriate parts of the body are prepared for hard work.

A warm-up should precede any physical activity, whether training or competing.

Reasons for warming-up:

1. Gradually increases the heart rate to nearer the working rate.
2. Gradually increases body temperature to nearer the working rate.
3. Gradually moves the muscles and joints in ways that will be used in the competition.
4. Introduces skills to be used in the competition.
5. Increases the intensity so that the body is prepared for competitive speed.
6. Systematically working through the routine will prepare the performer's mind for the competition. This may give them a better start than the opposition.
7. Allows players to work in small groups in the way they will in the game.

The warm-up time immediately before the main activity is crucial. This is the period when the body can prepare for the rigorous physical activity. There is no set time for a warm-up. It should be adapted to the demands of the sport and the age of the performer.

By warming-up, the body systems, muscles and joints gradually become used to working harder. This gradual increase of stress on the body reduces the risk of injury. The pulse and body temperature are also raised to nearer the working rate.

Concentrating on warm-up activities will help concentrate a performer's mind. By focusing in this way, an advantage may be gained over the opposition by having a better start to a match.

In the warm-up phase of team sports there needs to be an opportunity to practise the basic skills of the game and to start to think collectively as a team. The warm-up creates a link between rest and the main activity. The timing between the two is important: if there is too long a gap between the warm-up and the main activity, the effects of the warm-up will be lost. If actions stressing the muscles and joints, like sprinting, are used in the event then these should be included at the end of the warm-up session.

There are three phases to a warm-up: aerobic phase, stretch and flexibility phase, and skills and intensive exercise phase.

Aerobic phase
Light aerobic work, such as marching on the spot, jogging and side-stepping, starts a session off gradually and begins to work the heart and lungs harder.

Stretch and flexibility phase
The stretch and flexibility phase eases the muscles and joints into positions appropriate to the activity. There are different types of stretches so those performed in the warm-up should be performed in the following order for safety: static, assisted and dynamic.

Athletes using static stretches ease the muscles gradually into the stretched position and hold it there for ten seconds. Assisted stretching is when the action is helped by pushing against another person or a wall. A specialized way of stretching is often used in gymnastics and football. Here, the coach helps the performer by pushing the limb and so stretch the joint further. These are called proprioceptive neuromuscular facilitation (PNF) techniques. They should only be undertaken by an expert and with great care.

A coach using PNF stretching.

Dynamic stretches are the most complex to perform. Care needs to be taken as injury can occur if these are misused. The athlete moves into the stretch and position and 'bounces' the muscle. The movements reproduce the actions of the game or activity starting at half pace for two to three repetitions and gradually increases to full speed. These movements are used when the event or activity needs rapid, explosive movements.

Flexibility exercises increase the mobility of the joints of the body – rotating shoulders and hips, for example. Each joint should be given some time, although certain sports may need some joints warmed more than others.

After the aerobic phase, static stretches should be done.

Skills and intensive exercise phase
This phase contains slow stretching of muscles beyond their normal position, which are held for short periods of time. Including basic skills related to the sport in the warm-up can help coordination in the game. The exercises gradually increase in intensity. If the sport includes times when bursts of pace are necessary then, at the end of the warm-up session, some short sprints can be included.

By warming-up, a person will increase their awareness and reaction time ready for the game. Preparing the body will increase the level of work the person is capable of producing in the event. Note that professional football teams have set warm-ups, which they perform on the pitch before a match.

Main activity
The warm-up leads to the main activity. This can be a training session, skills session or a competition, match or performance. Once the body systems are trained they become fit enough to complete the skills practised. When the body is pushed to the limit in competition, the skills can be put to the test without breaking down because of inadequate fitness levels.

Warm-down
After the main activity, the body is given the chance of gradually returning to its resting state; the gentle aerobic warm-down helps to do this. In this phase the heart has a chance to gradually slow down and the muscles to relax. By completing a warm-down, the heartbeat reaches its resting rate sooner; this is called the 'recovery time'. The heart, therefore, does not have to work too hard for longer than it needs to. The speed of the recovery rate is influenced by several factors:

- The older a person is, the slower the recovery rate will be.
- If the exercise is new, then the new stresses will be harder to recover from.
- How 'in shape' the performer is: the fitter a person is, the quicker their recovery.
- Women tend to recover more slowly than men.

Like the warm-up, there is no set time for a warm-down. There are two phases to the warm-down: the gentle aerobic phase and the stretching phase. The gentle aerobic phase keeps the blood circulating and prevents the chance to 'pool' or collect in areas of the circulatory system. This prevents light-headedness.

Gentle stretching stops the build-up of lactic acid in the muscles and so prevents immediate cramp and aching and soreness the following day (know as DOMS – Delayed Onset Muscle Soreness). Stretches in a warm-down should be held for about 30 seconds and should concentrate on the muscles used in the event. Freestyle swimmers will concentrate on their arms; runners will stretch and flex their legs. A controlled, restful warm-down can have a calming effect on a person after the excitement of a competitive match.

Task 1

1 – Give three reasons why a warm-up helps a performer.

2 – List three types of exercise that would be included in a warm-up.

3 – Draw a spider diagram of the main points and reasons for a warm-down.

Precautions in outdoor and adventurous activities

Outdoor and adventurous activities can include mountaineering, climbing, caving, canoeing, mountain biking and sailing. Before setting out on an expedition, a detailed weather report should be studied. Any outdoor activity needs careful planning. The better the planning, the less likely it is that something will go wrong. Key factors to take into consideration are: experience and fitness levels of individuals, terrain, equipment and environment. The Met Office can supply weather information for the British Isles. The weather at sea or in the mountains can change rapidly, so preparations should be made accordingly. By obtaining the weather report, predictions can be made as to whether it is viable to go out in the first place or what possible weather changes may occur during the day. If the elements are too much to handle, then it is sensible to turn back, take a safety route home or not go out at all! In mountainous areas the weather can bring wind, mist, rain, snow, heat, sun and storms all in the same day. The key is to prepare for the worst.

The weather can dramatically change throughout the day so the key is preparation.

Effects of wind and temperature
Whatever the ambient temperature, the effect of the wind can reduce it by several degrees and leads to a cooling sensation of the body. This is called the chill factor and only affects living things. The wind cools the body in two ways; it takes away the warm layer of air around

the body and evaporates the moisture on the skin's surface. This can have a great effect on any performer or team playing outdoors. It can especially have a bearing on outdoor and adventurous activities.

Altitude also affects the temperature. At the top of a mountain it is colder than at the bottom. So whatever the temperature at the start of a hill walk it is going to get colder the higher you climb. Changes in the environment may cause extra risks. Good weather may encourage people to train more frequently so overuse injury may occur, and in hotter weather, dehydration is an issue. Working in the winter will change the way a training session is conducted as daylight disappears quickly, so the timing of training may change or be moved indoors. New safety considerations must also be taken into account, as working surfaces may become wet and icy, making them slippery to train on. Athletes should be aware of the need to change their footwear to combat the conditions or the session should be moved indoors.

Active challenge

Collect more information from the Internet on the effects of changes in the environment on sporting performances.

Experience of the leader and the group

A major factor in the safety of a party taking part in outdoor and adventurous activities is the experience, knowledge and ability of the leader. The leader should plan the route, taking into account the ability of each member of the group. They should have expertise in the use of a map and compass, carry safety equipment and know the safety procedures.

Leaders should be able to assess the group, encourage the weaker members and adapt the pace to suit the whole party. Their ability to make correct decisions under pressure to suit a situation can help ensure the safety of the party. For long expeditions, leaders should have the personal ability to keep the morale of the group high, even in difficult and demanding conditions.

Land drills help give instructions in a safe environment.

Map and compass work provides practical opportunities to apply geographical knowledge.

Environmental conditions

- Does the sailor or canoeist know the tides and currents?
- Wind may blow the party off course. Rain may dampen morale. Is the group equipped for snow?
- In mist, would they still know where they were going?
- In a storm, would they know what to do?
- Are they prepared for the heat?

Planning the activity

- Is the plan accurate?
- Are there any escape routes?
- Does the route include rests?
- Is it suitable for all members of the group?
- Will it stretch the abilities of the group too far?
- Has the route and planned times of return been left with a reliable source so the alarm can be raised if the group are not back on time?

Condition of the equipment

- Are the ropes too old?
- Is there a record of the equipment's use?
- Is the compass still reliable?
- Is someone taking the correct map?
- Has the torch got good batteries?
- Is the equipment in good order?

Factors affecting the safety of an outdoor activity

Experience of the leaders

- Do they know the area?
- Have they planned the route?
- Are they experienced in safety procedures?
- Can they use the safety equipment they have?
- Can they motivate the group?
- Will they set the pace to that of the slowest member?

Experience of the party

- Are they fit enough? Have they got the correct equipment?
- Have they enough experience for the degree of difficulty they may face?
- Have they the skills to finish the expedition?
- Do they know what is expected of them?

Degree of difficulty of the activity

- Is the group able to complete the route?
- Has the group got the correct equipment for the route?
- Will safety be compromised because of the difficulty of the activity?
- Is the route too difficult for the conditions?
- Are group members strong enough to last the distance?
- Has everyone got enough of and the right kind of protection for the activity?

Task 2

1 – Compile a list of five outdoor and adventurous activities.

2 – Name two specialized pieces of equipment required for each activity.

3 – Write two sentences about the job of the safety equipment.

Use the photographs in this section to help you as well as reference books and the Internet.

2 — Correct techniques and safe practice

Using correct techniques and safe practice are essential to all sports and physical activities. The coach is responsible for teaching these as well as giving the performer an understanding of the game. The skills learnt will be within the laws of the game and prepare the player for competition. The correct techniques are learnt, not only for success, but also to prevent risk. This is especially important for tackles and lifts.

Training improves the body so it is strong enough to deal with the stresses of the event. This reduces the possibility of fatigue, which often leads to injury. Coaching trains the performer to complete skills in a technically correct way. Body alignment is important in take-offs and landings, especially in activities such as gymnastics, trampolining and volleyball, to reduce the risk to the bones and tissues of the body. Knowledge and experience of how to control the equipment for the activity comes about through training. For example, a lacrosse stick used without training can become a danger to all on the pitch, not just the opposition.

How to use equipment safely

It is important in all activities to be able to safely use the equipment involved. Training on how to use the equipment is often required, especially for larger pieces.

Lifting
Applying safe techniques to lifting is essential for safety. Keep your back straight, grip the object firmly and bend your knees to lower your body. Lift the object by extending your knees.

Using the correct techniques can reduce the risk of injury.

Spotting in trampolining
Trampolining is a potentially dangerous activity. It is important that not only for the equipment to be in good order, but also for the spotters to be fully trained and their skills routinely refreshed before each session.

Their training could involve:

- Positioning around the trampoline –at least one spotter at the ends and two at the sides.
- Hand position whilst watching –on top of the protective cushion.
- Where to look whilst watching –at the upper part of the performer.
- An understanding of the weight distribution of the performer –top is the heaviest part.

Spotters need to be trained so they know to concentrate and be confident that they can do their job when required. More spotters are used in schools than are shown here.

- Hand position if the performer travels in their direction – contact wrist and upper arm.
- Easing a performer back to the trampoline centre –hold wrist and upper arm and gently push back onto trampoline.

3 — Clothing and equipment

In activities where there is physical contact, there is a danger of injury from impact with equipment or other players, or because excessive strain is put on the body. A performer should make sure they are protected by using the correct protective equipment.

The player should ensure that protective equipment:

- is the correct size and fits
- allows for adequate movement
- is always used
- is in good order (so it does not catch or scratch)
- is not damaged in any way, weakening its strength.

Each activity needs its own protective equipment. Each item of protection guards against a different kind of injury. These injuries could take the form of: impact of another player, the playing surface, the ball, forces put on the body by lifting, friction caused by repeating the skills of the event or injuries caused by external conditions.

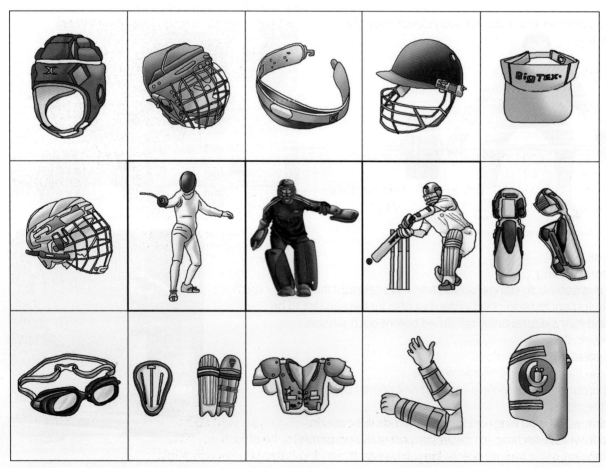

Some protective sports clothing and equipment.

Task 3

Choose a type of sportsperson and list the items they would need to dress for safety.

Use the illustrations on page 40 to help you with this task.

Active challenge

With a partner, discuss and decide on as many items of protection needed in as many sports as possible. Link each item of protection with an incident that could happen in a game.

Work from the head downwards.

Personal equipment in outdoor and adventurous activities

The clothing taken on any adventurous activity should suit every kind of weather possibility. The clothing mountaineers take on expeditions has to be appropriate for the extreme conditions they can face. These clothes range from undergarments to outer layers. Boots should be comfortable, waterproof and sturdy, with a good grip. An activity may begin in warm and sunny weather but, as the day goes on, the weather may change. As the altitude rises, the temperature drops on hills and mountains. Experienced mountaineers will be well equipped for this.

In addition to a compass and map, a mountaineer may also carry the following:

Personal safety kit:

- extra warm clothing
- extra gloves
- food and water
- bivvy bag (waterproof bag large enough for two people to shelter from the elements)
- whistle for distress call (a mobile phone would help but there are some areas where a signal cannot be picked up)
- torch.

Climbers such as Rhys Jones take a lot of protective clothing and equipment to make their climb safe. School groups also need to wear helmets.

Personal first aid kit:

- two crêpe bandages, one ankle and one knee-size tubular bandage for sprains
- army knife with scissors
- sterile wipes for dirty wounds
- various-sized plasters
- 12 pack of swabs for compression
- one roll of tape for holding the swabs in place
- safety pins.

The ability to use a map and compass correctly needs specialist training and much practice. If walking over a long distance and in hostile terrain then it is important to be able to navigate. A route plan should be worked out before the party sets off to include escape points at certain parts of the route in case there is an accident or the weather deteriorates. When visibility is zero, owing to mist coming down, it is possible, as long as you know your position, to navigate with a map and compass alone.

The safety equipment should suit all possible conditions of the day. This equipment may be bulky to carry, but it can be shared between members of the group. Often it will not be used but it is there should it be needed. If mountaineering or walking in the winter, specialized equipment is essential for safety, such as crampons and ice axes. Training and experience are necessary so that they can be used properly.

Regular checks on the condition of the equipment should be made. Ropes do not last forever; they have a life determined by the number of hours used. After this time they cannot be relied on to do their job and so should not be used for climbing again.

Wearing the correct gear and carrying appropriate safety equipment protects the performer from extreme elements and hazardous situations.

Jewellery

Before a team game begins, players are checked for any jewellery they may be wearing. This may seem petty, but each type of jewellery has its own hazards. Sometimes players put a plaster over earrings so they are not as dangerous. In games where physical contact regularly occurs, it is essential that there is no jewellery to mark the wearer or the opposition.

Having tidy hair and short fingernails reduces the risk of injury. Here, the England women's football team display their impeccable personal presentation.

- Rings – if fingers are jarred or a ball knocks the end of the finger (called 'stumped finger') and the finger swells, a ring could become stuck and cut into the flesh. Rings can also become caught and can cut the performer or an opponent.
- Necklaces – if caught and pulled they can cause a cut around the neck.
- Earrings – if caught they could injure the wearer or an opponent.

Personal presentation

Fingernails need to be clipped to prevent catching and scarring, especially in games such as netball and basketball in which reaching for the ball around head height is common.

Hair should be tidy and not in the performer's eyes so they can see where they are going and so it does not flick into another player's eyes.

If glasses are worn they should be made of plastic so if they break they do not shatter and injure someone.

Clothing worn for sport should be kept in good order. Ripped or frayed clothing can catch and be a danger.

Task 4

1 – Read the table of parts of sentences below.

2 – Link the beginnings of the sentences with the endings.

3 – Write out the complete sentences in your workbook.

Beginning of sentence	Ending of sentence
1. Players are checked for... 2. If a ball jars a finger... 3. Long fingernails can catch and scar... 4. Wearing correct clothing in gymnastics is important...	a. a player wearing a ring could cut their flesh. b. jewellery before a game. c. so the rules of netball state they should be short. d. so it does not catch on equipment.

4 — Rules and codes of conduct

Each game has its own set of rules or laws. These rules are connected to the type of equipment and competition involved. They are designed to make the event safer and fairer. Each set of rules helps to give the game its own individual style.

The governing bodies of the sports make the rules. The players play to the rules. The referee, umpire or judge makes sure the rules are kept. Within the rules are a series of stages of discipline; often the player is given one warning to stop any bad play. If the foul play continues, a player will be asked to leave the game.

It is important to understand the rules or laws of your chosen activities and how they help the game. There may be technical language to learn, correct procedures to follow and hand signals to perform when implementing these rules and laws.

Although there is often more than one official at a game, there will normally be only one official who has overall responsibility. However, in a full game of rounders, with two umpires, the responsibility is shared. Both umpires have joint responsibility for clearly announcing the decisions and scores, checking the pitch, equipment, players' clothing and keeping records of the score and batters out. Each umpire can dismiss players from the pitch for unsporting conduct. As well as these dual responsibilities, each umpire has a specific role to play and a position to adopt during the game.

A cricket umpire responds quickly to play and announces their decision clearly.

The batter's umpire:

* stands at the end of the batting line, so they can see the first post easily
* calls 'no-ball' if the bowler's action is not continuous, if the bowler bowls with a foot over the front line of the bowling square, if the ball passes above the head or below the knee of the batter, or for any bowl that hits the ground before reaching the batter
* calls 'rounder' or 'half rounder' when they are scored
* gives any decisions concerning the front line or back line of the batting square
* gives decisions on 'backward hits' and calls them when necessary
* gives decisions on the first and fourth posts
* gives decisions on all catches
* calls the next player (by name or number) to the batting square.

The bowler's umpire:

* stands behind, away and to the right of the second post so they can see the pitch
* calls 'play' at the beginning of each innings
* calls 'play' to restart the game after a deadball situation
* calls 'no-ball' for wide bowls, balls that hit or would have hit the player if they had not moved, or bowls passing on the non-hitting side of the batter
* gives decisions on the second and third posts
* calls 'no-ball' if the bowler's foot goes over the back line or side line of the bowling square
* ensures the waiting batters, and those batters that are out, stay behind their relevant lines.

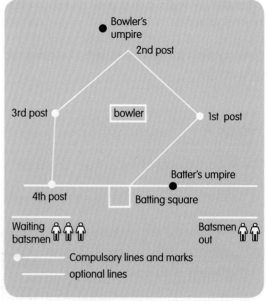

Position of the umpires in rounders.

The example of the two umpires in rounders highlights the importance of knowing what your responsibilities are in a game, so you know when, and what, to call. Your chosen sport will have direct guidelines as to each official's responsibilities in its rulebook.

Referees need a thorough knowledge and understanding of the rules and how they are applied in a game before beginning to referee. This allows them to use the correct terminology and hand signals when controlling the game. With practice and experience they gradually become more confident and efficient in applying rules appropriately.

To be a good professional official or referee takes time, practice and experience. They have to pass examinations, attend courses and keep up to date with developments in umpiring and refereeing in their sport to be the best they can be.

Task 5

Using the rounders example, state which rules or procedures fit in the following categories: safety, keeping order, making play fair.

Duties of a referee or umpire

The duties of a referee or umpire are the jobs they are expected to perform. An umpire should check that they have the correct equipment before each match so that their job can be completed effectively and efficiently. Such equipment may include:

- a watch to time the play (a back-up watch is recommended)
- a pencil to record the score or official decisions (spare pencils are recommended)
- a score pad set out for the particular game
- disciplinary cards to be shown for foul play.

In preparation for the game:

- Have a full knowledge of the rules of the game.
- Gain experience for the standard of the match.
- Make sure personal presentation is of a high standard.
- Have all necessary equipment.
- Achieve a level of fitness to meet the demands of the game.

Before the game:

- Check the condition of the playing surface for safety.
- Check equipment: match ball and goals.
- Check players: clothing, jewellery and equipment.

Duties of a football referee

During the game:

- Concentrate and watch play throughout the game.
- Keep up with play.
- Keep play within the laws of the game.
- Work as a team with the other officials.
- Make decisions efficiently.
- Communicate clearly with players and officials.
- Keep an accurate record of the score fouls.

After the game:

- Record the score.
- Make sure both teams know the final score.
- Write a match report (if necessary).
- Send scores (and report) to the relevant body.

Rules connected with correct skills and techniques

Some rules of an activity are there to make competition or performance safer. These rules often have a direct bearing on the technique permissible. The nature of some activities results in them having danger elements.

The form of danger can be due to the equipment. For example, a hockey ball or stick can be hazardous to others if not controlled. Therefore, within the rules of hockey there are clear restrictions on lifting the ball and stick. Certain footwear can allow the performer to maintain steady footing and change direction efficiently. Studs on football boots can also be dangerous to others. The laws of football are clear on dangerous play to do with raised boots and two footed tackles; infringements of this kind attract severe penalties.

The physicality of rugby makes it a joy to watch and play. Tackling can be spectacular to watch but if incorrectly performed it can be dangerous too. The rules on 'high tackles' (any tackles around the neck or above) protect the runner from being unfairly and dangerously brought to ground.

There are clear rules in hockey about lifting the ball and stick.

45

Each activity has its own rules affecting technique and skills. It is important to know and understand the rules of your chosen activities for safety purposes.

Active challenge

For one or more sports, think of rules that keep the game safe. Compare your choices with a partner.

Appropriate levels of ability and participation

In contact sports there are rules that keep similar age groups together and that separate the sexes at certain ages. This is an attempt to make the competition even and safe by keeping the experience and strength of the players at a similar level. Different factors are taken into account to ensure a balanced competition. These include:

- grading
- skill level
- weight
- age
- gender.

Codes of conduct

Codes of conduct, or **etiquette**, are the unwritten rules of behaviour a player stands by when competing. Each sport has its own code of conduct. A general example of this is shaking hands before and after a game. In tennis, new balls are used after the first seven games and every nine games after that. It is not a rule, but it is also good etiquette for a player about to serve to show the ball to the opposition by raising it in the air.

A player may throw or kick the ball away in anger after a decision by the referee. The referee can punish this demonstration of bad sportsmanship in an attempt to discourage such behaviour from other players. If a player is putting a ball in golf, the opposing player may show bad etiquette by coughing in an effort to break the putting player's concentration.

If a player becomes injured during a football game, the opposition may kick the ball out of play to stop the game so the player can receive treatment. When the treatment is complete, the throw on may then be passed back to the opposition. These actions are not rules, just good sportsmanship.

Umpiring in cricket is a fine art and even the best umpires cannot detect the slightest of touches that carry for a catch. Batters can take it upon themselves to 'walk', declaring themselves 'out', in such cases as only they will know if contact was made on the ball. This is sportsmanship of a very high order. At the end of rugby matches each team forms a tunnel to applaud the opposition off the pitch showing mutual respect for each other's efforts.

Tennis players show good etiquette by shaking hands after a match.

Key terms

Exercise – a form of physical activity done primarily to improve one's health and physical fitness

Warm-up – exercises that gradually put stresses on the body systems in preparation for the main activity

Warm-down – exercises after the main activity, which gradually bring the body systems back to near resting state

Technique – the way in which a skill is performed

Heart rate – the number of times the heart beats per minute

Etiquette – a code of polite behaviour

Summary

Rules not only give the activity its character but they also make competition fair and safe. Rules can have a direct bearing on the skills and techniques of an activity, often for the overall safety of the performers. Other ways of making a competition fair and safe are to have the competitors matched by age, weight, height and experience. This will even out the competition, making injury less likely and also create a more competitive match.

Exam questions

Multiple-choice question

1. Which of the following best describes common safety precautions for sport?

   ☐ **A** Playing in a balanced competition, using warm-ups and warm-downs properly, following the rules of the game, using the correct technique

   ☐ **B** Playing in a balanced competition, wearing the most expensive kit, following the rules of the game, using the correct technique

   ☐ **C** Using warm-ups and warm-downs properly, following the rules of the game, playing in an entertaining way, playing in a balanced competition

   ☐ **D** Following the rules of the game only when the referee is watching, using the correct technique, playing in a balanced competition, using warm-ups and warm-downs properly

   (1 mark)

Short answer questions

2. Protective equipment can be essential for safety. What factors should the user ensure of the equipment so it does its job correctly?

   (3 marks)

3. What dangers can jewellery cause if worn during sport?

   (3 marks)

4. Having a balanced competition makes the activity safe and fair. What factors would be considered when making an activity have balanced competition and why?

   (3 marks)

Longer answer questions

5. What are the **three** phases of a warm-up?

   (4 marks)

6. What is the purpose and effect of a warm-down?

   (4 marks)

3.1.1 ～ The range of physical activities and the different roles that the active participant can choose from

3.1.1c   The demands of performance: the difference between aerobic and anaerobic exercise

What you will learn about in this topic:

1 — Aerobic respiration
2 — Anaerobic respiration
3 — The function and role of the blood
4 — Oxygen debt
5 — The recovery process from vigorous exercise

Exercise affects breathing. The action of breathing is vital as it puts oxygen into the body and removes carbon dioxide. At rest, we take an average of 15 breaths per minute. The amount of air breathed in (inspiration) and out (expiration) is called the 'tidal volume'. This is enough breath for rest but when we start to exercise, greater amounts of oxygen are needed and greater amounts of carbon dioxide are produced, which then need to be removed. In extreme activity the breathing rate can go up to 50 breaths per minute.

Active challenge

Work in pairs, taking turns to be the active participant and the recorder. You will need a watch that counts seconds.

1 – Sit still for three minutes.

2 – Count the number of breaths taken in on the sixth minute.

3 – Jump on the spot for a minute.

4 – Now count the number of breaths taken in a minute.

5 – Record the difference.

As respiration increases, the amount of oxygen a person is able to take up will also increase. There is a limit to the increase in each person, called the VO$_2$ maximum. During exercise, the vital capacity (the largest amount of air that can be expired after the deepest intake of breath) will increase because of the demand for a greater intake of air. Both the residual volume (the amount of air that remains in the lungs after maximum expiration) and the tidal volume increase only slightly.

The body converts fuel (usually glucose) to energy and releases it into the body through **aerobic** and **anaerobic** respiration. The systems automatically kick in depending on the type and intensity of the exercise performed.

1 — Aerobic respiration

Energy released through aerobic respiration needs a sufficient supply of glucose and oxygen to the tissues. With enough oxygen present the activity can go on for long periods, as long as the difficulty or intensity does not become too great. This aerobic fitness allows us to keep going at a moderate level. The aerobic system is used in moderate to hard continuous activities that usually take place over a period of more than 60 seconds. The oxygen is breathed in and diffused into the circulatory system. In this type of activity, breathing becomes more regular and deeper. The muscles need oxygen to contract and in aerobic respiration this oxygen enters the body through the breathing process.

Long-distance runners, such as Dan Robinson, need aerobic respiration.

The formula for aerobic respiration is:

glucose + oxygen ⟶ energy + carbon dioxide + water

Extra air = aerobic respiration

2 — Anaerobic respiration

When energy is produced anaerobically no oxygen is used in its initial release, only glucose. Some sports wholly use anaerobic respiration. These are activities where there is a need for a single maximum burst of energy. Athletic field events are good examples of anaerobic exercise. In throwing and jumping events the actions used are explosive. They use one all-out burst of maximum effort to complete the event. The time it takes to complete the attempt is very short, so the energy is produced from the supplies already in the body.

Anaerobic respiration can only supply energy for a short time. If the demand for energy continues for over a minute then energy is released by breaking down carbohydrates. This is called the **lactic acid** system. Lactic acid is a mild poison produced in the muscles during strenuous activity. If lactic acid is allowed to build up in the muscles it can lead to fatigue and cramp.

Athletic field events use anaerobic respiration; Jessica Ennis demonstrates this in the Women's Heptathlon.

The formula for anaerobic respiration is:

glucose ⟶ energy + lactic acid

> No air = anaerobic respiration

3 — The function and role of the blood

Blood is the transportation system of the body and flows via the circulatory system (the heart and blood vessels). Its functions are as follows:

• To transport oxygen and nutrients to parts of the body and remove waste (toxic) products from the body. The body relies on this process to stay alive. The balance of nutrients keeps the body functioning properly.
• To control body temperature. The body is affected by changes of temperature, so keeping it in an acceptable range keeps the body functioning properly.
• To protect the body from infection. Antibodies in the blood fight disease and platelets help to clot the blood at the source of a cut and prevent other germs entering the body.

Blood is made up of four components: red blood cells, white blood cells, platelets and plasma.

Red blood cells

Red blood cells (erythrocytes) are small but there are many of them. Two million are produced and destroyed in your body every second! Their main job is to carry oxygen, but they also transport nutrients and waste products, such as carbon dioxide and salt. They are produced in the bone marrow of long bones. During exercise the blood increases in thickness as water is removed as waste.

Red blood cells contain **haemoglobin**. Oxygen chemically attaches itself to haemoglobin to make oxyhaemoglobin. It is in this way that oxygen is transported to the working muscles of the body and carbon dioxide is taken away to the lungs, transported in solution via the plasma.

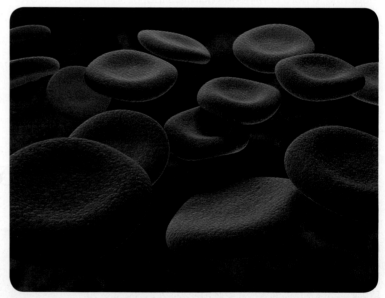

Human blood, showing red blood cells.

White blood cells

The job of the white blood cells (leukocytes) is to protect the body. There are five types of white blood cells. The main functions of leukocytes are to fight infection at its source, repair damaged tissue after an injury and destroy bacteria. When a cut or graze occurs, the white blood cells gather to stop bacteria entering the body. When a scab forms, it is made up of dead leukocytes. There are fewer white than red blood cells in the body. The cells are produced in the marrow of long bones and the lymph tissue of the body.

Platelets

Platelets are fragments of larger cells. They are in charge of clotting the blood. They clot at the surface of the skin after a graze or cut. They do the same job internally, on small, damaged blood vessels. Clotting is important to stop blood loss from the body and to stop internal bleeding.

Plasma

Plasma is straw-coloured and is 90 per cent water. It makes up 55 per cent of the volume of blood. It helps the blood flow more easily by the use of plasma proteins. The ten per cent of plasma that is not water contains a mixture of the following:

Active blood platelet cells.

salts, chlorine, amino acids, glucose, antibodies, **fibrinogen** (which helps clotting), hormones and waste products, such as urea and carbon dioxide. During exercise, hormones such as endorphins, cortisol, adrenalin and testosterone are produced and are transported in the plasma. Adrenalin can help a performer heighten their performance levels during competition.

Task 1

From your knowledge of the composition of blood, copy and complete each of the following sentences in your workbook:

a. Red blood cells are called _____

b. The main function of red blood cells is to _____

c. Red blood cells contain haemoglobin, this helps _____

d. White blood cells protect the body by _____

e. White blood cells are also called _____

f. White blood cells are produced in _____

g. The job of the platelets is to _____

h. Platelets are smaller parts of _____

i. Plasma is 90 per cent water and makes up _____

j. Plasma contains plasma proteins that help _____

Heart rate and exercise

At rest, the heart has a chance to slow down, as it does not have to work so hard against gravity to circulate the blood. The **resting heart rate** is about 72 beats per minute, which is sufficient to supply the muscles with the necessary blood and nutrients, although this varies with gender and age. The heart rate increases when extra demands are made on the body. The rate depends on the type of activity. If it is easy, the pulse goes up a little; if the activity is more intense, then the pulse rises further.

Performers can regulate the intensity of their training if they know their **maximum heart rate**. Usually, the heart rate needs to be raised to at least 60 per cent of the maximum to improve **cardiovascular fitness** levels.

To work out the maximum heart rate, the following formula is used:

220 – age = maximum heart rate

Sixty per cent of this amount will give the maximum heart rate. After exercise, the heart returns to its resting rate. The time it takes to do this is referred to as the **recovery rate**. A warm-down can help the body gradually return to the resting heart rate. This takes about five minutes depending on the individual's fitness level and the type of warm-down.

In prolonged events using aerobic respiration, it is vital that the blood controls oxygen and glucose levels, waste removal from the body and body temperature so that the athlete can sustain performance for the duration of the event.

In anaerobic respiration, glucose is utilized immediately, the demand controlled by blood circulation. After the high-intensity exercise, the removal of lactic acid via the circulatory system helps to relieve cramp and fatigue.

Immediate effects of exercise on the circulatory system:

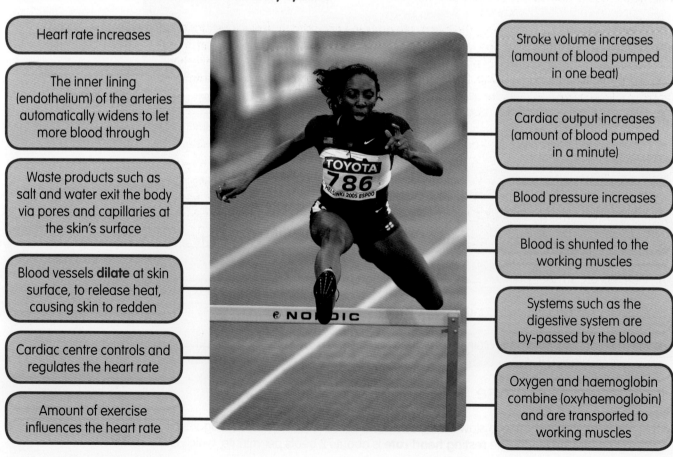

Heart rate increases

The inner lining (endothelium) of the arteries automatically widens to let more blood through

Waste products such as salt and water exit the body via pores and capillaries at the skin's surface

Blood vessels **dilate** at skin surface, to release heat, causing skin to redden

Cardiac centre controls and regulates the heart rate

Amount of exercise influences the heart rate

Stroke volume increases (amount of blood pumped in one beat)

Cardiac output increases (amount of blood pumped in a minute)

Blood pressure increases

Blood is shunted to the working muscles

Systems such as the digestive system are by-passed by the blood

Oxygen and haemoglobin combine (oxyhaemoglobin) and are transported to working muscles

Active challenge

1 – Find your carotid pulse at your neck by pressing your first two fingers to the side of your throat.

2 – Record your resting pulse.

3 – Now jump on the spot for one minute.

4 – Take your pulse again. How has it changed?

5 – Are you showing any other immediate effects of exercise?

6 – Record your results.

Effects of regular exercise and training on the circulatory system

Endurance training, commonly known as aerobic training, helps strengthen the heart. This type of training is progressive, over time. With aerobic training the general size of the heart gets bigger, the heart walls become thicker, stronger and more robust. The resting stroke volume increases and so does the cardiac output.

Whilst everything else is increasing, the heart rate does the opposite. A useful indicator of good fitness is the resting heart rate. The slower it is per minute, the more efficient the heart is as it can pump the required amount of blood with fewer beats. Therefore, the slower the resting heartbeat, the fitter the person. With good aerobic fitness, a person will usually be able to keep working efficiently without tiring or losing skill.

Task 2

Taking regular exercise affects the body in many ways. Using the two headings 'Immediate effects of exercise' and 'Long-term effects of exercise', make a list of the different changes that happen to the body.

Long-term benefits of exercise on the circulatory system:

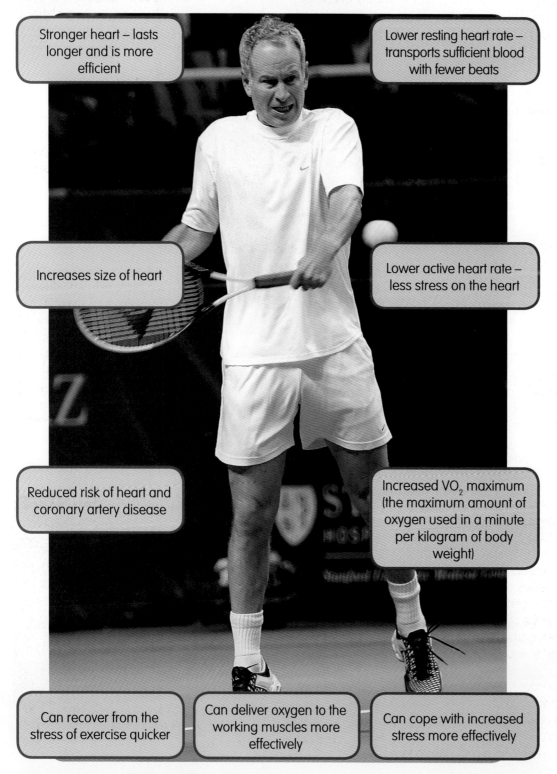

Stronger heart – lasts longer and is more efficient

Lower resting heart rate – transports sufficient blood with fewer beats

Increases size of heart

Lower active heart rate – less stress on the heart

Reduced risk of heart and coronary artery disease

Increased VO_2 maximum (the maximum amount of oxygen used in a minute per kilogram of body weight)

Can recover from the stress of exercise quicker

Can deliver oxygen to the working muscles more effectively

Can cope with increased stress more effectively

Monitoring heart rate

A person's pulse rate increases and decreases according to the stresses of the exercise they are doing. During an exercise or training session, monitoring and recording the pulse rate helps the performer in many ways:

Have knowledge of how quickly the blood is being pumped around their body

Indicates energy provision allowing the body to exercise

Safety – ensures the performer is working at the correct level for their ability

Monitoring and recording the pulse rate can show how training sessions should be adapted in the future

Monitoring heart rate

Varying the pulse can link with using the principle of overload (working harder than normal levels)

Monitoring the pulse rate in a training session ensures the work rate is at the correct intensity

Heart rate will show the zone the performer is working in and will vary according to the aims of the training (a light session (target zone) or demanding session (training zone))

The recovery rate after exercise reflects fitness levels

How fast the pulse rate returns to resting rate is an indicator of fitness

4 — Oxygen debt

Oxygen debt is a result of vigorous, anaerobic exercise. You can tell when a player has just used their anaerobic system from their breathing pattern. After working vigorously in the activity their breath may be shallow and gasping. This is due to insufficient amounts of oxygen going to the working muscles and so energy is released without the presence of oxygen. As a result, lactic acid, a mild poison, is built up in the muscles. Gasping for breath is an indication that there is an **oxygen debt**, and the body is making the effort to repay it.

Badminton players such as Nathan Robertson and Gail Emms require aerobic and anaerobic respiration.

This type of energy provision can only carry on for 45 to 60 seconds. After this, the lactic acid in the muscles becomes too high and prevents muscular contraction. The anaerobic system stops. The body then cannot keep running at its fastest speed or keep lifting heavy weights.

In all games, a combination of aerobic and anaerobic respiration is required. A player, while moving and positioning themselves correctly on the pitch according to the play, is using aerobic respiration. This is aerobic because the intensity of the exercise is moderate and will continue throughout the game. When the player takes a shot, for example, one maximum contraction is used. For this action, the anaerobic system comes into operation.

Badminton players, for example, use both types of respiration due to the need for a maximum effort whenever they strike the shuttlecock during a rally. Squash players will use more anaerobic respiration during their game, as they continually need maximum effort during the rallies to strike the ball.

Task 3

Study the comments below on the changes in respiration for an athlete in a sprint race. Put them into the order in which the athlete would experience them.

a. The oxygen debt is repaid.
b. An athlete breathes quickly and respires aerobically.
c. The athlete's muscles ache.
d. The lactic acid system begins to provide energy.
e. The athlete begins anaerobic respiration in their muscles.
f. The athlete breathes slowly and respires aerobically.

5 — The recovery process from vigorous exercise

Recovery after physical activity allows the muscles to become stronger, increases muscle proteins and helps to improve the lactic acid threshold. Eating carbohydrates just after the training session and then more within the following two hours not only adds to the energy stores (glycogen begins to build up again) but also helps the muscle proteins become restored too, helping the recovery of damaged tissue.

Recovery phases for performers are important. They:

- must be planned
- repair damaged tissue (including muscle)
- should improve level of fitness.

Recovery phases restore:

- energy producing enzymes in the muscle fibres
- stores of carbohydrates in muscle cells
- hormonal balance and the immune system.

Recovery can be monitored by using the Orthostatic Heart Rate test. The test requires a stopwatch and is conducted as follows:

1. Lay on the ground and rest for fifteen minutes.
2. Take your resting pulse and record (result one).
3. Stand up.
4. Fifteen seconds later take your pulse again and record (result two).
5. Calculate the difference between the two pulse readings and record the result.

If the difference between the two readings is greater than 15 to 20 beats, the athlete is unlikely to be recovered from the training. Possible adjustments should be made to the session in order to allow for recovery.

Active challenge

This task aims to show how the heart rate can indicate the rate of recovery.

In a group:

1 – Exercise for 20 minutes after a warm-up.
2 – Take your pulse and record your result.
3 – Wait a minute and take your pulse again. Record your result.
4 – Plot your results on a graph.
5 – Compare your results with two other people.

> Look for a reduction in your pulse after one minute. Notice which pulse reduces quickest.

Key terms

Aerobic – 'with oxygen'; when exercise is moderate and steady, the heart can supply all oxygen the working muscles need

Anaerobic – 'without oxygen'; when exercising in short, fast bursts, the heart cannot supply blood and oxygen to the muscles as fast as the cells use them, so energy is released without oxygen present

Lactic acid – produced in the muscle tissues during strenuous exercise, as a result of insufficient oxygen available

Haemoglobin – found in red blood cells, transports oxygen to body tissue

Fibrinogen – a protein found in blood plasma that helps clotting

Resting heart rate – number of heart beats per minute when the body is at rest

Maximum heart rate – calculated as 220 minus age

Cardiovascular fitness – the ability to exercise the entire body for long periods of time; this is dependent on the fitness of the heart, blood and blood vessels

Recovery rate – the time it takes for the heart and metabolism to return to resting rate after exercise

Dilate – open up or become wider

Endurance – the ability to keep working over a period of time without tiring or losing skill

Oxygen debt – the amount of oxygen consumed during recovery above that which would have been consumed in the same time at rest (this results in a shortfall in the oxygen available)

Summary

When a person exercises, their circulatory system needs to work faster as there is a greater demand by the muscles for oxygen. Exercising at a medium to high-intensity level for long periods uses aerobic respiration, whilst high-intensity, maximum bursts of energy require anaerobic respiration to release energy. With regular exercise, the body can be trained to make these adjustments quickly and efficiently. The blood helps to regulate body temperature and protect the body via the immune system. Blood transports oxygen, glycogen and waste products, aiming to keep each at a level where the body can work efficiently.

Exam questions

Multiple-choice questions

1. Which of the following best describes the function of the circulatory system?

   ☐ **A** Protects the body by transporting white blood cells to the site of injury, helps with breathing, is an indicator of fitness

   ☐ **B** Transports blood around the body, helps control body temperature, protects the body by transporting white blood cells to the site of injury

   ☐ **C** Helps control body temperature, works via the central nervous system, is an indicator of fitness, controls movement

   ☐ **D** Shunts blood to working muscles, helps with breathing, controls the intake of oxygen

   (1 mark)

2. Which of the following best describes the effects of exercise on blood flow?

   ☐ **A** Blood shunted to working muscles, stroke volume increases, heart rate remains constant, cardiac output increases

   ☐ **B** Heart beats harder, blood shunted to working muscles, stroke volume increases, blood changes colour

   ☐ **C** Blood shunted to working muscles, cardiac output decreases, heart rate increases, plasma is reduced

   ☐ **D** Heart rate increases, heart beats harder, blood shunted to working muscles, cardiac output increases

   (1 mark)

3. Which of the following best describes white blood cells?

   ☐ **A** Fight infection, repair damage, produced in bone marrow and lymph cells, are erythrocytes

   ☐ **B** Repair damage, main function is to carry oxygen, produced in bone marrow and lymph cells, are leukocytes

   ☐ **C** Are leukocytes, fight infection, repair damage, produced in bone marrow and lymph cells

   ☐ **D** Contain haemoglobin, repair damage, produced in bone marrow and lymph cells, are red in colour

   (1 mark)

Short answer questions

4. Aerobic respiration is one way energy is released.

   (a) Explain what aerobic respiration is.

   (1 mark)

   (b) Which athletes utilize this form of respiration?

   (1 mark)

   (c) Give the formula for this form of respiration.

   (1 mark)

   (Total 3 marks)

5. What are the immediate effects of exercise on the circulatory system?

   (3 marks)

6. What are the effects of regular exercise and training on the circulatory system?

   (3 marks)

7. What are the long-term benefits of exercise on the circulatory system?

   (3 marks)

8. How do red blood cells help in exercise?

   (3 marks)

9. After what type of exercise does oxygen debt occur?

   (1 mark)

Longer answer question

10. Describe anaerobic respiration using the correct formula. Link this to sporting examples and any issues that may occur including timing.

    (4 marks)

11. What is the importance of monitoring and recording pulse rates whilst training?

    (8 marks)

12. Why is it necessary to give the body a chance to recover after exercise?

    (6 marks)

3.1.1 ～ The range of physical activities and the different roles that the active participant can choose from

3.1.1d The demands of performance: characteristics and benefits of leisure and recreation

What you will learn about in this topic:

1 — Leisure
2 — Recreation
3 — Physical recreation
4 — Outdoor recreation
5 — Lifetime sports

Leisure and recreation can help a person achieve a balanced, healthy lifestyle. A person can choose to take part in a competitive sport or alternatively, a non-competitive leisure pursuit. The different opportunities non-competitive physical activities offer can provide a person with a lifetime of participation in sport.

1 — Leisure

Leisure time is the portion of the day a person has when they are free from the everyday duties of life such as work, study or child care and can do anything they choose. In this time, a person can voluntarily participate in physical activity or sport for pleasure and enjoyment. Although every one is different, a day can be split up approximately into time spent:

- sleeping, eating or carrying out bodily functions
- travelling
- working or studying
- domestic duties
- leisure time.

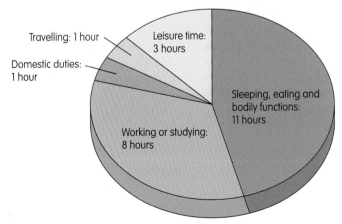

Approximate guide to how a person's day is filled.

2 — Recreation

Recreational opportunities give a person time to relax and actively take part in pursuits leading to a healthy lifestyle. **Recreation** provides a diversion from the normal day-to-day routine and can be amusing, relaxing or stimulating. Taking part in these types of activities is purely for fun and can be pursued individually or in a group. For example, a person who enjoys walking could join the Ramblers Association and follow recognized routes with other people who have the same interest.

There are many benefits to taking part in non-competitive activities:

- General fitness can be increased.
- Activities are not generally stressful on the body's cardiorespiratory and skeletal systems.
- Can be suitable for all age ranges.
- Participation can carry on throughout life.
- Group activities can provide social benefits by meeting and carrying out the activity with others.
- Completing activities can be done at the individual's pace.
- Being non-competitive can be appealing in itself.
- Some activities may specifically benefit health and fitness, for example, cardiovascular endurance.
- May involve club activities, which can motivate a person to regularly participate.

Active challenge

As a class, get into groups and think of three active, non-competitive pursuits a person can take part in during their leisure time. Exchange one of your ideas with someone else in another group. When you have ten activities, stop and record them in your workbook.

3 — Physical recreation

Taking part in a physical activity for recreation rewards the participant intrinsically rather than extrinsically. Intrinsic rewards are about how a person feels inside as a result of the physical pursuit and not about the league position, financial gain or how many trophies are won through sport, which are all extrinsic rewards.

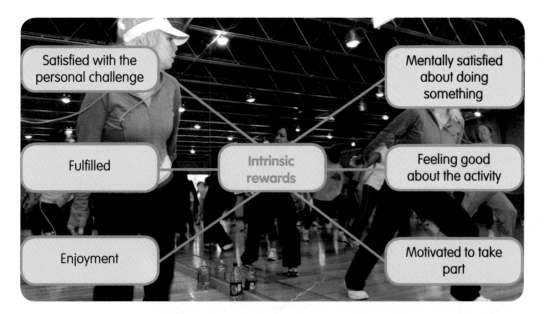

Satisfied with the personal challenge	Mentally satisfied about doing something
Fulfilled	Intrinsic rewards	Feeling good about the activity
Enjoyment	Motivated to take part

Active challenge

Think of different types of physical recreational pursuits. Decide on reasons why you would pursue that activity yourself. Share your views with three other people to build up your bank of reasons.

4 — Outdoor recreation

Outdoor recreation includes activities associated with challenges in the natural environment. Opportunities for outdoor recreation may be found locally or may require travel to parts of the country, or the world, providing specialized areas for these pursuits.

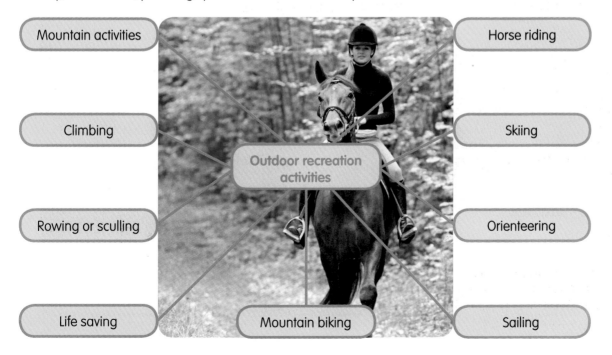

Mountain activities	Horse riding
Climbing	Skiing
	Outdoor recreation activities	
Rowing or sculling	Orienteering
Life saving	Mountain biking	Sailing

Taking part in outdoor recreation is geared towards fun, relaxation and stimulation, but, as with any involvement with nature, there is an element of danger so preparation is vital. For safety reasons, it is important that anyone pursuing outdoor recreation is ready for the challenges so they should:

- have specialist knowledge if necessary
- have experience appropriate to the challenge
- have the ability to use associated equipment effectively in any condition
- be able to make judgements under pressure
- be physically able to deal with different conditions
- be prepared to use a contingency plan.

5 — Lifetime sports

Certain activities can be carried on throughout life and are often non-contact sports. Non-contact sports often rely on judgement and accuracy, such as golf or bowls. In golf the handicap system creates a level playing field for all competitors – even if a person drives the ball a shorter distance, due to skill or age, their handicap compensates for this, enabling them to play in the same competition as other golfers of a different standard. Many sports have age categories. By grouping people of a similar age together a more balanced competition is possible. Athletics is a prime example of this type of grouping. For example, the Welsh Masters Cross-country Championships includes races for the 40 to 69 age group and for veterans aged 70 and over.

Continues to reach new physical and mental levels, such as in yoga

Keeps fit, maintaining a healthy lifestyle, which may prolong life

Keeps their mind focused and active with rules, procedures and new techniques

Puts into practise knowledge and understanding built up over the years

By pursuing sport throughout life, a person:

Remains determined to do well

Has the chance to enjoy the sport and be competitive through participation in different age groups

Works at their own pace

Keeps in social contact with others of similar interest

Summary

Changes in lifestyle over recent years have brought about a rise in leisure pursuits. People now have more control over their leisure time than ever before. Many people set aside time in their day or week for exercise. To help meet this increased demand for sports facilities, both the public and private sector have increased the amount of amenities available. Choosing physical recreation to fill available leisure time can provide a person with an active pursuit for the rest of their life.

Exam questions

Multiple-choice questions

1. Which of the following best shows the division of an average person's day?

   ☐ A Sleeping, eating, bodily functions = 11 hours; work, school = 8 hours; domestic duties = 1 hour; free time = 3 hours; travel = 1 hour

   ☐ B Sleeping, eating, bodily functions = 9 hours; work, school = 8 hours; domestic duties = 3 hours; free time = 3 hours; travel = 2 hours

   ☐ C Sleeping, eating, bodily functions = 12 hours; work, school = 4 hours; domestic duties = 1 hour; free time = 6 hours; travel = 1 hour

   ☐ D Sleeping, eating, bodily functions = 7 hours; work, school = 10 hours; domestic duties = 4 hours; free time = 2 hours; travel = 1 hour

   (1 mark)

2. Which of the following activities are non-competitive recreational pursuits?

   ☐ A Yoga, surfing, walking, aerobics, athletics

   ☐ B Climbing, orienteering, sailing, rowing, horse riding

   ☐ C Aerobics, walking, yoga, dancing, life saving

   ☐ D Orienteering, tennis, mountain biking, skiing, rowing

   (1 mark)

Short answer questions

3. Describe **two** leisure or recreational activities that are non-competitive.

   (2 marks)

4. Choose a non-competitive activity and state what the benefits are of taking part in that activity.

   (2 marks)

5. Describe what intrinsic rewards physical recreation can supply.

   (3 marks)

Longer answer questions

6. What are the benefits of continuing a lifetime of participation in sports?

   (4 marks)

7. Many people take part in outdoor activities. Describe the reasons why people are attracted to these activities.

   (6 marks)

3.1.2 ~ Linking physical activity with diet, work and rest for personal health and a balanced healthy lifestyle

3.1.2a Health, fitness and a healthy active lifestyle

What you will learn about in this topic:

1 — Fitness as one aspect of general health
2 — The adoption of a healthy active lifestyle
3 — Fitness components serving the body

1 — Fitness as one aspect of general health

The World Health Organization (WHO) gives the following definition for **health**: 'a state of complete mental, physical and social well-being, not simply the absence of disease or infirmity'.

Fitness is therefore one aspect of general health along with mental and social well-being, and a freedom from illness or infirmity.

For a person to be classed as healthy they have to have developed all the following components:

- **physical** well-being, which includes fitness – the ability to meet the demands of the environment with same comfort and without stress
- **mental** well-being – being able to concentrate and control emotions
- **social** well-being – being able to make and keep friends.

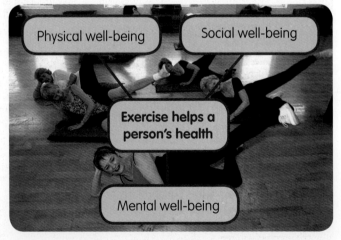

Physical well-being

Social well-being

Exercise helps a person's health

Mental well-being

Differences between health and fitness and how they are related

Health requires physical, social and mental well-being components and requires a person to have a balance of all these areas. Fitness concentrates on the physical. Training the body to meet the demands of a sport, by increasing the specific components required in that activity, will lead to fitness for that event. To be successful in that event requires fitness but also health. An athlete needs mental well-being to compete with the necessary levels of determination, concentration and self-belief. To work in a team, cooperating, supporting and encouraging others, needs social well-being. So, although fitness and health are different they are reliant on each other for maximum success.

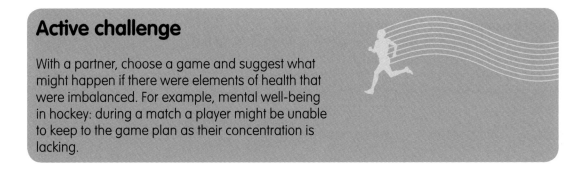

Active challenge

With a partner, choose a game and suggest what might happen if there were elements of health that were imbalanced. For example, mental well-being in hockey: during a match a player might be unable to keep to the game plan as their concentration is lacking.

Physical well-being

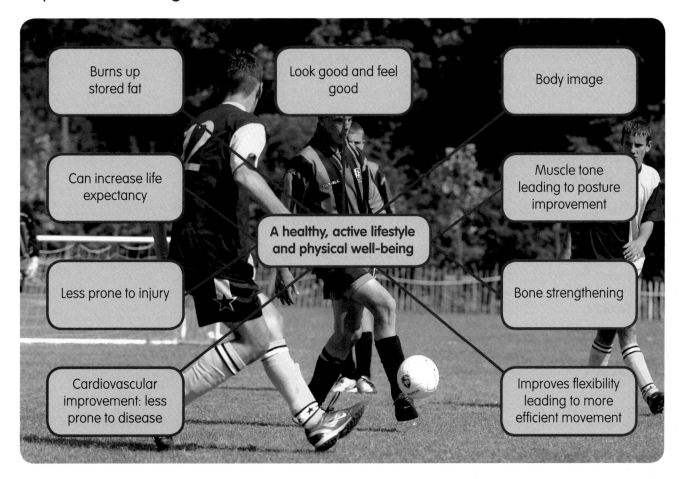

Burns up stored fat

Look good and feel good

Body image

Can increase life expectancy

Muscle tone leading to posture improvement

A healthy, active lifestyle and physical well-being

Less prone to injury

Bone strengthening

Cardiovascular improvement: less prone to disease

Improves flexibility leading to more efficient movement

Burns up stored fat
Exercise will put extra demands on the body. In turn, body fat will be burnt off, ultimately changing the shape of the person. Exercise at the correct level burns calories and as long as the dietary intake remains the same, a person may lose weight with the extra activity.

Look good and feel good
The effect of fat burning and the improvement it has on the shape of the body can in turn make a person feel good about themselves.

Body image

The changes to the body shape and the body's condition will not only change a person's feelings towards themselves but can affect the opinions of others towards them too.

Muscle tone and posture improvement

With regular exercise the muscles become toned. This is a tightening of the muscles in a state of readiness to work. The more muscles are toned the more they can do their job properly, which in turn can improve posture. Depending on the type of training programme, the shape and size of the muscle will begin to develop. Many people want greater muscle definition. 'Dynamic posture' can directly relate to the athlete in action and the application of correct technique.

Bone strengthening

Vigorous physical exercise stimulates the uptake of calcium to the bones. In young people this helps to build bone mass and in older people reduces the loss of bone mass. Bone mass density (BMD) is important as it reduces the risk of osteoporosis. Regular exercise can strengthen the bones as long as the effort gradually increases. There are two ways this can happen:

1. Impact: through the gravitational force of weight bearing exercises such as vigorous walking and jogging at the point of footstrike (when the foot contacts the ground) apply here.
2. Muscular pull: as muscles are attached to bone, those bones attached to the muscles involved in the exercise will be strengthened. Exercises such as rowing and weight training are examples of strengthening bone in this way.

A gymnast uses muscular pull in balances such as handstands and impact during landings such as during a tumble routine, and so has a high BMD.

A swimmer performs muscular pull without loading and therefore has good BMD, but not as high as a gymnast.

A weight trainer uses muscular pull and the stronger they are the greater their BMD. Weight training is a great way to increase BMD in the hip and spine.

Improves flexibility

Generally, the more a person exercises at suitable levels, the more readily the body is able to reach the demands of the exercise, making their movements more efficient. The body is able to perform tasks more efficiently with training and performers are able to reach their outcome with less effort. Training muscles and joints will increase strength and flexibility.

Cardiovascular improvement

The result of regular training on the heart and lungs improves the transport of blood around the body making it more effective and efficient. This allows a person to work more efficiently for longer. As the heart becomes stronger it can pump more blood with each beat. So, as you become fitter, the heart pumps enough blood but with fewer beats. Therefore, a fit person has a slower heart rate.

Less prone to injury

When exercise is carried out regularly the body begins to respond to the activity. The body may become stronger, more enduring and flexible. As a result, the body can work harder without becoming tired or breathless. With less fatigue and a stronger body, there may be less chance of injury.

Can increase life expectancy

When involved in physical activity, the stress a person may feel is forgotten for a time. This can have a positive effect on the functioning of the heart and so stress-related illnesses may be reduced, increasing the life expectancy of the person.

Research camed out by the Department of Medicine at the University of Dundee came to the following conclusions: 'Older people with better health habits live healthier for longer' and 'Regular physical activity in old age can rejuvenate physical capacity by 10–15 years.'

Task 1

1 – Study the information on physical well-being.

2 – Create a spider diagram of all the positive effects taking part in physical activity has on physical well-being.

> Use the Internet to find further information. Select a search engine and then type in 'physical activity' as a starting point.

Active challenge

With a partner, discuss what physical effects exercise has had on your body.

Social well-being

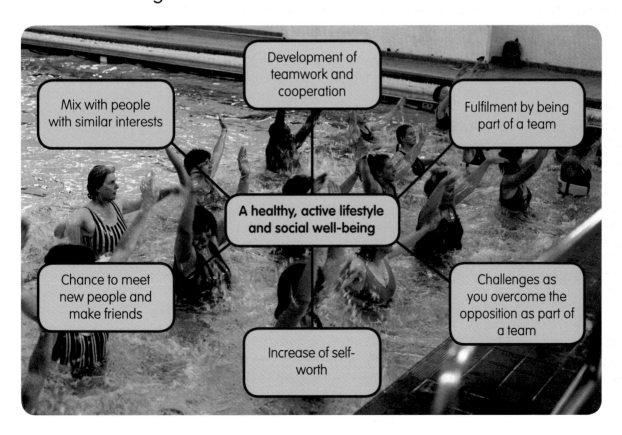

- Mix with people with similar interests
- Development of teamwork and cooperation
- Fulfilment by being part of a team
- A healthy, active lifestyle and social well-being
- Chance to meet new people and make friends
- Increase of self-worth
- Challenges as you overcome the opposition as part of a team

Development of teamwork and cooperation

Choosing a team or group activity relies on the individual's development of personal qualities. Situations may arise in group situations where certain demands may be put on its members. For example:

- being able to listen to instructions and carry them out
- being able to give instructions for others to carry out
- being able to think quickly for the good of the group
- being able to change and relay a change of strategy
- being able to encourage others to change what they are doing or to work harder.

Whatever the situation, cooperating and working for the whole group is necessary for success.

Fulfilment by being part of a team

Pursuing a physically active hobby may give a person the opportunity for regular exercise and so a healthier lifestyle. It can also fill a gap in their life that their work and family cannot. The activity chosen and the people they mix with may be such a change to their everyday experiences that they add a new dimension to their life.

Challenges as you overcome the opposition as part of a team

A person may start a sport as a novice performer, happy to learn new skills within a club, as part of a team. As their ability develops their confidence may grow in such a way that they desire competition and are confident to enter competitive events. This may develop further so they want to compete against other clubs too.

For some individuals, clearly set out goals and targets lead the performer through to higher levels of competition. Some people have the ability, desire and application to represent their local area, county and ultimately their country in their chosen sport.

Increase of self-worth

A good performance can lead to respect from peers. As a person learns, develops and applies their knowledge in an activity, personal confidence increases. Fellow players and peers also see this development: a good performance may earn respect for such achievements and further increase feelings of self-worth and popularity.

Chance to meet new people and make friends

Joining a group, club or society enables a person to increase the number of people they know and so increases the possibility of friendships being made.

Mix with people with similar interests

When people are in a team or a club for a particular activity there is a common interest. This provides an opportunity to share and develop ideas on a common theme in a social environment.

Mental well-being

Promotes the 'feel-good' factor

Can provide excitement

Gives enjoyment

Satisfaction of own performance

Improves self-esteem

Increases confidence in stressful situations

Personal development

Can relieve stress, tension and aggression

Develops a sense of being 'part of something'

Provides opportunity for success

Life's problems can be forgotten

Satisfaction of own performance
A person may take up physical exercise later in life for the first time since school or be a long-term regular exerciser. Whatever the circumstances, targets for development can be set so progress can be made. The satisfaction of reaching a higher standard through hard work, determination and effort can be the feeling that keeps a person continuing with exercise.

Promotes the 'feel-good' factor
The improvement to general body shape and posture can result in people feeling more positive about themselves. The fact that they have worked hard and got results increases their feeling of self-worth.

Can provide excitement
Some activities are attractive because they are exciting to perform. Skiing, climbing, skateboarding and BMX track racing are all examples of sports that attract people because of the thrill and adrenalin rush they provide.

Gives enjoyment
There are various reasons why a person enjoys an activity: it can be the physical challenge, the tactical battle to outwit the opponent, or the fun of playing as a team to achieve success. There is a sport suitable for everyone and those who seek exercise can usually find one they enjoy that satisfies them.

Can relieve stress, tension and aggression
Some activities are extremely competitive. These activities can act as a release valve for aggressive behaviour, possibly making a person's general life calmer.

Develops a sense of being 'part of something'

Many people look for physical activities that are team-, society-, or club-based. By doing so they automatically become integral members of a group and so part of that unit. A sense of belonging follows, satisfying the personal needs of the individual.

Provides opportunity for success

The challenging situations set by physical exercise can be the draw for a person's participation. Reaching a goal or winning an event can have a positive effect on a person, which encourages future participation. Many clubs arrange internal and external competitions. The competitive approach needed in some sports can link to qualities needed in everyday life. In the relatively safe environment of sport, a competitive, personal characteristic may develop that could help effectiveness at work.

Life's problems can be forgotten

Having a hobby, especially one which is physically demanding, is something to look forward to, and when taking part in a sport or activity, a person deals with a new set of challenges; this can take their mind off problems in their daily life.

Personal development

Starting a new interest can extend the knowledge of the individual. New tactics, skills, strategies and safety factors may have to be learnt. As the skills develop, personal pride in the new achievement is felt and so pleasure and satisfaction result.

Success in sport can lead to a positive and successful work life.

Increases confidence in stressful situations

As challenges become more demanding, greater resilience and application are required from the individual. As the new demands are met, a person's confidence will grow, safe in the knowledge that future demands will be met and overcome as before.

Improves self-esteem

Doing well and improving in a physical activity can enable a person to think favourably of themselves, thereby improving their self-esteem.

Active challenge

With a partner, link reasons for taking part in physical activity with the following people:

- a retired person
- a young mum
- a young, talented games player.

Task 2

1 – Link each sentence on 'health reasons for participating in physical activity' below with one of the following headings – physical, social or mental.

   a. My skills have improved in basketball and I have made the local county team; this makes me proud of my achievements.

   b. Despite my training sessions getting harder, I seem to be able to keep working for longer without tiring.

   c. I have met many new people since I joined a sports club.

   d. My pulse rate per minute is reducing; this means my heart is becoming more efficient.

   e. The rush of skiing downhill at maximum speed is what I really enjoy.

   f. I play right defender in the team; the right midfield player and I work well together in matches and we have a laugh after the game too.

2 – Copy out the table below in your workbook and write out each sentence under the correct heading: either 'physical', 'social' or 'mental'.

Physical	Social	Mental

2 — The adoption of a healthy active lifestyle

In order to be healthy you have to be physically fit. But as well as exercising in order to develop the physical component, you also need to be socially and mentally well adjusted in order to be healthy. If the social and mental components are lacking or underdeveloped you could still be physically fit, but not classed as healthy. Exercise is therefore the link between health and fitness.

Fitness is to do with the physical component, so your body may be functioning at a peak but the other aspects of health may not be present. The social component is to do with how well you interact, cooperate and deal with other people. The mental component is to do with how well you concentrate, think things through and approach life.

Your general health is the basis on which to train harder. A person who trains specifically for a sport has to 'raise the bar' of their state of good health and go beyond this level in order to keep improving their performance.

We all have the opportunity to lead a **healthy, active lifestyle** everyday. For example, going to work or school involves interaction with others for long periods of time, requiring a stable mental and social state.

Professional footballers continually train in order to improve their skills and fitness, which improves their health too.

71

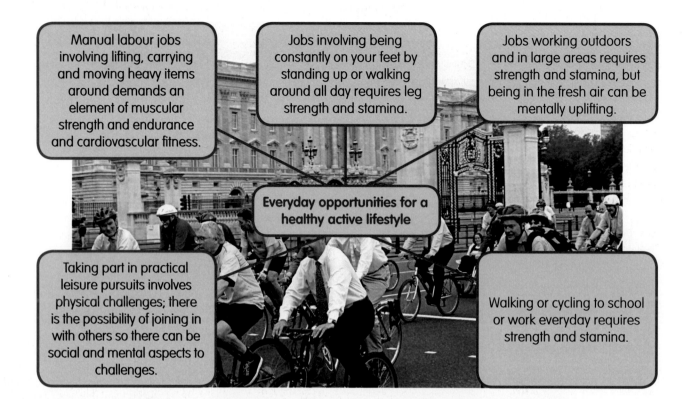

Manual labour jobs involving lifting, carrying and moving heavy items around demands an element of muscular strength and endurance and cardiovascular fitness.

Jobs involving being constantly on your feet by standing up or walking around all day requires leg strength and stamina.

Jobs working outdoors and in large areas requires strength and stamina, but being in the fresh air can be mentally uplifting.

Everyday opportunities for a healthy active lifestyle

Taking part in practical leisure pursuits involves physical challenges; there is the possibility of joining in with others so there can be social and mental aspects to challenges.

Walking or cycling to school or work everyday requires strength and stamina.

Active challenge

Give an example of specific jobs that would suit the job types stated above. Think of ideas of how people could be encouraged to cycle to work or school.

Give two examples of practical leisure pursuits you take part in and share your ideas with two other people.

Exercise is the key to being fit. A lack of exercise has an impact on a person's fitness and therefore their general health. For example:

Weight increase
If more calories are taken in than are burnt off, the result is weight gain. The effect on performance is that extra weight can increase fatigue as there is more fat to shift; fat takes up more space than muscle so the extra bulk may also get in the way and restrict flexibility. Following the guidelines for calorie intake can help a person keep the right balance.

A lack of exercise may cause an initial decrease in overall body weight, as muscle weighs more than fat. For performers who do not have a tendency to put on muscle and are relying on weight in their sport, such as forwards in rugby, this can be a disadvantage.

Less flexibility
If joints are not regularly moved to their full range then the ability to move them to their fullest extent will be lost. For example, this could inhibit a person rotating their arm in a tennis serve or kicking a ball in rugby or football.

Become breathless sooner

The body loses the ability to work for long periods of time without becoming breathless. A person will reach anaerobic capacity (VO_2 max) sooner. This is due to the cardiovascular system losing condition and being unable to work under certain levels of increased stress.

Aerobic capacity reduced

The body's ability to exchange gases efficiently reduces. A person will find that a lack of exercise prevents the body from working for long periods without tiring as the aerobic capacity is reduced. As a result, not enough oxygen reaches the working muscles so fatigue sets in. This is due to the insufficient transportation of oxygen to the working muscles making them tire, reducing skill levels and eventually preventing muscle contraction.

Loss of strength

Reduced stress on muscles allows them to become flaccid and weak. This gives rise to the saying 'use it or lose it'!

Task 3

For each of the effects of lack of exercise, give a detrimental effect each would have on a sporting example. Choose a different sport for each effect.

Key terms

Health – a state of complete mental, physical and social well-being

Physical – of the body

Mental – of the mind

Social – to do with the community and society

Healthy, active lifestyle – a lifestyle that contributes to physical, social and mental well-being, this includes regular physical activity

Summary

There are many advantages in following a healthy, active lifestyle. Physically, the body and its systems can increase in fitness and be able to meet the pressures of a more demanding environment. A stronger body and its systems could increase life expectancy. Socially there are opportunities to work as a team and meet different people. Mentally a person can develop through meeting the challenges of an active lifestyle by increasing their determination, courage, confidence and attitude.

3 — Fitness components serving the body

During physical activity the body must be able to cope with the demands put on it with ease and comfort and without stress. Fitness is the ability to meet the demands of the environment without undue stress or discomfort and still have energy left over for emergencies.

Because everyone has their own natural fitness level, everyone will have different requirements to maintain their own minimum level of fitness. If the demands of the environment become greater, the body can be trained to meet those demands.

Every sporting activity requires a different level of physical fitness ability. Some activities depend on the development of only a few fitness components; others need a combination of them all.

Having the minimum level of fitness will allow a person to meet the demands of everyday life without tiring. Fitness, therefore, is concerned with the physical condition of a person. Walking to the bus stop and completing tasks at work are both actions that should be completed without exhaustion. Each person has a different set of physical demands in their day, so each person's minimum level of fitness is different. If a person does not exercise and does not keep each of the components in good condition then daily tasks will become more difficult to complete.

Fitness and the environment

Everyone's level of fitness will be different as it is dependant on how people go about their daily lives and what particular sports they play. To take part in any sport requires a combination of fitness and performance. For example, a person might be fit to play badminton, but not fit in the same way to play tennis. Each activity has its own set of requirements that an individual must meet in order to succeed. As exercise is a series of physical activities that improve the body, the exercises in a training session will be different in order to fit the requirements of the particular sporting activity to be played. A person's performance will improve by choosing and working on the most appropriate exercises for a specific activity.

Different levels and combinations of fitness components that serve the body are required, but it is how well they are put into operation that will affect performance. The following are five of the main fitness components:

1. **Agility** – the ability to change direction quickly and still keep control of the body, such as dodging to escape a marker in netball.
2. **Balance** – the ability to keep the body stable whether still, moving or in a different shape by keeping the centre of gravity over the base, for example, a gymnast holding a handstand.
3. **Coordination** – the ability to use two or more parts of the body at the same time, such as striking the shuttle in badminton.
4. **Reaction time** – the time it takes to respond to a stimulus, for example, adjusting body position to tackle an opponent in rugby.
5. **Timing** – the ability to judge the time and place of an object's arrival and then to select, plan and execute appropriate movements. For example, in tennis, when watching an opponent's shot, moving into place and completing a successful return.

Daily activities demand different levels of fitness.

In order for any involvement in physical activity to be of any value to a person's physical fitness, the **FID** requirements must be met:

- Frequency – taking part in physical activity at least three to five times a week.
- Intensity – during these sessions the heart rate must be raised to above 60 per cent of its maximum (maximum heart rate = 220 – age).
- Duration – the heart rate should be raised to this level and sustained for no less than 20 minutes.

These requirements can also be referred to as FIT (frequency, intensity and time).

Task 4

1 – Consider your daily routine and the different fitness demands they have.

2 – For each hour between 8am and 4pm, state what daily activity you are doing and what level of fitness is required for that activity. Break each hour into 15 minute chunks.

> For example, 11am–11.15am – break – practice basketball shots on the playground – moderate level of fitness.

Fitness components are used to different degrees and at different times according to the demands made of them by a performer. Each component can be used separately or in combination.

The following are the other six main fitness components:
1. **Strength**
2. **Speed**
3. **Power**
4. **Cardiovascular endurance and stamina**
5. **Muscular endurance and stamina**
6. **Flexibility and suppleness**

Strength

Muscular strength is the ability of muscles to apply force and overcome resistance.

Strength can be measured by the ability to lift the maximum weight possible in one attempt. In itself, strength can be used to overpower an opponent. A player who can combine strength with speed can create power, which is especially useful when playing a forehand drive down the line in tennis, in order to pass an opponent at the net, for instance.

Having poor strength may prevent a player shooting with the required amount of power to beat a goalkeeper. In contact sports, such as judo, a weak player gives little resistance to an opponent with muscular strength.

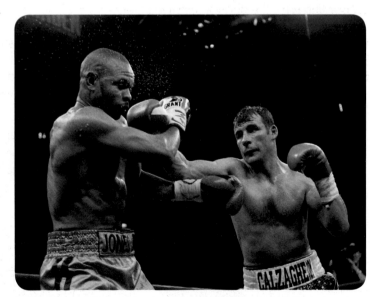
Jo Calzaghe uses his muscular strength to overpower Bernard Hopkins.

Active challenge

Make a list of sporting examples requiring strength. Compare your list with another class member and combine your ideas together.

> Look at the skills of the activity you have chosen. For example, jumping high for a ball shows leg strength.

A sportsperson uses different types of strength depending on the type of action required. Some sports can depend on one type of strength (such as tug of war), but most rely on a combination of different types. The type of strength needed for an activity needs to be identified and developed through training. There are three main types of strength:

- dynamic strength
- explosive strength
- static strength.

Dynamic strength

Dynamic strength uses prolonged, moving muscular contractions. Rowing is a good example as it shows the rhythmical pulling action of the oars and the prolonged period of activity. Middle- and long-distance runners and games players also benefit from this type of strength. Training for dynamic strength develops cardiovascular and cardiorespiratory systems and increases power and endurance. This type of strength is used in events that take a long period of time to complete, such as marathon running. There is a greater possibility of injury for the athlete though as the body is moving whilst the muscular contractions are taking place.

Rowing is a good example of dymanic strength.

Explosive strength

Explosive strength comes about when a burst of maximum effort is used, such as in athletic field events, striking a ball in tennis or kicking a penalty in football. This type of strength uses anaerobic respiration.

Static strength

Static strength takes place when the muscle length stays the same: it is used for stabilizing parts of the body or holding the body steady so that movement can take place elsewhere. For example, rugby players in a scrum and gymnasts in a balance use this type of strength. Static strength does not develop power or muscular endurance and the cardiovascular and cardiorespiratory systems are not improved. Only few sports require this type of contraction alone.

A jump in basketball and a return tennis shot are good examples of explosive strength.

Rugby players in a scrum and gymnasts both require static strength.

Task 5

1 – Study the information on static, explosive and dynamic strength.

2 – Think of two more examples for each type of strength.

Speed

Speed is the fastest rate at which a person can complete a task or cover a distance. Speed is necessary for almost all sports, whether a person is sprinting or playing a pass with pace to beat an opponent. Even what seems like a tranquil sport, such as fishing, will need speed at the 'strike' to secure a catch. As sporting activities vary so to do the areas of the body requiring speed – the sprinter will need leg speed whereas the shot-putter's arm speed is crucial to success.

Power

Power is the ability to apply a combination of strength and speed in an action. For power to be applied successfully to a sporting action there has to be a well-developed level of strength and speed. Power could be necessary throughout the activity, such as sprinting, or utilized at certain times as in when making a powerful shot is necessary for success.

Sprinters require speed of leg movement.

Combining strength and speed results in power, essential for the shot-putter Valerie Vili.

Task 6

1 – Study the information on speed and power.

2 – Chose a sport of your choice and link four situations in the game where speed and power are necessary.

> For example, speed is needed in hockey at a short corner; when the ball is stopped the player shooting has to make a quick movement and strike the ball before the defenders rush to block.

Cardiovascular endurance and stamina

The cardiovascular system deals with the heart and blood vessels of the body. A cardiovascular system in good condition allows for efficient transportation of blood to the necessary parts of the body in order that the body can meet the extra demands of exercise.

In training, if the cardiovascular system is not fit then the ability to keep working is reduced and so the required skill level is less likely to be reached. In competition, fatigue and breathlessness would prevent a person playing to the required standard or even continuing the activity in some instances.

To exercise effectively for any length of time, without tiring or becoming less efficient, requires the training of the cardiorespiratory system. The better the heart and lungs work – the better a person's cardiovascular endurance and stamina – the more efficiently the body gets oxygen to the working muscles and removes waste products from the body.

Marathan runners like Emma Archer and Melanie Ellis need good cardiovascular endurance to transport oxygen to their working muscles.

Active challenge

With a partner, make a list of sporting activities that require cardiovascular endurance and stamina.

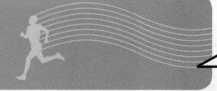

> Use the length of time of the activity to help your choices.

Muscular endurance and stamina

Muscular endurance and stamina is the muscles' ability to move weight over a long period without tiring and losing effectiveness. Muscular endurance is essential for long-distance events such as 10,000m racing. The body is able to keep working for a long time without tiring and so the performer has more chance of winning.

Good muscular endurance prevents Jody Cundy's body tiring quickly.

Flexibility and suppleness

Flexibility is movement at a **joint** to its fullest range. With regular practice, the range of movement around a joint can get nearer to its maximum. Controlled use of the full range of movement available at a joint can allow for the execution of the correct technique, improving performance and lessening the risk of injury. Where resistance to a force is necessary, the muscles must be strong enough to prevent overextension beyond the fullest range. For example, players in a rugby scrum must have muscles strong enough to prevent overextension of their shoulders.

A knowledge of the skeletal system – bones and joints – and how they work together with the muscular system will show their role in allowing flexibility.

Louis Smith needs to move his joints through the full range to be effective.

Bones

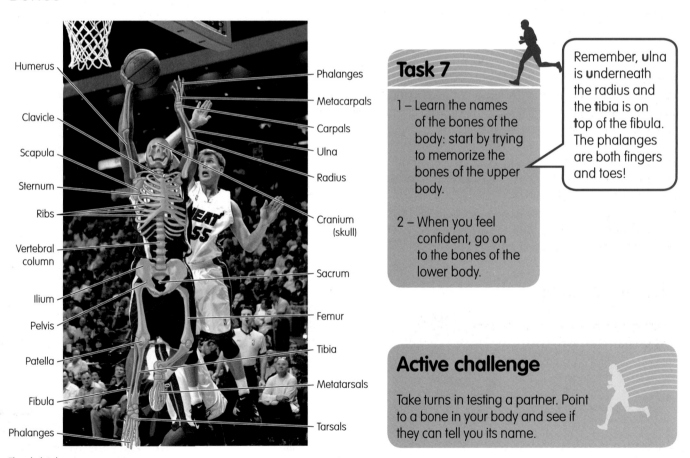

The skeletal system.

Task 7

1 – Learn the names of the bones of the body: start by trying to memorize the bones of the upper body.

2 – When you feel confident, go on to the bones of the lower body.

Remember, **u**lna is **u**nderneath the radius and the **t**ibia is on **t**op of the fibula. The phalanges are both fingers and toes!

Active challenge

Take turns in testing a partner. Point to a bone in your body and see if they can tell you its name.

Bones have a number of functions: they protect the delicate parts of the body such as the heart and lungs; they give the body shape and support the rest of the skeleton, for example, vertebrae support the head; the skeleton is joined together to allow movement and red and white blood cells are made in bone marrow.

Joints

The meeting of one or more bones creates a joint. There does not have to be movement there. Freely moveable joints are called **synovial joints**. These types of joint are common in the human body and are important to the sportsperson as they allow the greatest range of movement and flexibility. The components of synovial joints have built-in safety factors to help guard against injury. These joints are designed to reduce wear and tear, absorb shock and reduce friction. These factors are especially important when performing skills at pace and with power.

The following are examples of synovial joints:

- ball and socket
- hinge
- pivot
- condyloid
- gliding.

Active challenge

Using the Internet, find examples of synovial joints and their components.

Each type of synovial joint is different. This is due to where it is in the body, how many bones are located at the joint and the types of bones involved. Each different type of joint will allow a different type of movement and range of flexibility.

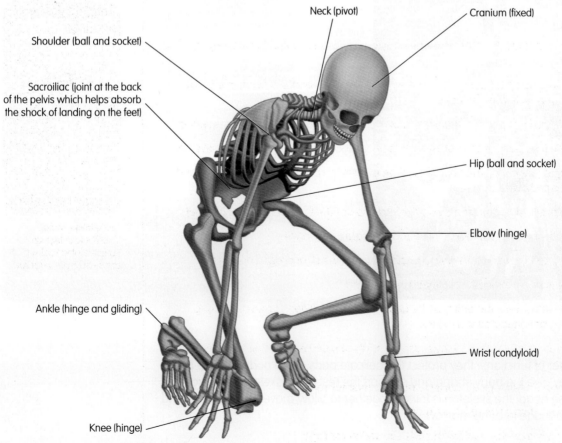

Neck (pivot)

Cranium (fixed)

Shoulder (ball and socket)

Sacroiliac (joint at the back of the pelvis which helps absorb the shock of landing on the feet)

Hip (ball and socket)

Elbow (hinge)

Ankle (hinge and gliding)

Wrist (condyloid)

Knee (hinge)

The main synovial joints of the body.

Whenever a sportsperson is involved in an activity, they are relying on the joints of the body to help the action. For example:

- In cricket, the bowlers rely on the joints of the fingers to move forward and spin the ball.
- Playing a forehand drive in tennis involves the shoulder rotating as the racket is swung forward.
- Volleyball players rely on the joints of the leg to cushion their landing after performing a smash.

Hinge joints – metacarpals and phalanges in fingers – spinning a ball.

Ball and socket joint – scapula and humerus in the shoulder – throwing a ball in rugby.

Task 8

1 – Use the examples on this page to help you create your own joint – bone – action chains using different types of bones.

2 – Remember to include: type of joint, type of bone, location of the bone and the linked action relating to a sporting activity.

Gliding – ankle – passing the ball.

Condyloid – wrist – golfer at 'wrist break' phase of swing.

Key terms

Agility – the ability to change the position of the body quickly and to control the movement of the whole body easily

Balance – the ability to keep the body stable whether still, moving or in a different shape by keeping the centre of gravity over the bone

Coordination – the ability to perform complex moves using two or more body parts together

Reaction time – the time between the presentation of a stimulus and the onset of a movement

Timing – the ability to judge the time and place of an objects arrival and then select, plan and execute appropriate movements

FID – frequency, intensity, duration (can also be referred to as FIT – frequency, intensity, time)

Strength – the ability of muscles to apply force and overcome resistance

Speed – the fastest rate at which an individual can complete a task or cover a distance

Power – the ability to apply strength and speed in an action

Cardiovascular endurance – the ability of the heart to provide oxygen to muscles during physical activity for a prolonged period of time

Muscular endurance and stamina – the muscles' ability to move weight over long periods of time without getting tired

Flexibilitys and suppleness – joints' ability to move to their full range

Joint – the point where two or more bones meet

Synovial joints – freely movable joints with ends covered in cartilage

Hinge joint – femur tibia/fibula in legs and humerus/ulna/radius in arms – swinging a racket.

Muscles

Voluntary muscles, also known as skeletal or striated muscles, are important to the movement and flexibility of the body. These muscles attach to the skeleton and as they pull, movement at a joint occurs.

Task 9

Learn the names of the muscles of the body. Start by trying to memorize the muscles of the upper body. When you feel confident remembering these, go on to the muscles of the lower body.

Link the muscles with a bone you already know, this may help you to remember them.

The following diagram gives the name, location and action of muscles:

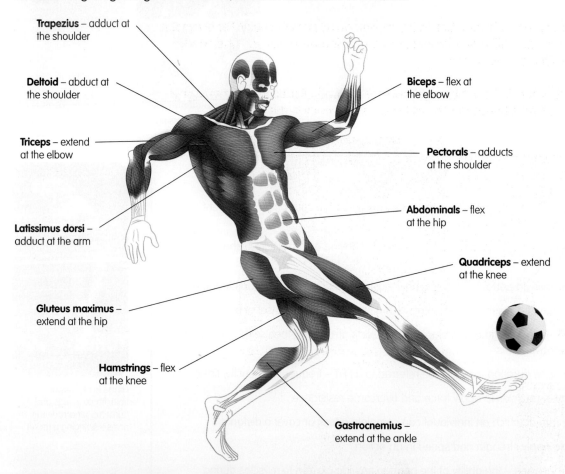

Trapezius – adduct at the shoulder

Deltoid – abduct at the shoulder

Triceps – extend at the elbow

Latissimus dorsi – adduct at the arm

Gluteus maximus – extend at the hip

Hamstrings – flex at the knee

Biceps – flex at the elbow

Pectorals – adducts at the shoulder

Abdominals – flex at the hip

Quadriceps – extend at the knee

Gastrocnemius – extend at the ankle

Active challenge

Work with a partner and take turns testing each other. Point to a muscle in your body and see if your partner can tell you its name.

Task 10

Link each of the muscles listed below with a sporting action and example. Use the examples of movement from the muscle diagram and the photographs on page 81 to help you.

- biceps
- triceps
- deltoid
- pectorals
- trapezius
- abdominals
- gluteus maximus
- quadriceps
- hamstrings
- gastrocnemius
- latissimus dorsi

> For example: abdominals – raise the knee so flexing at the hips – used prior to take-off in the high jump.

Flexion takes place when the angle at a joint decreases. This happens when arms bend at the elbow in preparation to make a chest pass.

Extension takes place when the angle at a joint increases. This happens when a tennis player in the service action makes contact with the ball with their arm at full stretch.

Abduction takes place when limbs and bones are moved away from the body. For example, a gymnast performing a vault will reach forward, moving their arms away from their body, reaching for contact with the vaulting box.

Adduction takes place when limbs are brought towards the body. For example, a swimmer performing the butterfly stroke brings their arms towards their body in the pull phase.

Is the right leg flexed or extended?

Is the arm adducting or abducting when the ball is brought into the body?

As the leg is driven back, is it flexed or extended?

Are the arms adducting or abducting in the reach phase of the row?

Muscles' relation to bone

Voluntary muscle is attached to the bone by tendons. The muscle at the point where it moves is called the **insertion** and at the point where it is fixed is called the **origin**. For example, when the arm flexes at the elbow the movement is at the elbow, so the fixed point – the origin – is the shoulder. The following diagram shows flexing at the elbow:

The origin for the triceps and biceps is at the shoulder.

Insertion for the triceps and biceps is at the elbow.

The insertion is at the elbow and the origin is at the shoulder.

Task 11

1 – Copy the picture of the arm above, showing the muscles clearly.

2 – Label all of the parts.

3 – Add in the origin and insertion of the muscle in another colour.

Muscles are attached to bone by tendons; it is this attachment that creates an anchor for the muscles to pull and so move the body.

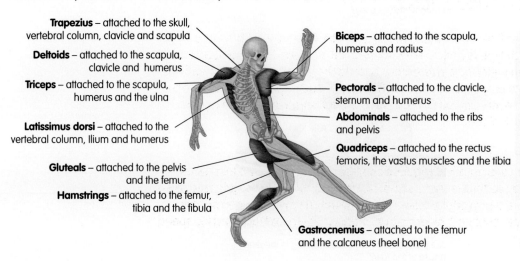

Trapezius – attached to the skull, vertebral column, clavicle and scapula

Deltoids – attached to the scapula, clavicle and humerus

Triceps – attached to the scapula, humerus and the ulna

Latissimus dorsi – attached to the vertebral column, Ilium and humerus

Gluteals – attached to the pelvis and the femur

Hamstrings – attached to the femur, tibia and the fibula

Biceps – attached to the scapula, humerus and radius

Pectorals – attached to the clavicle, sternum and humerus

Abdominals – attached to the ribs and pelvis

Quadriceps – attached to the rectus femoris, the vastus muscles and the tibia

Gastrocnemius – attached to the femur and the calcaneus (heel bone)

Task 12

Study the diagram above. Look on the Internet and for each example, find out which bones are attached forming the origin and which are attached forming the insertion.

> For example, biceps are attached to the scapula and the humerus (origin) and the radius (insertion).

Antagonistic pairs of muscles

The body is moved by muscle groups, not by individual muscles. Muscles work in pairs. As muscles can only pull, they need to work in partnership so movement can occur. Muscles are attached to bone at fixed points and produce movement of body parts in relation to each other. Understanding the relationship of muscle to bone is important when looking at movement and flexibility. The pulling muscle is called the **prime mover** (agonist). When a muscle pulls, it contracts or becomes shorter. The muscle that relaxes is the **antagonist**, and opposes the prime mover. When a muscle relaxes it lengthens. When muscles work as a pair, their ability to relax and contract affects the range of flexibility at the joint.

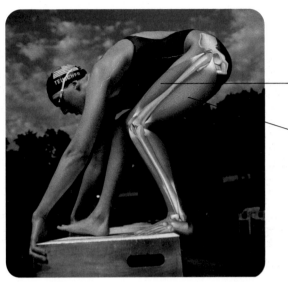

Quadriceps are relaxed.

Hamstrings contract.

Muscles work in pairs. Here, the quadriceps and hamstrings are working.

Task 13

In your own words, describe how muscles work.

Fast and slow twitch muscle fibres

There are two different types of fibre in muscles. There are fast twitch muscle fibres and slow twitch muscle fibres. Each type is better suited to different activities. Every person has a natural combination of both in their body. This amount cannot be changed, although with the correct training, improvements can be made to the efficiency of each type. Games and racket sport players will have a fairly even distribution of them both, but some will have a higher percentage of fast twitch muscle fibres.

Fast twitch muscle fibres

When the nervous system decides an event requires short bursts of energy, the fast twitch muscle fibres are used. These are for the more explosive activities which need quick reactions. They contract fast and produce a powerful action. They have only a limited oxygen supply and so tire quickly. Under a microscope they are white in colour. They are best used for speed events, throwing and jumping.

Slow twitch muscle fibres

The nervous system can detect when an event is slow and prolonged and will activate the slow twitch muscle fibres. These are more suited to endurance activities. They can contract many times and stay efficient over long periods. They have a very good oxygen supply, which gives them their energy. Under a microscope they are red in colour. They are suited to events that take a long time to complete, such as long-distance running, cycling and swimming.

Explosive events such as the discus, performed here by Shelley Drew, rely on fast twitch muscle fibres.

Slow twitch muscle fibres are needed in long-distance events, as demonstrated by Olympic gold medallist, Nicole Cooke.

Task 14

Make two columns headed fast twitch muscle fibres and slow twitch muscle fibres and list four main points for each type of fibre.

Active challenge

In pairs, take turns in naming a sport. Your partner should say whether it needs fast or slow twitch muscle fibres for greatest success.

Muscle tone and posture

Muscle tone is voluntary muscles' readiness to work and be in a prepared state to react. Each muscle has slight tension, waiting to be used. A person's muscles never completely rest. The nearest they come to resting is when a person is asleep. The muscles' state of slight contraction helps with posture. The toned state of the abdominals helps keep in place the internal organs of that area.

Posture relates to the way the body is supported by the muscles, whether standing, sitting or moving. In some activities where the look of the performer is important to the result, such as gymnastics, diving and dance, good posture is vital. It increases the marks awarded to the performer and enhances the performance. When muscles are trained, their tone increases and this can help posture. Having poor muscle posture and tone can affect the balance and agility of a person as their muscles are out of alignment and do not contract efficiently to change direction quickly.

There are several advantages to having good posture:

- When breathing, there is more room for the lungs to expand and operate; round shoulders make it hard to breathe properly.
- The heart needs to be given enough space to function properly and beat without hindrance.
- The digestive system works well if it has the space to do its job properly.
- Bone alignment prevents strain and injury – poor posture can strain the bones, tendons and ligaments, such as fallen arches.
- There is more energy available when the body is in alignment, as the muscles do not have to work so hard to keep the body stable. (Like carrying a ladder, if it is vertical it is easy to carry, if it is at an angle more energy is required to carry it.)
- Maintaining good posture can help the shape of a person. In turn, self-esteem is increased if a person feels good about the way they look. A person standing or sitting well can give a good impression to others.

Task 15

1 – Look carefully at the illustrations below showing two different postures. Describe what you see, thinking about the head, shoulder, stomach and hip positions.

2 – Complete a spider diagram which includes information on good muscle tone and posture.

Good posture.

Bad posture.

Key terms

Flexion – decreasing the angle at a joint

Extension – increasing the angle at a joint

Abduction – moving a limb or bone away from the body

Adduction – moving a limb or bone towards the body

Insertion – the point where a tendon attaches a muscle to bone where there is movement

Origin – the point where the tendon attaches the muscle to a fixed bone

Prime mover – contracting muscle that causes movement

Antagonist – a muscle whose action counteracts that of another muscle and so allowing movement

Summary

The fitness components can be applied to different physical activities. Some activities rely heavily on one component, whilst others need a combination of all of them. Fitness can be improved by increasing the frequency, intensity and duration (FID) of exercise undertaken. The variety of actions required in a physically active lifestyle relies on the bones, joints and muscles working together to allow movement and flexibility.

Exam questions

Multiple-choice questions

1. Health is:

   ☐ **A** The ability to meet the demands of the environment

   ☐ **B** Working towards improving all areas of the body

   ☐ **C** A state of complete physical fitness and calmness

   ☐ **D** A state of physical, mental and social well-being
   (1 mark)

2. Which of the following best describes why people take part in sport?

   ☐ **A** Gives enjoyment, encourages friendship, helps pay bills, encourages cooperation

   ☐ **B** Changes diet, gives enjoyment, provides excitement, encourages cooperation

   ☐ **C** Encourages friendship, gives enjoyment, provides excitement, encourages cooperation

   ☐ **D** Provides excitement, encourages friendship, is a training principle, encourages cooperation
   (1 mark)

3. Which of the following best describes physical effects of taking part in physical activity?

   ☐ **A** Strengthens bones, relieves stress, improves muscle tone, improves flexibility

   ☐ **B** Burns stored fat, strengthens bones, improves muscle tone, improves flexibility

   ☐ **C** Improves muscle tone, burns stored fat, encourages cooperation, improves flexibility

   ☐ **D** Improves flexibility, burns stored fat, strengthens bones, provides excitement
   (1 mark)

4. Which of the following bones are linked with throwing a ball?

   ☐ **A** Humerus, ulna, fibula

   ☐ **B** Metacarpals, tibia, radius

   ☐ **C** Phalanges, humerus, carpals

   ☐ **D** Scapula, sternum, femur
   (1 mark)

5. Which following statement best describes a joint?

   ☐ **A** A place where bones are close

   ☐ **B** Where several bones and muscles meet allowing movement

   ☐ **C** Where the production of movement occurs

   ☐ **D** Where two or more bones meet, but where there is not necessarily movement
   (1 mark)

Short answer questions

6. What are the consequences of being unfit on general health?
   (2 marks)

7. Explain the differences between fitness and health.
   (2 marks)

8. State **three** physical benefits of taking part in physical activity.
   (3 marks)

Longer answer questions

9. Agility helps both in daily life and sporting activities.

   (a) What is the definition of agility?
   (1 mark)

   (b) Link agility with a daily physical activity and a sporting activity.
   (2 marks)

   (c) Give a sporting example of agility in practice.
   (2 marks)

   (Total 5 marks)

3.1.2 ~ Linking physical activity with diet, work and rest for personal health and a balanced healthy lifestyle

3.1.2b Aspects of training

What you will learn about in this topic:

1 — Training considerations
2 — The principles of training
3 — Repetitions, sets, rest and recovery
4 — Monitoring and testing a training programme

1 — Training considerations

When a coach or athlete designs a fitness training session there are guidelines to keep to in order to ensure the training suits the performer and the desired results can be achieved. These guidelines are called 'principles of training' and are the rules to follow when exercising, to safely improve the body through physical activity.

Any training must consider the following:

• regularity
• moderation
• peaking.

Regularity

To make the body work harder than the minimum level of fitness, exercise should be repeated more regularly, with more intensity and for longer. For example, training sessions could be increased to five times a week instead of three. The intensity of the exercise could raise the pulse rate to 70 per cent of the maximum instead of 60 per cent to make the body work harder. The duration of the exercise could be 30 minutes rather than 20 minutes.

By adapting the training programme in this way it more than doubles the FID principles (frequency, intensity and duration) for the minimum level of fitness guideline (20 minutes for a minimum of three times a week). This is also known as FIT (frequency, intensity, time). Increasing training in this way takes an athlete to an even higher level of fitness.

Moderation

Reaching greater intensities of exercise is a gradual process. All athletes should find their own balance between exercises. If they train too little then progress will not be made, if they train too much then injury may occur. Moderation is crucial. Frequently changing the intensity will help to moderate training.

Peaking

The effects of training will create peaks in an individual's performance – the point at which they reach their best possible level of performance. Athletes try to peak at the time of an event. However, an athlete can plan for the peaks in their performance. This needs careful consideration, but when an athlete does reach their peak, they are physically, mentally and emotionally at their best. After this peak period has passed, loss of peak performance during an event may result in poor form and bad results.

Athletes aim to reach their peak performance in competitions.

2 — The principles of training

The principles of training are rules to follow when undertaking physical activity programmes to improve fitness. Each person has a different reason for exercising. It may be for leisure or competitive reasons, or for professional or personal pride. A person trains to improve performance and their body. When the principles are applied, improvements in cardiovascular and respiratory condition, fitness, strength, endurance and skill might be expected. For example, top-class athletes have a final competition in mind when training so their training process is systematically planned so they reach a peak performance to coincide with that event. A person training for general fitness would have their personal goals in mind, which could include weight loss, an increase in distance covered or ability to train for longer.

The principles of training are:

- **Specificity** – matching training to the needs of the physical activity
- **Progression** – gradually increasing the stresses put on the body
- **Overload** – exercising the body more than normal
- **Reversibility** – when training stops, any gain to the body is lost.

Each of the principles show the way in which the body is affected by the degree and type of exercise undertaken. If these basic rules are to be adhered to, each stage should be followed and planned carefully. As everyone's fitness level differs, **systematic training** (training planned as a result of the effect of previous training on an individual) must take into account the **individual needs** of the performer. An understanding of body systems is vital: knowing the existing capabilities of the heart, lungs and muscles sets the degree of difficulty of the training plan. For training to succeed, the degree of difficulty or intensity is set at a personal level. Setting the demands and intensity of the exercise at the right level ensures it is safe for the performer. If the demands are set too low, there will be no improvement, but if set too high, injuries might occur.

Task 1

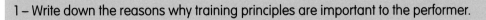

1 – Write down the reasons why training principles are important to the performer.

2 – What considerations should be made when creating a training schedule?

Details of the principles

Each of the main principles of training influences the training of the performer in a different way. Good training takes into consideration all of the principles and their effects on the body. These principles are essential to the planning of a systematic training programme so that an individual can improve their fitness. The FID components are directly linked with the overload training principle and are also key to developing fitness.

Specificity

This principle requires an understanding of the needs of the activity. For example, a goalkeeper will need to include lots of reaction work in their training in order to be able to perform well in a game. When applying this principle, the activity is usually practised at the pace required for the sport. If a person trains too slowly then their skills will only be reproduced at the slower pace and the action will be unable to match the requirements of the game. At a school practice for your team, if you repeat the skills slowly then when you get to the game the other team may be quicker than you are. So, speed up your practices!

The actions in training should copy the actions used in the game. If a person needs good leg strength, simply making them strong may not be enough. A cyclist will train their legs whilst cycling in a different way from a long-distance runner: both need muscular strength, but the method of training is different. In order to become a better swimmer a person needs to spend most of their time in the water!

Progression

Exercising at the same level of difficulty all the time will only maintain current fitness levels. As training starts to change a person's body tolerances, the same session will not have the same effect. An athlete's body needs to be gradually and systematically put under slightly more pressure to continue to improve. The need to increase the amount of difficulty of exercise gradually is reflected by the ease with which an athlete completes tasks for cardiovascular fitness; the same amount of exercise will not bring the pulse rate into the target zone. After about five to six weeks there may be a need to change the programme. A decreased resting heart rate also indicates improvement as it shows how much fitter a person is becoming.

Overload

The training principle of overload involves having the body work at a greater rate than normal and then gradually increasing the stress on the body as it adapts to the exercise training levels.

Muscle strength can be improved by making the muscles work harder than normal. Putting greater demands on the body by exercising can improve fitness. The point where exercise is demanding enough to have an effect on the body is called the **threshold of training** – where the pulse is raised higher than 60 per cent of its maximum.

Whether a person is training for muscular endurance or muscular strength, their aim is to train between 60 and 80 per cent of their maximum heart rate. This is the 'target zone'. Working between these levels will put enough stress on the athlete to bring about improvement. For older people the threshold of training decreases. Working at 50 per cent of their maximum heart rate will often have a positive effect on their cardiovascular fitness.

Meeting the FID requirements will ensure a performer meets the **minimum level of fitness**. Training can be adapted by changing any one or more of the FID (or FIT) principles.

FREQUENCY Frequency is the number of times exercise is undertaken in a week. The more times a person exercises the more often their body is put under stress. Three to five times a week is the recommended number of times exercise should be repeated to reach the minimum level of fitness. However, top-class sportspeople have to train a lot more frequently than this to achieve results good enough for their aspirations.

Monday 8–9am

But remember, the body also needs time to recover from training. Training very hard, every day, may be harmful even to a top-class athlete.

INTENSITY Intensity is the level of difficulty of the exercise. For instance, during cardiovascular fitness, your pulse rate can show you how intensely you are working.

Working in a target zone of 60 to 80 per cent of the maximum heart rate is the level where fitness will usually increase. When training for strength the intensity is calculated in the same way. A person trains within the target zone by finding the maximum weight they can lift and working between 60 and 80 per cent of that weight. As the amount of weight lifted increases with training, this adds to the intensity.

Monday 6–7pm

DURATION This is the length of time the exercise session lasts. Keeping your pulse at 60 to 80 per cent of its maximum for 20 minutes is the target. Warming-up is not included in the 20 minutes. The 20 minutes begins during the main activity when the pulse is at 60 per cent of its maximum.

Reversibility

Just as the body will increase in strength, tone and skill with exercise, it will lose them without it. The body needs to be stressed frequently in order to maintain and increase strength. After an injury or illness an athlete may have lost their strength and skill. Although a person can quickly improve their endurance capability, it can be lost three times faster than it can be gained. Remember, if you don't use it you lose it!

Wednesday 7–8pm

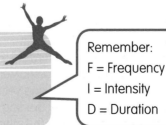

Task 2

Write three sentences for each of the training principles. Include FID in your answer.

Remember:
F = Frequency
I = Intensity
D = Duration

Saturday 2–4pm

A person training for general fitness will vary the activities they do. If the intensity of the exercise is at 60 to 80 per cent of their maximum heart rate, fitness will improve.

Threshold

There are different threshold levels a person can work to when exercising. When the levels are actually reached depends on the fitness of the performer, measured by their heart rate. (Generally, a fitter person will have a slower resting heart rate and recover more quickly from exercise.) The threshold of training (the aerobic threshold) is the level at which exercise starts having an affect on your body: between 60 and 80 per cent of the maximum heart rate. Working below 60 per cent of the maximum heart rate will make no improvement to a person's fitness.

Exercising in the **target zone** (the range within which an individual needs to work for aerobic training to take place) will work the cardiovascular system and improve endurance and stamina.

Working above 80 per cent of the maximum heart rate (anaerobic threshold) is classed as the **training zone**. In this zone the body is worked anaerobically and improves strength, power and muscular strength.

A graph to show the changes in pulse rate of a 16 year old when training in the target zone.

60–80% of maximum heart rate

Training zone
Threshold of training
Target zone
Threshold of training
Resting heart rate

Heartbeats per minute

Time in minutes

The type of activity a person is training for will govern the threshold the performer will work. If a sport requires more bursts of high intensity effort then working in the training zone would be appropriate. Activities requiring both aerobic and anaerobic training (such as rugby and football) will vary the zone worked in accordingly.

A person's fitness will also have a bearing on the level of effort and the zone in which they exercise. A less fit performer will often work in the target zone, at 60 to 80 per cent of their maximum heart rate, gradually building up to increased intensity work.

3 — Repetitions, sets, rest and recovery

Repetitions are the number of times an individual action is performed. For example, lifting a weight ten times or dribbling around cones and finishing with a shot ten times. Sets are the completed number of prescribed actions (ten repetitions make one set for example). Repetitions and sets can be adapted to several methods including interval training, circuit training and weight training. Adapting the repetitions and sets can increase the intensity and stresses on the body so further progress to the area being trained (such as strength) can be made:

• The number of repetitions in a set can be increased.
• The intensity of the repetition can be increased – such as lifting more weight in one repetition.
• The number of sets in a session can be increased.

During their training, an athlete will incorporate repetitions, sets, rest and recovery time to their programme to get the result they want.

Rest and recovery

For training to be effective there should be a balance between exercise and rest and recovery. Damage and injury can result if recovery phases are not planned and incorporated into a training programme. Rest and recovery gives time for restoration of:

• energy-producing enzymes in muscle fibres
• stores of carbohydrates in muscle cells
• hormonal balance and immune systems.

Overtraining results in poorer results from performance and training. It can also increase the risk of injury and illness and decrease the desire to exercise.

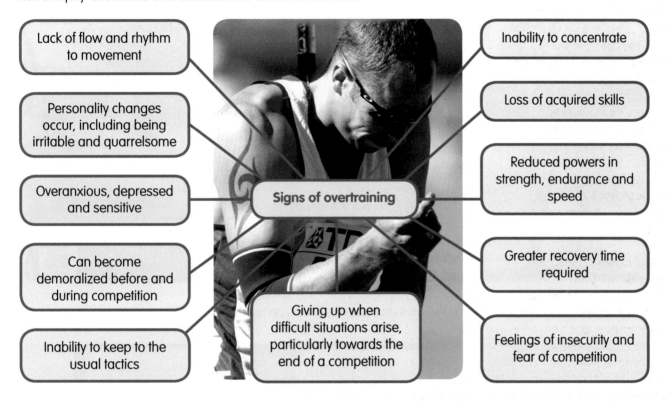

Lack of flow and rhythm to movement

Personality changes occur, including being irritable and quarrelsome

Overanxious, depressed and sensitive

Can become demoralized before and during competition

Inability to keep to the usual tactics

Signs of overtraining

Giving up when difficult situations arise, particularly towards the end of a competition

Inability to concentrate

Loss of acquired skills

Reduced powers in strength, endurance and speed

Greater recovery time required

Feelings of insecurity and fear of competition

Planning the training year should enable the athlete to reach peak performance for certain events or games. Periodization reduces the risk of overtraining and involves:

• designating times for rests, giving adequate time for recovery between training sessions
• applying a variety of types of training and session content to keep the performer motivated
• varying the way the same muscles are exercised, but keeping the same effect.

4 — Monitoring and testing a training programme

In order to plan and prepare a programme of exercise for an individual, a clear picture of their fitness level should be identified. This is called a 'fitness profile'. This can be a general understanding of the heart rate and lung capacity or it can be made more detailed by testing aspects of skill. It is useful when assessing games players as they will need many different skills to play their game properly and the test can be designed to include all skills.

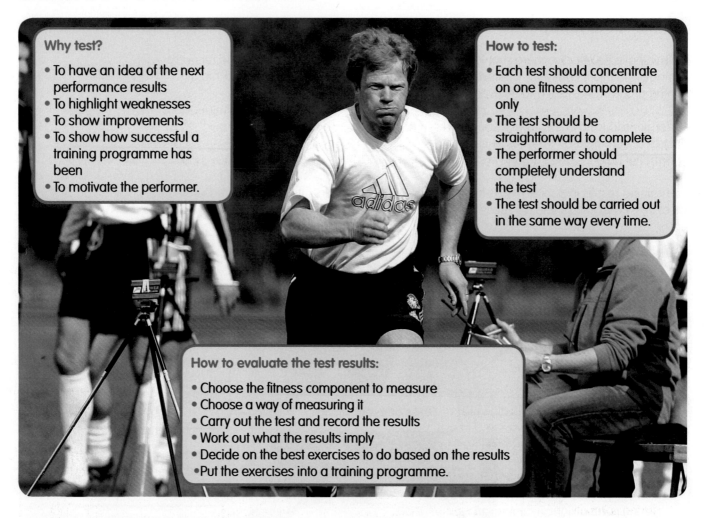

Why test?

- To have an idea of the next performance results
- To highlight weaknesses
- To show improvements
- To show how successful a training programme has been
- To motivate the performer.

How to test:

- Each test should concentrate on one fitness component only
- The test should be straightforward to complete
- The performer should completely understand the test
- The test should be carried out in the same way every time.

How to evaluate the test results:

- Choose the fitness component to measure
- Choose a way of measuring it
- Carry out the test and record the results
- Work out what the results imply
- Decide on the best exercises to do based on the results
- Put the exercises into a training programme.

There are a number of tests that can be carried out to test specific fitness components:

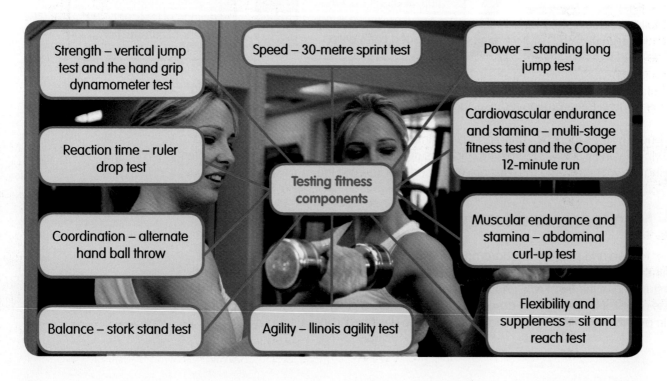

Strength – vertical jump test and the hand grip dynamometer test

Speed – 30-metre sprint test

Power – standing long jump test

Reaction time – ruler drop test

Testing fitness components

Cardiovascular endurance and stamina – multi-stage fitness test and the Cooper 12-minute run

Coordination – alternate hand ball throw

Muscular endurance and stamina – abdominal curl-up test

Balance – stork stand test

Agility – Ilinois agility test

Flexibility and suppleness – sit and reach test

Testing strength

Muscular strength is the muscles' ability to apply force and overcome resistance.

Power or explosive strength testing
The vertical jump test measures explosive leg strength. There are other tests measuring arm and leg strength too, for example, the standing broad jump test and the pull-up test. Explosive leg strength is vital to athletes and games players needing to jump, whether it is for distance or height. Games players also need to be able to jump for a ball in a challenge or to play a shot.

VERTICAL JUMP TEST

Equipment needed

- A wall
- Measuring tape
- Chalk
- Recorder
- Recording sheet
- Pen

Protocol

1. Performer stands sideways to a wall.
2. While standing with feet flat, the performer reaches up with their arm nearest to the wall.
3. The height where the stretched fingers reach is measured.
4. The performer chalks their fingers to mark the wall.
5. Standing slightly away from the wall (for safety), the performer chalks their fingers then jumps vertically, as high as possible, using arms and legs for maximum height.
6. They touch the wall at the highest point possible (by chalking the fingers first a clear mark is left to measure).
7. The distance between the two chalk measures is recorded.
8. The performer has three attempts at achieving a good result.

Vertical jump test results table in centimetres

Gender	Poor	Below average	Average	Above average	Excellent
Male	<30	30–39	40–49	50–65	>65
Female	<26	22–35	36–46	47–58	>58

Source: www.brainmac.co.uk

Static strength testing

The hand grip dynamometer measures the force generated by the performer's hand in one grip action. This is an easy test to administer and is used as a measurement of general strength.

HAND GRIP DYNAMOMETER TEST

Equipment needed

- Hand grip dynamometer
- Recording sheet
- Pen

Protocol

1. Adjust the hand grip dynamometer to the size of the performer's hand this is important as the accuracy of the adjustment will affect the results.
2. The performer grips the dynamometer with their dominant hand.
3. The arm hangs by their side with the dynamometer in line with the forearm.
4. Maximum grip strength is applied without any swinging of the arm.
5. The performer has two attempts for each hand with the best result recorded.
6. The best results are added together and divided by two to reach a score.

A hand grip dynamometer with the performer's arm by their side.

Hand grip dynamometer test results in kg							
Gender	Very poor	Poor	Below average	Average	Above average	Very good	Excellent
Male	<40	40–44	44–48	48–52	52–56	56–64	>64
Female	<20	20–22	22–26	26–30	30–34	34–38	>38

Testing speed

Speed is the fastest rate a person can complete a task or cover a distance. Most sports rely on a performer to move their whole body at speed, so tests for this component are appropriate to all.

30-METRE SPRINT TEST

Equipment needed

- Flat, even running surface
- 30m tape measure
- Recording sheet
- Two cones
- Stopwatch
- Pen

Protocol

1. The 30m straight is measured out.
2. The performer sets off as quickly as possible from a standing start – at the same time, the stopwatch starts.
3. The performer sprints to the finishing line as quickly as possible.
4. As the performer crosses the finishing point, the stopwatch is stopped.
5. The time is recorded to 100th of a second.

30-metre sprint test results in seconds					
Gender	**Excellent**	**Above average**	**Average**	**Below average**	**Poor**
Male	<4.1	4.3–4.1	4.5–4.4	4.7–4.6	>4.7
Female	<4.6	4.7–4.6	4.9–4.8	5.1–4.10	>5.1

Task 3

1 – Choose either speed or strength and write down how you would recognize accomplishment in your choice.

2 – Choose a sport and give two examples of how your choice improves the skills or performance of the activity.

> For example: speed – basketball – team makes a defensive rebound and player sprints into position to receive an outlet pass.

Testing power

STANDING BOARD JUMP TEST

Equipment needed

- Long jump pit
- Recording sheet
- Tape measure
- Assistant recorder
- Pen
- Teacher or coach to take measurements

Protocol

1. The athlete positions themselves at the end of the jump pit.
2. The athlete should stand with both feet together and with feet up to the edge.
3. They then crouch, lean forward, swing their arms for momentum to jump as far horizontally into the jump pit as possible. The start of the jump must be from a static position.
4. They should land with both feet in the sand.
5. A measurement should be taken from the edge of the jump pit to the nearest point of contact into the sand.

Standing long jump test results table for 15 to 16-year-old athletes

Gender	Poor	Below average	Average	Above average	Excellent
Male	<1.65m	1.75–1.65m	1.85–1.76m	2.00–1.86m	>2.01m
Female	<1.35m	1.45–1.35m	1.55–1.46m	1.65–1.56m	>1.66m

Source: www.brainmac.co.uk

Testing cardiovascular endurance and stamina

Having strong and efficient heart and lungs will help a player keep working hard throughout a game without losing breath and lowering performance. The bleep test, for example, can measure heart and lung efficiency reflecting the oxygen uptake (VO_2 – the maximum amount of oxygen that can be transported to, and used by, the muscles during exercise in one minute).

Multi-Stage Fitness Test

This test uses VO_2 as an indicator of fitness.

Equipment needed

- 20m length course set out between cones
- Four cones
- A CD of the test
- A CD player
- Recorder
- Recording sheet
- Pen

Protocol

1. The athletes listen to the CD.
2. They run to a cone and return only on the beep. The time between the beeps gradually lessens.
3. If an athlete fails to reach the cone on the beep twice in a row then they are out.
4. The level they reached at that point is recorded as 'their level'.

Multi-stage fitness test results, VO_2 maximum

Age	Very poor	Poor	Fair	Good	Excellent	Superior
13–19	<25.0	25.0–30.9	31.0–34.9	35.0–38.9	39.0–41.9	>41.9
20–29	<23.6	23.6–28.9	29.0–32.9	33.0–36.9	37.0–41.0	>41.0

Source: The Physical Fitness Specialist Certification Manual, The Cooper Institute for Aerobics Research, Dallas TX, revised 1997 printed in Advance Fitness Assessment & Exercise Prescription, 3rd Edition, Vivian H. Heyward, 1998. p48

A note of caution: These tests were originally designed for mature athletes and are not suitable for all students. Serious injuries can occur if students push themselves too hard.

Active challenge

The Harvard step-up test is another method of measuring cardiovascular endurance. Use the Internet to research the protocol for administering this test.

COOPER 12-MINUTE RUN

Equipment needed

- Flat area for the course with 100 metre distances marked
- A whistle
- Stopwatch
- Recorder
- Recording sheet
- Pen

Protocol

The performer must complete the test without stopping, whatever their pace, and will achieve a better score the further they go.

1. A whistle is blown to start the test.
2. At the same time, a stopwatch is started.
3. The performer runs, jogs or walks the designated course.
4. Each time the performer reaches a 100-metre mark, the time is recorded.
5. The test finishes after 12 minutes.

Cooper 12-minute run results table in meters					
Age	**Gender**	**Excellent**	**Very good**	**Good**	**Fair**
13–14 years	Male	3300	3000	2700	2400
	Female	2700	2400	2100	1800
15–16 years	Male	3400	3100	2800	2500
	Female	2800	2500	2200	1900
17–18 years	Male	3500	3200	2900	2600
	Female	2900	2600	2300	2000

Task 4

1 – Choose an appropriate sport.

2 – Using the sport you have chosen, answer the question: what is good cardiovascular endurance?

3 – Give two examples of how good cardiovascular endurance improves the performance of the sport.

Testing muscular endurance and stamina

Performers working for lengthy periods need muscular endurance and stamina so they can keep their skill level high throughout the game.

ABDOMINAL CURL-UP TEST

Equipment needed

- Flat surface
- A partner
- Recorder
- Pen
- Mat for safety
- Stopwatch
- Recording sheet

Protocol

1. The performer lies on their back and bends their knees to a 90-degree angle.
2. Their feet should be flat on the floor.
3. Their hands should be resting on their thighs.
4. Their head should be resting on the back of their partner's hands.
5. The performer curls up slowly (using abdominal muscles) sliding their hands up their thighs to their knees.
6. They return slowly to the starting position (a complete curl takes three seconds).
7. They repeat as many curls as possible, keeping to the same rate of these seconds per curl.
8. The number of curls made are recorded.

Abdominal curl-up test results

	Males		
	Aged <35	Aged 35–44	Aged >45
Excellent	60	50	40
Good	45	40	25
Fair	30	25	15
Poor	15	10	5

Abdominal curl-up test results

	Females		
	Aged <35	Aged 35–44	Aged >45
Excellent	50	40	30
Good	40	25	15
Fair	25	15	10
Poor	10	6	4

A note of caution: These tests were originally designed for mature athletes and are not suitable for all students. Serious injuries can occur if students push themselves too hard.

Another test for muscular endurance is the press-up test.

Active challenge

Find the press-up test on the Internet and write out the protocol for its administration.

Testing flexibility and suppleness

Players need to move their joints to their full range without hurting themselves. In football, tackling effectively needs flexibility and suppleness. The sit and reach test is the most common test for flexibility.

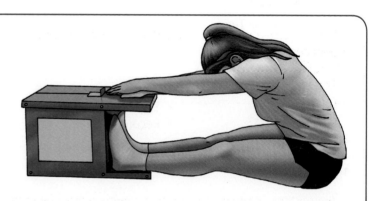

SIT AND REACH TEST

Equipment needed

• Indoor area
• Wooden block or a bench and ruler
• Measure

Protocol

1. The person sits, straight-legged, with feet touching the start of the measuring block (or bench).
2. They reach forward and place their hands on the block to be measured.
3. If they reach as far as their toes this measures 0cm, beyond their toes it is +0cm and if it is not as far as their toes it is –0cm.
4. A recorder (or ruler) measures the distance that the hands reach along the block.

Sit and reach test results for 16 to 19 year olds in centimetres					
Gender	Poor	Below average	Average	Above average	Excellent
Male	<4	4–6	7–10	11–14	>14
Female	<4	4–6	7–11	12–15	>15

Testing agility

Agility is the ability to change direction quickly and still keep the body under control. This component fitness is needed in most sports including team games, gymnastics and skiing. The Illinois agility test is a good way of measuring this.

Task 5

1 – Choose either agility or strength and write down how you would recognize accomplishment in your choice.

2 – Choose a sport and give two examples of how your choice improves the skills and performance of the activity.

For example: agility in netball: 1. Wing attack changing direction to dodge marker. 2. Goal Defence changing direction, turning and moving to recover shot off the netball post's ring.

ILLINOIS AGILITY TEST

Equipment needed

- Flat surface to set the course: approximately 15m x 8m
- Eight cones
- Whistle
- Stopwatch
- Recorder
- Recording sheet
- Pen

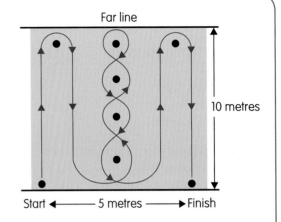

Protocol

1. The performer begins by lying face down on the floor at the starting point.
2. On the whistle, the performer jumps to their feet and makes their way around the course to the finish.
3. A stopwatch should be used to time how long it takes for them to reach the finish.

Illinois agility test results for 16 year olds in seconds

Gender	Excellent	Above average	Average	Below average	Poor
Male	<15.9	15.9–16.7	16.8–17.6	17.7–18.8	>18.8
Female	<17.5	17.5–18.6	18.7–22.4	22.5–23.4	>23.4

Testing balance

Balance is the ability to keep the body stable whether still, moving or in different shapes by keeping the centre of gravity over the base.

STORK STAND TEST

Equipment needed

- Any warm and dry space
- Stopwatch
- Recorder
- Recording sheet
- Pen

Protocol

1. The performer stands upright on both feet in a comfortable position, with their hands placed on their hips.
2. One leg is lifted and the toes of that foot are placed on the knee of the other leg.
3. When directed to do so, the performer raises the heel of their standing foot and stands on their toes.
4. At the same time, the stopwatch is started.
5. The performer balances for as long as possible without putting their heel on the ground or moving the other foot away from the knee.
6. A record is made of how long the balance was held.
7. The test is repeated using the other leg.

Stork stand test results for 15 to 16 year olds in seconds				
Poor	**Below average**	**Average**	**Above average**	**Excellent**
<11	11–25	26–39	40–49	>50

Testing coordination

Coordination is the ability to use two or more body parts together. It can also be defined as the ability to carry out a series of movements smoothly and efficiently.

ALTERNATE HAND BALL THROW

Equipment needed

- Smooth wall
- 2m measure
- A tennis ball
- Stopwatch
- Recording sheet
- Pen

Protocol

1. A 2m distance is measured from a smooth wall.
2. The performer stands that distance away from the wall.
3. The performer holds a tennis ball in their dominant hand and throws the ball against the wall.
4. The performer catches the ball in their other hand.
5. They then throw the ball from that hand and catch it in the dominant hand.
6. The performer should repeat the catch and throw as many times as possible in 30 seconds.

Alternate hand ball throw results for 15 to 16 year olds

High score	Above average	Average	Below average	Low score
> 35	35–30	29–25	24–20	< 20

Task 6

1 – Write down which test you would use to recognize coordination accomplishment.

2 – Choose a sport and give two examples of how coordination improves the skills or performance of the activity.

3 – Work together in a small group (about five to seven people). One person should conduct a coordination test, while the rest take the test.

4 – Collate your results and create a bar chart.

Testing reaction time

Reaction time is the time it takes for a performer to react to a stimulus. If there is one stimulus, the reaction time is called the simple reaction time. When a performer is presented with two stimuli, each requiring a different response, this is known as choice reaction time.

RULER DROP TEST

Equipment needed

- A 1m ruler
- An assistant
- Recording sheet
- Pen

Protocol

1. The assistant holds the ruler, with their arm outstretched.
2. The ruler is held between the outstretched thumb and finger of the assistant's dominant hand.
3. The performer's thumb should be level with the '0' on the ruler.
4. The assistant should instruct the performer to catch the ruler between their thumb and finger as soon as the ruler is released.
5. The assistant records distance between the bottom of the ruler and the top of the performer's thumb at the point of the catch.

Ruler drop test results: national norms for 16 to 19 year olds

Excellent	Above average	Average	Below average	Poor
<7.5cm	7.5–15.9cm	15.9–20.4cm	20.4–28cm	>28cm

Key terms

Specificity – matching training to the needs of the physical activity

Progression – gradually increasing the stresses put on the body

Overload – exercising the body more than normalReversibility – when training stops, any gain to the body is lost

Systematic training – planning a programme for an individual as a result of the effect of previous training

Individual needs – personal requirements for training

Minimum level of fitness – the resulting fitness level over a period of weeks of three to five exercise sessions of 20 minutes, raising the heart rate to between 60 and 80 per cent of its maximum

Target zone – the range within which an individual needs to work for aerobic training to take place (60 to 80 per cent of maximum heart rate)

Training zone – working above 80 per cent of the maximum heart rate (anaerobic threshold)

Summary

Individuals need their own programme of exercise as everyone is different and has their own reasons for training. Testing a person's capabilities first gives a clear idea of the level of training needed. By applying the training principles (specificity, progression, overload and reversibility, and applying FID to overload), both beginners and top athletes can be catered for. The key is to work the heart above the threshold of training. Working in the target zone will help general fitness whilst working in the training zone is for more serious athletes. It is important to keep to the 'ten per cent' rule when changing the intensity of the exercise – any increase to the programme should be ten per cent or less of the current activity. For example, if a person is lifting 20lbs, the intensity should be increased by a maximum of 2lbs. This might take an athlete longer to reach a goal but it helps to avoid injury.

The principles of training create guidelines for improving the body. Progression should be planned carefully by reviewing the improvements made by the athlete. Systematically planning new programmes and increasing the intensity of the exercises is necessary when the body has adapted to the training and the effort required fails to continue to reach the desired threshold of training.

Exam questions

Multiple-choice questions

1. Overload is:

   ☐ **A** Matching the exercises to the activity

   ☐ **B** The degeneration of the muscles after exercise has stopped

   ☐ **C** Working the body harder than normal

   ☐ **D** Allowing the body to recover to maintain a high level of performance

   (1 mark)

2. Specificity is:

   ☐ **A** Allowing the body to recover to maintain a high level of performance

   ☐ **B** Matching the exercises to the activity

   ☐ **C** The degeneration of the muscles after exercise has stopped

   ☐ **D** Working the body harder than normal and then increasing the intensity gradually

   (1 mark)

3. FID stand for:

   ☐ **A** Fitness, intensity, duration

   ☐ **B** Frequency, intensity, determination

   ☐ **C** Frequency, increased, duration

   ☐ **D** Frequency, intensity, duration

   (1 mark)

4. Reversibility is:

   ☐ **A** Increasing the amount of exercise undertaken

   ☐ **B** The body adapting to exercise

   ☐ **C** The benefits of training being lost when exercise stops

   ☐ **D** The exercises in training relating to the chosen sport

   (1 mark)

5. Regularity is important when exercising. Which of the following best describes what regularity is?

   ☐ **A** Changing the intensity levels in the training session

   ☐ **B** Reaching the best level of performance

   ☐ **C** Losing fitness when exercise stops

   ☐ **D** Sometimes increase the amount of training sessions

   (1 mark)

Short answer questions

6. Between what percentages of the maximum does the heart need to beat in order to work in the target zone?

   (1 mark)

7. There are recognized training principles, one of which is overload. What is meant by overload when training?

   (2 marks)

8. Describe how a person would use repetitions and sets to increase the intensity of a training session.

   (3 marks)

Longer answer questions

9. Signs can occur to indicate when an athlete is overtraining. What are these signs?

   (8 marks)

10. Name a test that measures power and explosive strength. Describe how it works in relation to a specific sport.

    (6 marks)

11. Name a test that measures flexibility and suppleness. Describe how the test works and which sports would benefit from it.

    (6 marks)

3.1.2 ～ Linking physical activity with diet, work and rest for personal health and a balanced healthy lifestyle

3.1.2c Training

What you will learn about in this topic:

1 — Weight training
2 — Circuit training
3 — Interval training
4 — Fartlek training
5 — Continuous training

There are many training methods open to the performer. Each method works the body differently. The reason for training and the type of activity being trained for will steer a performer to a particular training method. When training over a long period, varying the methods used will reduce the risk of overuse injury and keep the athlete interested and fresh for each session. The aim of training is to improve some or all of the following:

- fitness
- skills
- techniques.

So choosing the correct method to fit the activity is important. The different training methods include: **weight training, circuit training, interval training, Fartlek training** and **continuous training**.

For each of the training methods you will learn about:

- The training method
- What the training develops
- How the method works
- The exercises involved
- How the training principles apply
- Disadvantages of the method.

1 — Weight training

Weight training uses anaerobic respiration when shifting heavy weights with few repetitions.

The training method
The training involves shifting weight to increase the strength of muscles, using a programme of repetitions and sets.

What the training develops
A person setting up a weight-training programme needs to think about the following questions: what is the reason for doing the training? Is it for aerobic (endurance) or anaerobic

(strength) development? Which parts of the body are to be exercised? The answers to these questions will shape the whole programme.

Weightlifting can develop different types of strength. Lifting lighter weights many times develops muscular endurance so uses aerobic respiration. This way of adapting weight training can help a person who is rehabilitating after injury. By moving light weights, the muscles gradually get used to working and taking weight again in a safe and controlled way. This adaptation to the method would also suit long-distance athletes.

Weight-training machines are always set up and are fully adjustable.

Lifting heavy weights with few repetitions develops strength and power. This will build up strength, increase muscle size and use anaerobic respiration. Long jumpers, javelin throwers and sprinters would use the adaptation.

Lifting medium to high numbers of repetitions and shifting medium to high weights builds strength and increases the size of the muscles, and uses aerobic respiration. Rugby players would benefit from this combination.

Lifting maximum weights in a single repetition builds strength. A shot-putter would benefit from this combination. This uses anaerobic respiration.

Rest and recovery times are essential to the weightlifter. The length and frequency of rest and recovery times depends on the following:

- The athlete's weight
- The athlete's condition – strength of muscles
- Whether large or small muscle groups are used – small muscle groups can require more recovery time
- The loads shifted in the session – different loads can require different recovery times; heavier loads take longer to recover from
- The type of strength being developed – are they endurance or strength training (anaerobic or aerobic?); aerobic work takes longer to recover from.

Usually two days' rest is needed between sessions, especially when muscular endurance is the type of strength being developed, as it takes this long for glycogen levels to be restored.

How the method works
A weight-training programme relies on good testing to find the correct level of intensity at which to work. Keeping to the planned number of repetitions and sets is important for a safe, appropriate training session. Often, the space and equipment used for the sessions is shared by others, so some coordination and flexibility in the order of the exercises may be necessary.

When organizing a weight-training programme:

Number of exercises – the usual range is between eight and 12.

Assess – the performer's strength and fitness. Once the maximum a person can lift is known, the programme can start to develop.

Safety factors – using straps, adjusting the seat, setting the correct weight and using the correct technique are essential for safe weight training.

Review – when the body has adapted to the stresses of the programme, changes are made. The strength of the performer is re-tested. If the programme has been set at the right level, the performer will have increased in strength.

Repetitions – complete 12 to 17 repetitions at 60 to 70 per cent of maximum lifting ability for an anaerobic beginner. Use many repetitions for lighter, aerobic work.

Weights – light for aerobic (endurance), heavier for anaerobic, (strength and size).

Rest between sets – about two minutes.

New programme – changes are made to the programme. As a result, a combination of weights, repetitions and sets increases slightly.

Number of sets – a beginner might complete one set for anaerobic, building up to two sets after two weeks. More repetitions are completed for aerobic training.

Training to get the best results – speed of exercise for greatest benefit: lifting and lowering takes two seconds to achieve the maximum benefit of the action.

Number of sessions per week – three to four sessions every other week should show an improvement with up to 48 hours between each session.

Weight-training cards

Weight-training cards can be helpful to the performer in many ways. They can be used to check on the frequency of training, they show the specific repetitions and weights used, they help the performer to focus on the different sessions within the training session and they show the level from which progressions can be made:

% of maximum lift	Repetitions
60	17
65	14
70	12
75	10
80	8
85	6
90	5
95	3
100	1

Good for beginners.
Complete one set of above.
After three weeks, increase sets.

Weight-training repetitions: the performer works through the card from 60 per cent to 100 per cent in a session.

Lift 70 per cent of maximum
8 repetitions
3 sets completed

Good for beginner.
Level of effort required means weights are lifted properly.
Little risk of injury.

Simple sets: the performer works at the same intensity throughout the session, completing three sets of eight repetitions.

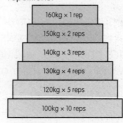

160kg × 1 rep
150kg × 2 reps
140kg × 3 reps
130kg × 4 reps
120kg × 5 reps
100kg × 10 reps

Pyramid sets: the performer starts at the easiest weight, working their way to heavy weights but with fewer repetitions.

The exercises involved

There are two ways of weight training: machine weights and free weights.

MACHINE WEIGHTS   Using machines weights can be a safer way of weight training. They are technically designed to move in the correct way and are adjustable for different sizes of user. They are safe as they are steady and do not vary position apart from the designed range. However, this also has the effect of not training the stabilizing muscles that may be needed for a sport. Machine weights usually have supports and belts to make sure the body is prepared in the correct position to shift the weight. They are always set up, so are ready to use. Users starting a weight-training programme find them easy to work.

A variety of exercises can be performed using machine weights.

FREE WEIGHTS   Free weights can be used in a weight-training programme. The use of such weights is specialized and needs lots of training so that the performer works safely. Many top sportspeople use free weights. A person training with heavy weights must always use a spotter; this is a person who helps steady the performer and is ready to catch the bar or assist if the performer is struggling.

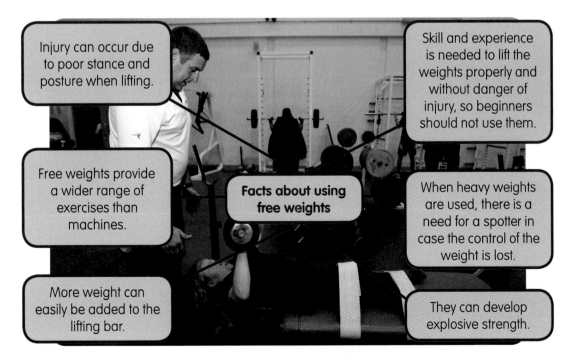

Injury can occur due to poor stance and posture when lifting.

Skill and experience is needed to lift the weights properly and without danger of injury, so beginners should not use them.

Free weights provide a wider range of exercises than machines.

Facts about using free weights

When heavy weights are used, there is a need for a spotter in case the control of the weight is lost.

More weight can easily be added to the lifting bar.

They can develop explosive strength.

How the training principles apply

With both types of weight training, regular training improves the muscles' ability to move the weight. As the body adapts, the progression, overload and FID principles are applied and the weights, repetitions and sets are gradually increased. This allows improvement of the muscles to continue. Lifting 60 to 80 per cent of the maximum weight a person is able to lift will keep the performer within the target zone. Each session should last for no longer than 45 minutes.

A weight-training card helps the performer to train safely and see progress:

Name:	Personal trainer:		Date programme started:	
Visits	1 2 3 4 5 6 7	8 9 10 11		12 13 14
Warm-up option	Jog 5 mins	Cycle 5 mins	Easy row 5 mins	Stepper 5 mins
Then:	Stretches	Arms/shoulders	Legs/hips	Abdominals
Exercise	Starting point	Progression 1	Progression 2	Progression 3
Tricep pulldowns				
Squats				
Hip flexors				
Lateral pulldown				
Hamstring curls				
Hip extensors				
Bench presses				
Seated leg extensions				
Warm-down options	Walk/jog 5 mins	Easy cycle 5 mins	Easy row 5 mins	
Finish with stretches				

Disadvantages of the method

Disadvantages of using machine weights:

• No extra weight can be added to the machine, limiting the advanced performer.
• The movement performed is isolated.
• Isolated exercises do not improve core strength (muscles between groin to shoulders).

Disadvantages of using free weights:

• Difficult to use.
• Training is required.
• Spotters required for heavier weights.
• Correct lifting technique is essential to avoid injury.
• Skill is required to lift the weights properly.

Task 1

1 – What makes machine weight and free weight sessions different?

2 – How do free weight training sessions compare to machine weight training sessions?

> The training principles change in the sessions. When comparing each type think of the special features each method has.

2 — Circuit training

The training method
Circuit training is a series of exercises, completed for a certain amount of time, one after another.

What the training develops
Circuit training can be useful in different ways. Depending on how the circuit is set up, it can develop power, strength, flexibility and endurance. At a basic level it can improve the general fitness of the heart and lungs as long as the rests in between the activities are kept short. It can be adapted to incorporate skills for a particular game. Top-class performers, however, do not benefit much from circuit training as it does not allow them to achieve a high enough level of skill.

Circuit training can develop aerobic and anaerobic respiration. When using large muscle groups at each station (moving the whole body), aerobic respiration is in operation and this will develop the cardiovascular system. If exercising small muscle groups (such as the biceps and triceps) in turn at the stations, this is anaerobic respiration, which builds strength.

How the method works
A circuit is made up of several activities. Each activity is given its own space in the gym or sports hall; this space is called a 'station'. Each activity is completed as many times as possible, these are called 'repetitions'. There is a set time for each activity, usually between 30 and 60 seconds. In this time as many repetitions of the activity are performed as possible. When all exercises at each station are completed, the circuit is finished. By repeating the circuit or by adding exercises, the session increases in intensity. For general fitness the sequence of exercises works different muscle groups at each station. Whether a beginner or not, three circuits is usually enough.

Each activity in a circuit is completed as many times as possible.

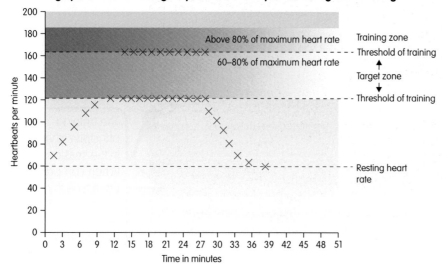

The exercises involved

Circuit training can be adapted to different sporting activities by including exercises that can be repeated and match the skills of the chosen sport. If an activity requires a dominance of leg strength then more stations can include exercises working the lower limbs: training for skiing would suit such adaptation.

How the training principles apply

A circuit can be set for individual needs. Each person doing the circuit can have their own targets, but completing a circuit three times should be the minimum as the third circuit is the one when a person's fitness will be visible. This means that beginners and fitter people can work at the same time because they can work within the same time limits, but they each complete a different number of repetitions. Completing a circuit can be competitive and can motivate people to work harder and achieve more repetitions. Even with inexpensive equipment, a successful general fitness circuit can be set up.

Circuit training in school.

Active challenge

Cover the numbered list below without reading it. With a partner, study the circuit training illustration on page 116 and try to name some of the exercises in the circuit.

1. Step-ups
2. Skipping
3. Sit-ups
4. Bench lifts

5. Bench astrides
6. Leg raises
7. Push-ups
8. Squats

9. Star jumps
10. Shuttle runs

Disadvantages of the method
Disadvantages of circuit training:

- Can only improve general fitness at a basic level.
- Skills could be performed incorrectly.
- Top-class performers cannot achieve a high enough level of skill with this method.

Task 2

1 – List the advantages and disadvantages of circuit training.

2 – Look at the circuit training picture on page 116. Change four exercises from general fitness to skills used in a sport of your choice.

3 — Interval training

The training method
Interval training involves times of work followed by times of rest.

What the training develops
Interval training can be adapted to develop different types of fitness. Short bursts of pace, using anaerobic respiration needed in games play, uses short interval training. Prolonged moderate to hard pace, using aerobic respiration needed in middle-distance running events, uses long interval training.

Interval training is suited to individuals working on their own, small groups of people and to larger numbers, like teams of players. Many sportspeople can benefit from interval training. The sessions can be adapted to practice the skills used in a particular game. Whether a runner, swimmer, footballer or netball player, interval training can be adapted to your sport.

Athletes use interval training to improve their workload. Interval training involves:

- periods of running fast – here lactic acid builds up and the state of oxygen debt (the amount of oxygen taken in during activity, above that which would have been taken in ordinarily) is reached

- periods of slow jogging to recover – here the heart and lungs work hard to pay back the oxygen, which in turn breaks down the lactic acid.

The stresses of training results in:

- the heart being strengthened
- more capillaries being formed
- more oxygen being taken up, which helps break down the lactic acid.

The result is improved performance especially of the cardiovascular system. The work is intensive and should be performed with accuracy and at competition pace. The times of rest allow performers to regain energy so they do not become too tired and can no longer carry on training. The times of work are repeated to form repetitions. Four or five repetitions make up a set. There may be four or five sets in a session.

Interval training is made up of repetitions and sets.

The table below shows an example of an interval training activity for hockey or football.

Complete four sets of the following in the time limit	Time limit for return
6–10 seconds dribble and shoot	60–120 seconds jog, return and rest
6–10 seconds dribble and shoot	60–120 seconds jog, return and rest
6–10 seconds dribble and shoot	60–120 seconds jog, return and rest
6–10 seconds dribble and shoot	60–120 seconds jog, return and rest

How the method works

Interval training can be adapted for different types of athlete and event as the working periods copy those in the event. The rest periods allow time for recovery in the same way that there would be quieter times during a game.

LONG INTERVAL TRAINING Work time is 15 seconds to three minutes. Games players and middle-distance athletes benefit from this type of training. The training copies the events in the need for bursts of maximum effort within the 15-second and three-minute time spans. Even the best athletes cannot work at full pace for longer than 60-second periods so, when using this method, performers work at between 80 to 90 per cent of their maximum heart rate in their training zone.

A graph to show the change in pulse rate of a 16 year old during interval training.

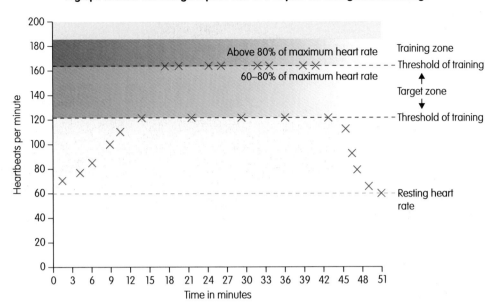

The resting times match the working times so the longer the athlete works, the longer they rest. The resting times are important to enable a performer to recover and continue the session. When working in larger groups it is more difficult for everyone to keep together due to the longer time limit and the variation in ability.

A four-minute-mile runner could use interval training in the following way: repeat 10 × 60 second 375m distances with two minute rest between each run.

Short Interval Training   This training works on short bursts of maximum effort. The working time may be as short as 15 seconds. The performer aims to work all out for the whole of this time. Sprinters and racket sport players use this method to match the short bursts of maximum effort used in their events. A sprinter goes all out to reach the line as fast as possible and a squash player hits the ball with a burst of maximum effort. Due to the effects of the intensive effort on the body, rests of two minutes are necessary. In this time, the body has a chance to recover enough to carry on training.

The exercises involved
You will have used interval training in school already. Shuttle runs, dribbling relays, lay up shot drills and swimming 25 metres are all examples of exercises used for interval training. In a games or athletics lesson, you will have used shuttle runs. As you complete your shuttle run, that is one repetition. You rest while your teammates complete their shuttle run. You may complete four repetitions before you are stopped; these make up a set. The teacher may give you another chance to complete the shuttle run after resting and so you will have then completed two sets.

How the training principles apply
As the periods of work and rest imitate the game, the principle of specificity is applied. To keep the performer improving

Swimming, athletics and many games, such as football, use interval training. Here, Jolean Lescott practises his dribbling skills.

when using interval training, the principle of progression is used. There are several ways to do this:

- The amount of recovery time may shorten and the pace you would work at competitive training is increased.
- The intensity or difficulty of the work may increase; this could be increasing the distance covered or amount of time run.
- The number of repetitions or sets completed may increase.

Disadvantages of the method
Disadvantages of interval training:

- Recovery periods are essential.
- Unsuitable for endurance events.
- Careful timing of work and rest periods is essential.
- Long interval training is hard to carry out with large groups due to the variation of ability.

Task 3

Choose a sport and design a 30-minute interval training session for that sport.

> If designing a session for long interval training, include five repetitions and four sets. If using short interval training, use more repetitions and sets.

4 — Fartlek training

The training method
Fartlek is a Swedish word meaning 'speed play'. Fartlek training involves exercise, often running, varying in time, distance and effort.

What the training develops
Due to the changes of intensity of the exercises, Fartlek training works on both aerobic and anaerobic fitness. The athlete becomes increasingly capable of meeting the changes of pace in a competition or game.

How the method works
Speed, distances covered and the amount of time spent exercising change. In general, the session has work of varying intensity taking place over a minimum of a 20-minute period. Fartlek can be an introduction to interval training and sometimes both can be combined to form a programme of exercise, owing to their similar content.

This method of training would suit a games player. The type of exercise should be adapted to suit the movements in a game. The speed will vary and the direction of movement should vary too. Players in most games will backtrack and change direction so running backwards and slalom running will be important factors to include.

The content of the session is flexible. Therefore the repetitions in the sessions are made different to add interest to the training. Rest periods or periods of less strenuous exercise gives time to recover so training can continue. For example, in a 45–minute session:

0–15 minutes	Warm-up
	Sprint ten seconds on flat
	Jog on flat
	Sprint ten seconds uphill
	Jog/walk downhill then on flat
	Run 150m on flat for one minute
	Jog on flat
	Sprint 80m on flat
15–35 minutes	Jog
	Sprint 20m uphill
	Jog downhill then on flat
	Sprint ten seconds on flat
	Jog/walk uphill
	Jog/run downhill then on flat
	Sprint ten seconds uphill
	Jog/run downhill on flat
35–45 minutes	Warm-down

The exercises involved

The exercises that make up the session are sprints, jogs and runs. These may have times set for them or may be for a certain distance. The session can be continuous with periods of intense work followed by easier work, which gives the body a chance to recover. Sometimes the session can include periods of complete rest.

In Sweden, where this method originated, athletes use the surrounding hills and forests to train in. Many areas large enough to run in can be used to vary the training session. It could take place in a park, at the beach or in the countryside. Fartlek training can be adapted to running, cycling and swimming.

How the training principles apply

The principles of FID adapt to keep the performer improving.

A graph to show how the heart rate of a 16 year old rises and falls regularly in a Fartlek training session

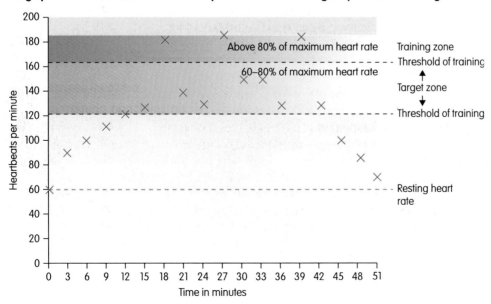

Disadvantages of the method

The disadvantages of Fartlek training are:

- Fartlek training is governed by the local area, terrain and facilities.
- Travelling to suitable outdoor areas may be necessary.
- Fartlek training does not help with the specific skills of a game.

Task 4

Devise your own Fartlek training session using the terrain in your local area. The session should last for 20 minutes.

Remember, the session should include a warm-up and a warm-down.

5 — Continuous training

The training method

Continuous training exercises the body at a moderate rate, keeping the pulse at a constant level above the training threshold (between 60 and 80 per cent of the maximum so working in the target zone).

What the training develops

This training works the body aerobically and keeps the pulse at a high rate. Its effect is to improve the cardiovascular and respiratory systems. It can be adapted for both the health and fitness performer and the top athlete.

Running at different intensities has different effects:

- 60 per cent of the maximum heart rate for 60 minutes or more, burns fat: is good for joggers.
- 60 to 70 per cent of the maximum heart rate for 45 to 90 minutes burns glycogen and fat, improves cardiovascular system (increases capillaries): is good for marathon runners.
- 70 to 80 per cent of the maximum heart rate for 30 to 45 minutes burns glycogen, improves cardiovascular system (increases capillaries): is good for 5km to marathon distances.

Increasing the intensity further works the body anaerobically, but can only be carried out for shorter periods of time, helping with lactic acid tolerance.

How the method works

After a gradual warm-up, the person training works their body at a moderate level throughout the session. The heart rate is above 60 per cent of its maximum but below 80 per cent. By keeping in this zone the work is aerobic and can carry on for a long time. Continuous training suits a person who is training for the first time or returning to exercise after a period of non-activity, such as after injury. A person who specializes in long-distance events can use this type of training out of season to maintain a good level of cardiorespiratory fitness. At the start of the season, continuous training can adapt as a gentle way to re-establish the cardiorespiratory levels. To begin with, the work is moderate, but can be adapted to be harder at a later time.

A variety of machines, such as rowers, treadmills and exercise bikes, can be used for continuous training.

A graph to show the change in pulse rate of a 16 year old during continuous training.

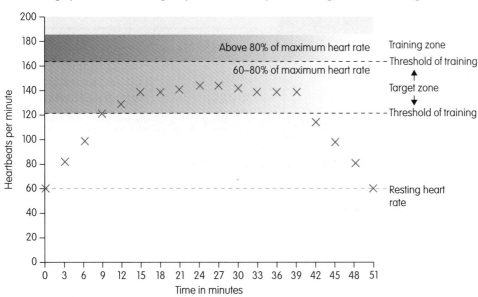

The exercises involved

The types of activity that suit this training include cycling, swimming, exercise classes (aerobics), running and jogging. Many sports centres and gyms have specialized machines that adapt to continuous training. Treadmills, exercise bikes, rowing machines and steppers all lend themselves to this type of training. The activities are a good way of developing general fitness and can be adapted to suit both individuals and groups of people. If running is the exercise chosen, then it is inexpensive to start, and changing the place of training is easily arranged, which adds interest to the session.

How the training principles apply

After several training sessions, the body will have adapted to the strains of the exercise. Checking the pulse rate during exercise will show if it is in the 60 to 80 per cent zone, showing that the heart has become stronger as a result of the exercise. The speed of the exercise should be increased, in order to get the pulse rate into the target zone so the training continues to have an effect on the performer.

For the more advanced performer, greater stresses and demands are made on their body. By keeping in the training zone of 80 to 90 per cent of their maximum heart rate and working for 15 to 20 minutes, the training will be effective. An endurance athlete, such as a marathon runner, would use this method as part of their training programme.

Marathon runners use continuous training within their training programme.

Disadvantages of the method

Disadvantages of continuous training are:

- Careful monitoring is required so that improvement continues through regularly increasing the intensity.
- The use of machines may be required for variety and to keep interest, which may incur expense.
- Continuous training is adapted to endurance events only.

Task 5

1 – Write down six facts about continuous training.

2 – How can the training method be adapted for beginners and more competitive performers?

Think about: how hard the body works, what effect the exercise has on the heart, the types of activity that can be adapted to this method and who would use this method of training.

Key terms

Weight training – progressively lifting heavier weights to improve strength or lifting weights more often to improve stamina

Circuit training – a series of exercises completed in order and for a certain time limit

Interval training – mixing periods of hard exercise with rest periods

Fartlek training – 'speed play', changing speed, distances and times of exercise, with rests in the same session

Continuous training – aerobic exercising, at a moderate to high level, with no rests, lasting for a sustained period of time

Summary

The method of training used can be a personal choice or it can be sport specific. Some methods suit certain kinds of events or games better than others. People exercising for leisure can make any choice they want. People needing specialized training must choose the method that will improve their body systems and skills to the best of their ability. In this case, knowledge of the requirements of the sport is essential. By combining the knowledge of the sport and the abilities of the individual, an appropriate programme can be designed.

Exam questions

Multiple-choice questions

1. Which of the following statements describes circuit training?

   ☐ **A** This method of training involves times of work followed by times of rest

   ☐ **B** A series of exercises, completed for a certain amount of time, after one another

   ☐ **C** Exercising, often running, varying time, distance and effort

   ☐ **D** Involves shifting weights to increase the strength of muscles, using a programme of repetitions and sets

   (1 mark)

2. Which of the following statements describes interval training?

   ☐ **A** This method of training involves times of work followed by times of rest

   ☐ **B** A series of exercises, completed for a certain amount of time, after one another

   ☐ **C** Exercising, often running, varying time, distance and effort

   ☐ **D** Involves shifting weights to increase the strength of muscles, using a programme of repetitions and sets

   (1 mark)

3. Which method would a sprinter most likely use to improve performance?

   ☐ **A** Weight training

   ☐ **B** Cross training

   ☐ **C** Interval training

   ☐ **D** Continuous training

   (1 mark)

4. Fartlek training depends on varying:

   ☐ **A** The people in the training session

   ☐ **B** The sports played

   ☐ **C** The weights lifted

   ☐ **D** The time, distance and effort in the session

   (1 mark)

5. Which training method is a triathlete most likely to use?

   ☐ **A** Cross training

   ☐ **B** Weight training

   ☐ **C** Circuit training

   ☐ **D** Fartlek training

   (1 mark)

Short answer questions

6. What kind of athlete would use interval training as part of their programme and why?

   (3 marks)

7. What type of sportsperson would use Fartlek training in their programme and why?

   (2 marks)

8. How would someone using weight training as part of their training programme increase the intensity of the session?

   (2 marks)

Longer answer questions

9. Interval training is used in training sessions and can be adapted to many activities. Devise an interval training session lasting 30 minutes for an activity of your choice.

   (5 marks)

10. Explain why a person would use cross training in their training programme.

    (5 marks)

3.1.2 ～ Linking physical activity with diet, work and rest for personal health and a balanced healthy lifestyle

3.1.2d Further aspects of training

What you will learn about in this topic:

1 — Environment and training
2 — The training year

1 — Environment and training

Training can be affected by the athlete changing the environment in which they are working. Working at altitude for example can change the air quality, terrain and heat conditions, but, with careful monitoring, can bring about positive adaptations to the body.

Changes in altitude and temperature can impact on the exercising athlete both positively and negatively. Adjustments can be made to the conditions, which benefit the performer.

Effects of altitude on the athlete

Runners experience extreme heat when taking part in the Sahara Desert marathon.

Endurance athletes will source areas that allow them to train at altitudes between 1.8 kilometres and three kilometres above sea level to see improvement. It takes up to 21 days for the **altitude training** to have an effect on the athlete.

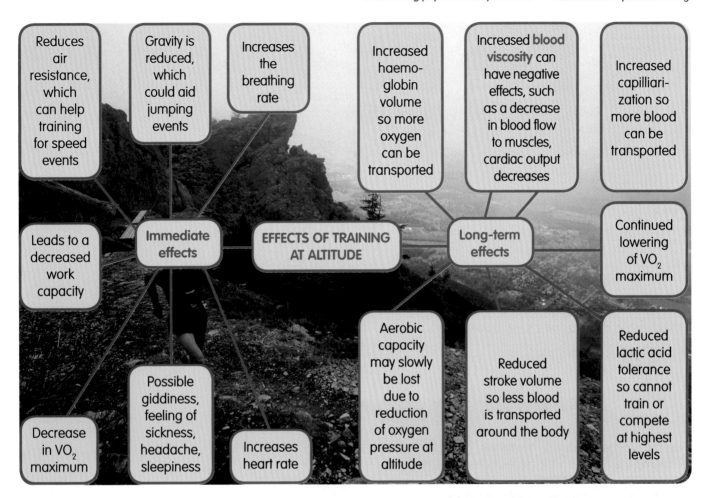

Reduces air resistance, which can help training for speed events

Gravity is reduced, which could aid jumping events

Increases the breathing rate

Increased haemo-globin volume so more oxygen can be transported

Increased **blood viscosity** can have negative effects, such as a decrease in blood flow to muscles, cardiac output decreases

Increased capilliari-zation so more blood can be transported

Leads to a decreased work capacity

Immediate effects

EFFECTS OF TRAINING AT ALTITUDE

Long-term effects

Continued lowering of VO_2 maximum

Possible giddiness, feeling of sickness, headache, sleepiness

Decrease in VO_2 maximum

Increases heart rate

Aerobic capacity may slowly be lost due to reduction of oxygen pressure at altitude

Reduced stroke volume so less blood is transported around the body

Reduced lactic acid tolerance so cannot train or compete at highest levels

Active challenge

Using the Internet, search for suitable sites that give advice to athletes who train at altitude. Pay particular attention to information given about the height and terrains of areas.

Training effects

The negatives effects of training in a different environment can include:

- Travel – can be expensive and take time
- Cultural differences – an athlete may have to adapt to unfamiliar local ways of life
- Dietary differences – in foreign countries an athlete would have to eat different food such as spices, there would also be differences in preparation and ways of cooking
- Homesickness – periods away from family and friends
- Poor facilities – may not be up to usual standards
- Unfamiliar surroundings – finding places and shops, and so on, can be stressful.

The positive effects of training in a different environment can include:

• When the athlete returns and performs at sea level their performance will peak 19 to 21 days after they have finished their altitude training
• Their performance improves on days 36 to 48 after their return as altitude training improves the red blood cell production: increasing three per cent in week three and seven per cent in week four, so more oxygen is taken up during exercise.

Effects of warm weather on the athlete

In warm weather, athletes should maintain carbohydrate and fluid levels (through water and sports drinks) in order to stave off early fatigue. Wearing lose, lightweight specialist clothing can help keep the body cool. The position of the clothing helps by 'wicking' the sweat away from the body – moisture is moved away from the body through the fabric to the exterior where it evaporates. Using an appropriate factor suncream can help prevent the risk of sunburn. In long-distance events there is a danger that the body may overheat, so an athlete may pour water over their head to help cool their body down.

Sportspeople cannot continue vigorous exercise in high temperatures because of a number of hindrances:

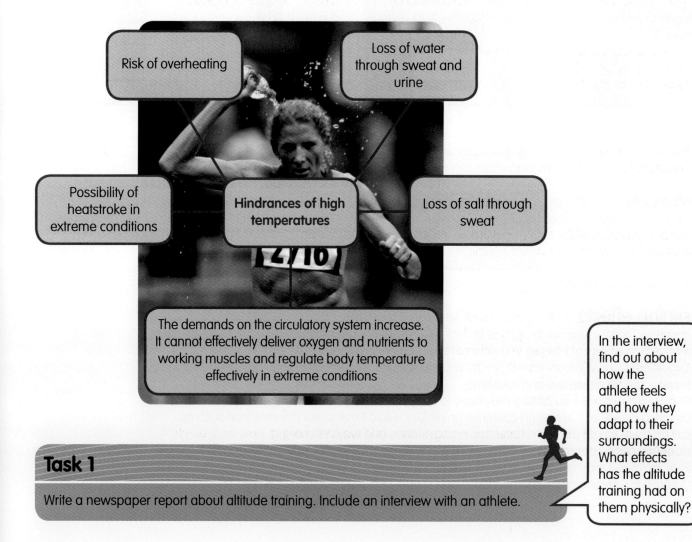

Risk of overheating

Loss of water through sweat and urine

Possibility of heatstroke in extreme conditions

Hindrances of high temperatures

Loss of salt through sweat

The demands on the circulatory system increase. It cannot effectively deliver oxygen and nutrients to working muscles and regulate body temperature effectively in extreme conditions

In the interview, find out about how the athlete feels and how they adapt to their surroundings. What effects has the altitude training had on them physically?

Task 1

Write a newspaper report about altitude training. Include an interview with an athlete.

2 — The training year

An athlete's training programme for the year needs detailed planning. The plan will change according to the sport, the individual and the facilities available. The performer's coach should make the team or individual familiar with the plan and, although it may have to change due to injury or postponed fixtures, the general outline should create goals to achieve which will keep the performer motivated. Training differs greatly depending on whether it is taking place pre-season, peak season (competition) or out of season (closed season) periods – the type of training and its intensity will differ according to the season, due to the different needs of the athlete and the demands of the activity.

The performer will need to consider the following when creating their yearly plan:

• What is the overall aim of the training?
• When does the training year start?
• What results are they working on: personal best or qualifying performance?
• When is the competition they are training for?

Yearly plan for team games

A team game with a seasonal playing time may include the following in their pre- and peak season training:

• Progressive development of the energy systems that are needed for the activity
• Practice of basic skills
• Teamwork for effective play.

Pre-season

• Working on fitness, strength, mobility, power, speed, skills and strategies to improve the condition of the body systems and to raise the level of fitness.

Early season

• Increased work in skills, tactics, mental approach and diet in order to improve the physical and mental condition of the body to meet the challenges of the competition.

Peak season (competition)

• Emphasis on speed, working at competitive pace, experiencing game situations and improving fitness in order to apply a skilled performance to competitive situations.
• Improving skill and strategies with maintenance of pre-season fitness.
• Supplementing skill sessions with more intensive weight, sprint or endurance training.

Out of season (closed season)

• Resting from the efforts of the season, keeping a level of fitness, continuing to work on strength, flexibility, aerobic fitness and skills to maintain a level of fitness and condition of the body.

- Monitoring body fat and activity levels so that players begin pre-season training at or close to their 'playing weight'.
- Undergo specific weight training.
- Undergo specific skill development programmes to remedy any diagnosed weaknesses.

The following is a yearly programme that has been adapted to netball:

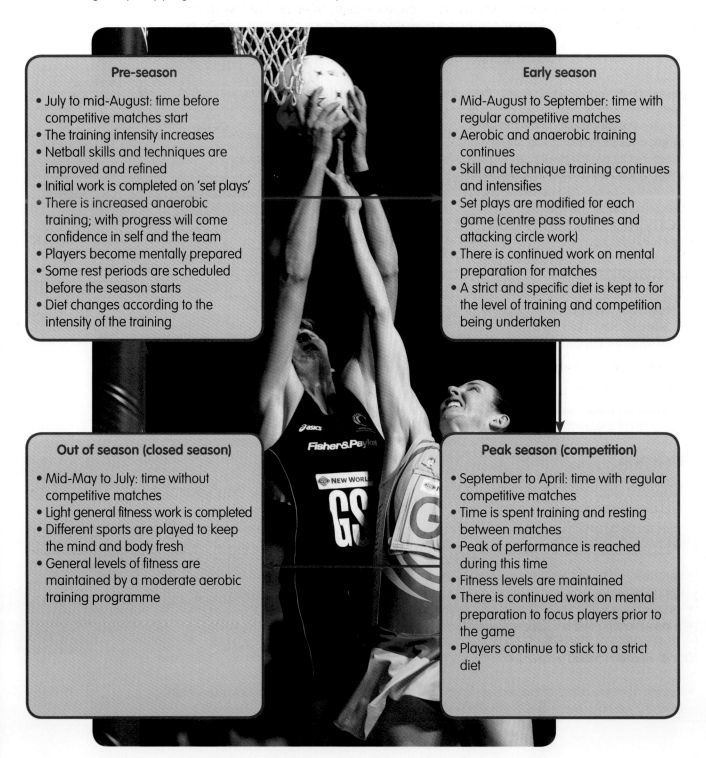

Pre-season

- July to mid-August: time before competitive matches start
- The training intensity increases
- Netball skills and techniques are improved and refined
- Initial work is completed on 'set plays'
- There is increased anaerobic training; with progress will come confidence in self and the team
- Players become mentally prepared
- Some rest periods are scheduled before the season starts
- Diet changes according to the intensity of the training

Early season

- Mid-August to September: time with regular competitive matches
- Aerobic and anaerobic training continues
- Skill and technique training continues and intensifies
- Set plays are modified for each game (centre pass routines and attacking circle work)
- There is continued work on mental preparation for matches
- A strict and specific diet is kept to for the level of training and competition being undertaken

Out of season (closed season)

- Mid-May to July: time without competitive matches
- Light general fitness work is completed
- Different sports are played to keep the mind and body fresh
- General levels of fitness are maintained by a moderate aerobic training programme

Peak season (competition)

- September to April: time with regular competitive matches
- Time is spent training and resting between matches
- Peak of performance is reached during this time
- Fitness levels are maintained
- There is continued work on mental preparation to focus players prior to the game
- Players continue to stick to a strict diet

Yearly plan for an individual event

If an athlete is training for a competition taking place in August, then their training needs to start in the previous October. Their training is divided into six phases, each with their own goals.

The timetable sets out specific plans to develop each of the following areas: condition of the body, strength, technique, mobility, endurance and speed. The activities are building blocks worked on to ensure there is no injury. The goals or objectives of each phase are as follows:

- Phase 1 – starts in October for 16 weeks: general development of strength, mobility, endurance and basic techniques.
- Phase 2 – starts in mid- to late January for eight weeks: development of specific fitness and advanced technical skills to do with the event.
- Phase 3 – starts in mid-April for eight weeks: competition experience and achievement of indoor objectives, helping to bring an edge to performance.
- Phase 4 – starts in mid-May for eight weeks: adjusting technique for the event and preparation for the main competition.
- Phase 5 – starts in mid-July for eight weeks: competition experience and achievement of outdoor objectives.
- Phase 6 – starts in early September for four weeks: active recovery from the season's efforts, changing the intensity, amount and type of training. Planning preparation for the next season is done.

Key terms

Altitude training – training at a place situated between 1.8km and 3km above sea level

Blood viscosity – thickness of the blood

Summary

When training at altitude, athletes need to understand the effects it will have on their body. They should be aware that the decreased oxygen pressure might reduce aerobic fitness. They may also become 'overtrained' as they work to the training zone based on their heart rate at sea level, and their heart rate will change at altitude. It is roughly 19 and 36 days after training at altitude that the effects can be realized. Training in warm weather requires attention to the intake of carbohydrates and fluids required. Water and sports drinks can replace these fluids, helping to starve off fatigue and poor performance.

When an athlete works on their training programme they should be confident that it has been planned correctly according to their fitness levels. They should be secure in the knowledge that the exercises being performed are within their capabilities and unlikely to lead to injury. Knowledge and training may be required when undertaking certain training methods for the safety of the performer and should be followed as a matter of course for each session.

Exam questions

Multiple-choice questions

1. Which of the following best describes the personal drawbacks of training at altitude?

   ☐ **A** Homesickness, dietary changes, travel expense, cultural differences, eventual increased performance

   ☐ **B** Increased blood viscosity, dietary changes, travel expense, cultural differences

   ☐ **C** Travel expense, homesickness, dietary changes, effects could be immediate, aiding jumping events

   ☐ **D** Homesickness, dietary changes, travel expense, cultural differences

   (1 mark)

2. Which of the following best describes activity for inclusion in out of season training?

   ☐ **A** Monitor body fat, maintain level of aerobic fitness, work on speed, work on specific skills that may be weak

   ☐ **B** Work on intensive weight-training programmes, work on strength and flexibility, monitor body fat, work specific skills that may be weak

   ☐ **C** Maintain level of aerobic fitness, work on strength and flexibility, monitor body fat, work specific skills that may be weak

   ☐ **D** Work on strategies, maintain level of aerobic fitness, work on strength and flexibility, monitor body fat

   (1 mark)

Short answer questions

3. What are the dangers of an athlete training in high temperatures?

   (3 marks)

4. Even out of season an athlete should continue training. What kind of work will be in this training session?

   (3 marks)

Longer answer questions

5. What immediate effects on the body can athletes experience when they start altitude training?

   (4 marks)

6. What are the **four** main phases to consider when planning training for the year?

   (4 marks)

7. What phase of the year does the photograph below illustrate? What parts of training does it show?

   (2 marks)

FA Cup fifth round between Watford and Chelsea.

8. At different times of the year, the type of training in a programme changes. What is the likely content of for the following training sessions for a team game?

   (a) Pre-season.

   (2 marks)

   (b) Early season.

   (2 marks)

   (c) Peak season.

   (2 marks)

   (d) Out of season.

   (2 marks)

   (Total 8 marks)

3.1.2 ～ Linking physical activity with diet, work and rest for personal health and a balanced healthy lifestyle

3.1.2e Diet

What you will learn about in this topic:

1 — A balanced diet
2 — Understanding nutrients
3 — Causes and results of dietary imbalance and deficiency
4 — Special diets for active participation

1 — A balanced diet

Exercise, diet, work and rest influences a person's health and well-being, with each aspect linking together. Exercise prepares the body so it is physically capable of completing tasks without becoming exhausted. In order to exercise, the body needs to be fuelled by food. A good, balanced diet will see that the correct amount of calorie intake provides the body with enough energy to complete tasks. Work and rest create a mental and physical balance for the individual, providing times which are demanding and times when the body systems can recover and adapt to the demands made of it. The correct balance of these aspects enables the body to function at its optimum level.

The food you eat fuels your body just like petrol fuels a car. As the human body is more complex than a car engine, there are different types of food to keep the various parts of the body functioning properly. Food does the following:

- provides energy
- helps our bodies grow
- repairs injured tissue
- contributes to good general health.

It is important to have a balanced diet consisting of seven types of food. Eating the correct quantities and combinations of food will keep the body's systems functioning properly, keep hair and skin in good condition and reduce the chances of obesity. In general, a balanced diet is important, but by changing the amounts of each nutrient eaten, a diet can be adapted to have a specific result for a sportsperson training for a particular event.

2 — Understanding nutrients

There are seven parts to a balanced diet, which fulfil the requirements necessary for a healthy, functioning body.

Food type	About the food	Aid to the sportsperson
1. Carbohydrates (sugars and starch) 	• Carbohydrates can be found in: fruit, cakes, beer, sweets, granulated sugar, bread, pasta, rice and potatoes. • They are stored in the liver and muscles as glycogen. They convert to glucose and are used as energy for muscles of the body, brain and other organs. • Any excess is converted and stored as fat. • Carbohydrates should provide over 47 per cent of daily energy requirements and if training hard, this should rise to 65 to 70 per cent.	• Provides a ready source of energy when the muscles require it. • Carbohydrates in the highly processed form of sugars, provide energy, but no other nutrients, so it is better to eat more starchy carbohydrates. • Any excess is stored in the body as glycogen and, on demand, releases energy slowly. Athletes in long-distance events can take advantage of this.
2. Protein 	• Protein can be found in: meat, fish, pulses (chick-peas, lentils and beans), nuts, eggs and poultry. • Builds body muscle, repairs tissue, enzymes and hormones. • Proteins are broken down in the body as amino acids: 21 types are needed for our bodies to work properly. • Our bodies can produce 13 types of non-essential amino acids, but the other eight (essential amino acids) come from protein in foods. • Any excess is converted and stored as fat.	• Builds muscle and repairs tissue within the body. • Proteins are essential to help the body heal after injury. • Sportspeople who need large muscle size will take in extra proteins for this effect.
3. Fats 	• Fats can be found in: milk, cheese, butter, oils, chocolate, fatty meats, soya beans and corn. • Fats provide energy. • The recommended daily intake of fat is 30 per cent, made up of a combination of saturated, polyunsaturated and monounsaturated fatty acids. • Fat can be stored in the body.	• Increases size and weight of the body. • Important for performers who benefit from having extra bulk, shot-putters for instance. • Unnecessary weight can inhibit performance and lead to high cholesterol levels. • Fats are a form of stored energy, released slowly when there is a lack of carbohydrates.

4. Vitamins	• Vitamins can be found in: fruit (vitamin C), liver and carrots (vitamin A), whole grain and nuts (vitamin B1) and vegetable oil (vitamin E). • Vitamins help with the general health of vision, skin condition, forming of red blood cells and blood clotting, and bones and teeth. • There are a total of 13 vitamins.	• The general health of an athlete is important if they are to perform well. When training hard, vitamins from the B group are used more and so need to be replenished. This can be done by eating more vitamin B foods or using supplements.

5. Minerals	• Minerals can be found in: milk, saltwater fish (iodine), red meat, liver, green vegetables (iron), cheese and cereals (calcium). • Calcium helps bones grow, iron helps the making of red blood cells and the way oxygen is carried in the body by haemoglobin. • The more exercise a person does, the greater the need for minerals, provided by a varied diet or supplements. • Excessive amounts of the mineral salt can lead to high blood pressure.	• Minerals increase the body's ability to efficiently carry oxygen to the working muscles. • Iodine aids normal growth, essential for an athlete's ability to produce energy. • Iron helps produce red blood cells and so carries more oxygen around the body, helping to prevent fatigue. • Calcium helps blood to clot, aiding recovery from injury and strengthens bones and muscles.

6. Fibre and roughage	• Fibre can be found in: leaves, seed cases, cereals and whole grain. • Fibre helps digestion, but contains no nutrients. • There are two types of fibre: insoluble which adds bulk to food helping it to keep moving through the digestive system, preventing constipation and soluble which helps to reduce cholesterol, keeping the heart healthy.	• Less cholesterol in the body makes the heart more efficient, which is important for transporting blood to the working muscles. • By keeping the digestive system functioning regularly, the body retains less waste products.

7. Water and fluids	• Water and fluids can be found in: sports drinks, watermelon, orange juice, and so on. • Two-thirds of the body is made up of water. • Everyone needs regular intakes of fluid to replenish what is lost in urine, sweat and condensation through breath.	• Water allows blood to flow more easily around the body. This is extremely important when exercising, as the body demands more oxygen, nutrients, heat control and waste removal. • In endurance events, or when exercising in hot weather, water is lost quickly and can lead to dehydration and heatstroke if not replenished. • However, recent cases have shown drinking excess water during exercise can be fatal. If in doubt, medical advice should be sought.

135

Task 1

Answer the following questions on nutrients.

1 – What is the major role in the human diet of:
   a. Carbohydrates   **b.** Protein   **c.** Fat   **d.** Vitamins?

2 – Give three examples of foods that are good sources of:
   a. Vitamins   **b.** Carbohydrates   **c.** Protein.

3 – What two types of carbohydrates are there and in what form are they stored in the body?

4 – How does the sportsperson use the following:
   a. Carbohydrates   **b.** Protein   **c.** Water   **d.** Fats

3 — Causes and results of dietary imbalance and deficiency

There are many factors that change the energy requirements of individuals. At different stages of life, greater or lesser levels of energy are needed. For instance, teenagers need more energy than adults. Women, on average, need less energy than men as they have a smaller build. As people get older their pace of life slows down and their energy requirements reduce. Even same age, same gender people rarely have the same energy needs owing to variations in their lifestyles and build. Some of these factors are out of our control, but what does dramatically change our energy requirements and is in our control is the amount of activity we undertake and the amount of food that we take in.

Below is an approximate calculation of the daily intake requirements for people of different ages:

15-year-old boys	11,500kJ (approx. 2700kcal)
15-year-old girls	8800kJ (approx. 2100kcal)
Adult men	10,500kJ (approx. 2500kcal)
Adult women	8400kJ (approx. 2000kcal)
Older men	8800kJ (approx. 2100kcal)
Older women	8000kJ (approx. 1900kcal)

Active challenge

Discuss with a partner four different reasons why people have different energy requirements.

How energy is calculated

The body needs energy all of the time, even when sleeping. This is because the body is still functioning – the heart is beating, blood is circulating and the body is breathing. This lowest form of energy requirement is called the basal metabolic rate (BMR).

Each sport then has a different energy requirement depending on the length of the activity, the intensity of the activity and the level of the opponent (easy game or lower level opponent). Each food type has an energy value, which can be calculated in two ways:

• Joules are calculated by a moving force – energy needed when one kilogram is moved by one metre by a force of one Newton.
• Calories are calculated by a rise in temperature – the amount of energy needed to raise the temperature of one gram of water by 1°C.

The main ways we understand these calculations are as kilojoules (kJ) and kilocalories (kcal). This is because diets and nutritional information on food packaging deal in large quantities and so the equation is multiplied by 1000 to make the figures more manageable.

The table below shows the energy per hour needed to perform different activities:

Activity	Approx. energy (kJ)	Activity	Approx. energy (kJ)
Weightlifting	676	Cycling	1806
Mowing the lawn	1016	Swimming	1357
Housework	790	Circuit training	1806
Walking	903	Tennis	1579
Ice skating	376	Water aerobics	903
Gardening	1016	Running	2033

Strenuous cycling uses high amounts of energy

Dietary imbalance and deficiency

There are different causes of dietary imbalance and deficiency including stress, illness, injury and not eating the correct nutrients. When a person starts to train, more energy is required but they may not adapt their diet accordingly.

Experiencing weight gain? You have decreased exercise and training and your calorie intake exceeds energy expended.

Want to maintaining your weight? Balance your calorie intake with energy used.

Degrees of being overweight

An **overweight** person can be said to be heavier than the average person of that gender, height and build. The extra weight, however, is not necessarily a threat to the person's health because sometimes a lot of it is muscle.

Being **overfat** can have a direct effect on a person's health. In this category a person will have a high level of fat in comparison to their total **body composition**. Having this amount of fat can lead to obesity-related diseases: problems may include high blood pressure, strokes, cancer and heart attacks.

When a person reaches the stage of being **obese**, they are abnormally fat (more than 20 per cent over the standard weight for their height). At this stage the health risks become more dangerous and can include diabetes, high blood pressure, heart disease, osteoarthritis and early mortality.

Being overweight is a problem of the twenty-first century. Many nations now record more than 20 per cent of their population as clinically obese and well over half the population as overweight. This trend has increased throughout the world as fast food chains reach various areas. In the USA, 66 per cent of the population is overweight, giving America the nickname 'the fat capital of the world'.

Experiencing weight loss? You have increased exercise and training but are not consuming enough calories to fuel the exercise increase.

Underweight

To be classed as underweight a person has to be ten per cent under their **optimum weight**. Some athletes are naturally underweight, others succumb to pressures to be a certain weight to be the best they can be at their chosen sport. When people are unnaturally small, there are consequences:

- Some suffer from osteoporosis in later life.
- Low food intake leads to malnutrition and greater risk of injuries.
- Insufficient vitamins and minerals are taken in to maintain a healthy body.
- Lack of eating leads to an energy drain, affecting performance.
- Women have irregular periods.
- Women have loss of bone mass leading to injury.

How to minimize the risks of weight loss

The risks of weight loss can be minimized by making weight loss realistic and gradual. Any weight loss should be planned, carefully monitored and related to the optimal weight of the individual. Consulting specialist dieticians will keep the weight loss safe. Losing weight should be attempted at the beginning of the season or out of season, as high-energy requirements will increase as the training builds up and competition arises.

Possible dietary problems

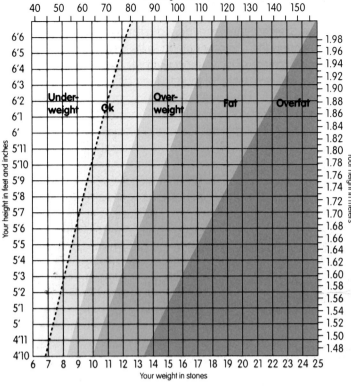

This chart provides a guideline for adults showing what their correct weight should be depending on their height.

Some athletes put pressure on themselves in an attempt to reach and maintain a low body weight that is ideal for their sport but unnatural for themselves. In some cases this may lead to an eating disorder such as anorexia nervosa. An anorexic person does not eat because they see themselves as fat. Their obsessive state of mind forces them to severely reduce their intake of food. This condition leads to excessive weight loss. A person who is bulimic eats a lot and then forces themselves to vomit. This also has the effect of weight loss.

Both eating disorders can lead to bouts of depression and many severe medical problems, including kidney and liver damage, and even death. Both men and women can suffer from an eating disorder.

Task 2

1 – Choose five different types of sportsperson.

2 – Write a sentence on what they may say about their diet and how it affects them.

> You should include ideas on energy needs of the activity and weight demands of the activity.

4 — Special diets for active participation

An increase in demands on the body from exercise means an increase in energy requirements. This should result in a change of diet to compensate for the new demand. The general diet for an athlete is high in carbohydrates, low in fat, with a high fluid intake, including energy drinks and/or water. These provide energy and keep fluid levels balanced.

Diets can be organized around an exercise programme. This will involve timing when meals are taken, the content of the meal depending on the activity and the quantity of food to be eaten. A top-class athlete acquires knowledge of how to use the different types of food to their best advantage. Each sportsperson's diet will vary due to individual differences of build, demands of the sport, position played in the team and any injury incurred.

Diet plays an important part in an athlete's performance. It is seen to be so important that many sportspeople are guided by specialist dieticians and follow strict eating habits. The dietician will play their part in the performer's success just as the coach does. There are crucial times when a sportsperson can adapt their diet to help performance. By adapting their diet over the following periods, the athlete can get the best results out of their performance:

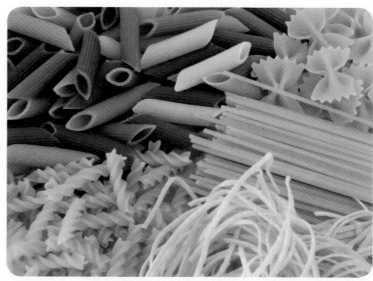
Pasta meals are suitable for long-distance events because they provide a slow energy release.

- the week before the event
- the day of the event
- during the event
- after the event.

High-protein diet

This diet requires the intake of a large amount of protein. Weightlifters and athletes needing a loss of weight over a fairly short period of weeks can adopt this diet. High-protein diets can also be used in a rehabilitation programme after injury for the repair of damaged tissue. A bodybuilder or a rugby player will use this type of diet to burn fat and increase muscle size. Taking creatine supplements (a form of protein) increases the effect. A rugby league player can eat as many as six meals a day taking in mainly proteins, some carbohydrates, but little or no fat. Throughout the day, they are encouraged to drink plenty of fluids and eat fruit as well as the prescribed meals. The protein will build up the muscle, carbohydrates will provide energy, and fluids will keep the body hydrated.

High-protein meals help repair and build muscle tissue – great for rugby players.

Eating a high-protein diet has the effect of reducing the storage of fat in the body. Some performers, who need to lose weight quite quickly, can use this type of diet. However, there is now evidence of long-term problems with this type of diet. For example, when a bodybuilder takes in a high level of animal proteins this raises the cholesterol levels in the body leading to a possibility of heart disease, diabetes, stroke and cancer. A performer using a high-protein diet to control their weight can develop kidney damage in the long term.

Carbohydrate loading

Traditionally, **carbohydrate loading** is linked with long-distance events but other competitors can benefit too such as swimmers. Carbohydrates are important to an athlete, as they are easy to digest and provide an instant source of energy. By eating more carbohydrates, a store of glycogen is built up in the body. In competition this store will reduce levels of fatigue and so help to maintain a standard of performance.

The week before the event

The week before an event a runner's training routine and diet change. Due to the excesses of previous training, carbohydrates are low in the body while proteins are high. This combination is not appropriate for a long-distance athlete. So, four or five days before the race, many more carbohydrates are eaten in order to build up these energy stores for the event.

The training programme is now tapered so fewer miles are covered, allowing energy levels to build up and the speed of the shorter runs increases, preparing for a burst of speed during the race. By taking in extra carbohydrates and fewer fats, together with reducing the intensity of the training programme, the body is able to store these nutrients, as glycogen, for use in the race.

The usefulness of carbohydrates is so widely recognized by long-distance athletes that 'pasta parties' are organized for the athletes two days before the London Marathon. Eating foods such as noodles, rice, potatoes and even beans on toast will have a similar effect.

Carbohydrate loading can be useful for long-distance athletes, such as Sandra Graf, winner of the 2008 women's wheelchair London Marathon.

The day of the event

On the day of the event athletes will choose, from preference and experience, either a large meal three to four hours before the race, or a lighter one up to two hours before the race. This is the final chance before the competition to make sure that carbohydrates are stocked up and fluid levels are high.

During the event

The prolonged, moderate to hard intensity of a long-distance race reduces the amount of water in the body. Low water levels reduce performance and prevent correct circulation and temperature control. Regular water intake is essential to the athlete to prevent dehydration. Energy drinks help the body to work hard for longer by using the carbohydrates in them.

Taking in fluids during an endurance event is essential.

After the event

An athlete must continue to drink fluids and energy drinks to replace the fluids and carbohydrates lost. High-energy food can be eaten immediately after the race. Depending on the training programme following the event, a sensible meal including various carbohydrates is usual.

1. Week before competition: eat complex carbohydrates to build glycogen stores.

2. Last three or four days: eat small snacks every two to three hours that are high in carbohydrates plus smaller portion of protein.

3. Morning of competition: eat high complex carbohydrates, low fat, protein and fibre.

4. Pre-competition: consume carbohydrates in solid or liquid form as glycogen is only stored for 12 hours – helps with energy in the latter stages of long-distance events.

5. Just before competition: eat a small amount (50g) of fast absorbing carbohydrates to keep blood-sugar levels high.

6. During competition: for long-distance events, take in carbohydrate drinks – in tournaments, eat carbohydrates between matches.

7. After competition: drink fluids to rehydrate the body – eat small amounts of carbohydrates (2g per kg of body weight) to replenish glycogen stores and speed up recovery time.

Task 3

Make a ten-point list about carbohydrate loading and the procedure for food and fluid intake for a long-distance event.

Active challenge

With a partner, discuss high-protein diets and then design three different meals for this type of diet for a sports performer.

Key terms

Balanced diet – daily intake of food containing the right type and amounts of nutrients

Overweight – having weight in excess of normal (not harmful unless accompanied by overfatness)

Overfat – a term used to describe a person who has more body fat than is recommended for their gender and height

Body composition – the proportion of body weight that is fat, muscle and bone, normally measured as a percentage

Obese – a term used to describe people who are very overfat

Optimum weight – ideal weight for a person, giving them the best chance of success in an activity

Energy drinks – fluids containing carbohydrates

Carbohydrate loading – building up carbohydrate levels in the body to use in endurance events

Summary

For general health, a balance of all seven nutrients in the daily diet is important. Different types of food provide these nutrients, helping the body to function properly.

Each food has a different energy value and use. A person who strikes a balance between food intake and energy output according to activity levels will maintain a constant weight. When an athlete understands the different qualities of food, they can use them to their best advantage and build special diets into the training programme. By eating certain foods in the correct quantities, athletes can change their natural shape (changing their fat ratio and muscle size), energy levels and recovery period, so helping them to be more effective in their sport. Any reduction in weight should be carefully planned and monitored. Adapting the type of diet consumed and exercise undertaken can change the tissue ratio. However, extreme diets can badly affect the health of an individual.

Exam questions

Multiple-choice questions

1. Which of the following does not describe a function of food?

   ☐ A Provides energy

   ☐ B Increases fast twitch muscle fibres

   ☐ C Repairs injured tissue

   ☐ D Contributes to general healthy growth

   (1 mark)

2. Which of the following are examples of carbohydrates?

   ☐ A Pasta, beer, bread, meat

   ☐ B Rice, cheese, fruit, milk

   ☐ C Pasta, rice, potatoes, bread

   ☐ D Bread, milk, cheese, beans

   (1 mark)

3. Which combination of food would best help tissue repair?

   ☐ A Fish, nuts, eggs, poultry

   ☐ B Fish, lentils, bread, eggs

   ☐ C Beans, eggs, butter, fruit

   ☐ D Eggs, cereals, liver, nuts

   (1 mark)

4. Which of the following best describes carbohydrate loading?

   ☐ A Eating foods that allow a store of glycogen to build up in the body

   ☐ B Eating foods that are high in bulk to fill you up

   ☐ C Eating foods that give a balance of all nutrients

   ☐ D Eating foods that will reduce weight and build muscle

   (1 mark)

5. Sportspeople will use a high-protein diet for different reasons. Which of the following is not one of them?

   ☐ A To help with weight loss

   ☐ B To burn fat and increase muscle size

   ☐ C To store energy

   ☐ D As an aid to rehabilitation after injury

   (1 mark)

6. Which of the following is not a direct danger of being overweight?

   ☐ A High blood pressure

   ☐ B Being run over by a car

   ☐ C Diabetes

   ☐ D Stroke

   (1 mark)

Short answer questions

7. What possible risks to a person's health could there be if a person reached the stage of obesity?

   (3 marks)

8. When a person is lower than ten per cent of their optimum weight they are classed as underweight. What are the risks to health of being underweight?

   (3 marks)

9. Anorexia is an eating disorder. What are the mental and physical effects this disorder can have on the sufferer?

   (3 marks)

Longer answer questions

10. A balanced diet helps a person in many ways in everyday life. State **four** functions of eating a good balance of food.

    (4 marks)

11. There are seven constituents of a balanced diet. Vitamins and water/fluids are two, what are the other **five**?

    (5 marks)

3.1.3 ～ Making informed decisions about getting involved in a lifetime of healthy physical activities that suit their needs

3.1.3a School influences

What you will learn about in this topic:

1 — National Curriculum requirements
2 — The healthy schools programme and PSHE
3 — Healthy eating
4 — Physical activity
5 — Extra-curricular opportunities and provision

Physical education (PE) can play a major part in bringing all aspects of a school together. The range of skills and tasks involved in a challenging, active programme can provide lifelong competence and proficiency skills. There are recognized career pathways in sport, which involve not only the performer but also leaders, coaches, officials and volunteers.

1 — National Curriculum requirements

The National Curriculum aims to develop:

- successful learners who enjoy learning, make progress and achieve
- confident individuals who are able to live safe, healthy and fulfilling lives
- responsible citizens who make a positive contribution to society.

(National Curriculum 2007)

The National Curriculum sets out key concepts for learning in PE. An understanding of these concepts allows for the maximum learning and application.

In relation to PE, the Key Stage 4 key concepts are:

- Competence
- Creativity
- Performance
- Healthy, active lifestyle.

Schools help to promote a healthy lifestyle.

PE has a high status in school curriculums. It is a foundation subject with statutory programmes of study at all Key Stage levels. It is recommended that each student undertake two hours of PE per week. At Key Stages 1 to 3 competitive games are a compulsory part of the PE curriculum. At Key Stage 4 engaged learning aims to motivate young people so they continue to learn, train and understand the available employment opportunities after finishing their school career.

Task 1

1 – Search the QCA website and find the Programme of Study for PE Key Stage 4.

2 – Write down and explain what is involved.

3 – Add what is involved in each area to each of the Key Stage 4 key concepts headings on page 145.

Benefits of a school PE programme

There are many factors that affect why a person takes part in sport. What we see on the television or read in newspapers and magazines may sway us in our thinking. The more we are in contact with an influence, the more it may affect us. School, consequently, can have an important part to play in the encouragement of exercise.

Sports day brings the whole school together through physical activity.

Promotion
Schools actively encourage participation in sport. As PE has foundation subject status, its importance is recognized in the school curriculum. A school's PE programme can encourage participation on many levels and by giving the opportunity to enjoy sport in school, a student may decide that they want to do more in their own time.

Demonstrates fitness levels
Schools provide up to two hours of PE lessons a week for all students. Statistically this is insufficient to improve a person's fitness. However, PE lessons can educate young people about the amount of exercise that can be undertaken to have a positive effect on fitness.

Encourages a healthy lifestyle
Some PE lessons involve general instruction on a balance of exercise, diet and the need to avoid harmful substances for a healthy life. A good health education can help young people make sound life choices, which can continue throughout adulthood. A good PE programme can show students how to be healthier and fitter; this knowledge can be used in the future to avoid obesity and other eating problems.

Offers a range of activities
By offering a wide range of activities, schools provide a variety of experiences for students where progress and achievement can be made. Providing a mix of sports will give students more chance of finding an area of interest and, hopefully, the confidence to continue taking

part in physical activity after they have left school. A mix of competitive and non-competitive activities on the timetable provides a balance that may also suit a wider variety of personalities. By being given the chance to take part in activities they like, young people may voluntarily choose to do more in their own time. A school PE programme can present students with unique opportunities: they may have the chance to experience sports camps and various other outdoor activities not usually readily available. Residential visits develop both physical and social skills. Whilst knowledge, understanding and application of new activities progress outside of the school environment, students also learn to deal with others in both a learning and social situation.

Extends skills learnt in class

Many schools offer students the chance to join a school club or team. This provides an opportunity to improve and extend skills learnt in lessons in a competitive environment, although sometimes participation is purely for fun. Some clubs may be set up for a completely new activity not on the PE timetable to further extend students' interest. Using local facilities as part of the PE programme helps to show students what is available locally to them, what is expected there and whom they are going to meet. This experience can equip students with enough knowledge, understanding and confidence in an activity that they have the self-assurance to pursue it on their own, in their own time, independent of school.

Leisure pursuits

By providing a wide variety of activities on the timetable and during extra sessions after school, students may be sufficiently interested in exercise to continue participation after they have left school. The experience of visiting a local gym or sports centre whilst at school may provide them with the knowledge and confidence to go to these centres independently. Well over half the adults that ski had their first skiing experience through their school.

Experience different ways to enjoy sport

Schools recognize the importance of giving students a chance to not only play games, but to take part in different ways too. Members of a class may regularly experience how to judge, coach, observe, officiate, captain, lead, organize or choreograph through other activities they take part in. These different experiences may appeal to

Orienteering provides a different type of challenge for students.

students and lead to an interest in sport beyond actually playing the game.

Experience healthy competition

Some activities provide the opportunity for competition. The rules governing a particular game will allow for healthy competition whilst supplying a framework for safe and fair play. The players know the boundaries and rely on the umpire or referee to implement them consistently.

Develop a variety of skills

By providing a balanced curriculum, a full range of skills can be learnt. From experience and knowledge of a variety of activities, a person may choose their favourites – those providing the most satisfaction and enjoyment – and pursue them throughout adulthood, such as coaching or performing.

Develops social skills and friendships

Many activities involve people coming together to train, organize or compete. Meeting people with similar interests can develop social skills and help to create friendships. The skill of team work can also be learnt, such as in game situations where each person has their own role to play. Team members learn that working hard individually contributes to group success. Each player relies on the others to do their job and when necessary. For example, in football a midfield player may have to run back to cover the defender.

Often after a match, all involved in the game meet together socially. This gives a chance not only to talk about the game, but also to chat socially and to maintain old friendships and establish new ones.

Education for lifelong learning

A long-term aim of PE is to see young people take part in physical activity into adulthood. Schools aim to give everyone a positive experience of exercise and provide students with knowledge, skills and understanding, thereby giving them confidence to apply this to their lifestyle after they have left school. Students should be shown how they can use physical activity for leisure, recreation or a career and should aim for sport to be a lifelong learning experience.

Positive experiences

For most people PE provides both winning and losing situations. Any success can boost a person's self-esteem: for that moment their standing in the group rises and they can take that feeling away and build on it for the future.

Positive experiences in school can lead to a lifelong enjoyment and participation in sport.

The chance to learn about, and cope with, losing is also a valuable lesson. In this way, sport prepares people for coping with high and low situations, possibly helping them with the ups and downs of life they may experience as they get older.

Develops stars of the future

At school level a teacher can recognize early on a student's ability and potential to do well. These skills can be nurtured and developed within lessons and extra-curricular activities.

Through school, staff can point a student in the direction of a club or coach so that their skills can be further advanced. Linking different institutions at this stage gives the performer the opportunity to experience a higher level of coaching and competition. In the long-term, this progressive development can prepare performers for major events and competitions.

PE teachers

By relating their enthusiasm for the subject, a PE teacher can show all of the good reasons for taking part in exercise. Although some students are not enthusiastic about PE, a positive approach by staff can encourage them to join in. By using different ways to deliver information and encouraging more than just the acquisition of skill, the teacher can plan their lessons to inspire enthusiasm in their class. However, there may be some occasions when a teacher has favourite sporting activities, which may lead to less time being spent on other sporting options. In these instances students could miss out on the chance to learn about the full range of sporting activities available.

Skills that are nurtured and developed at school can lead to the sporting stars of the future.

Teachers bring their own expertise and experience to their lessons. This greater in-depth knowledge can be passed on to students for their benefit and success. The teacher may play particular sports themselves and be able to reproduce quality demonstrations, further helping students to increase their level of interest.

Task 2

1 – Using the headings from the section 'Benefits of a school PE programme', create a spider diagram to help you to remember the main points.

2 – Under each heading, write a sentence in your own words to expand the idea.

2 — The healthy schools programme and PSHE

The National Healthy Schools Programme

The **National Healthy Schools Programme (NHSP)** is a long-term government initiative aiming to create children who:

- are happier
- stay safe
- are healthier
- do better in learning and life.

The initiative involves students, parents, young people, school staff and the whole school community working together in an effort to equip children with the skills and knowledge for them to make informed choices about healthy living.

The majority of schools are involved (95 per cent in 2008) and the government aims that 75 per cent will achieve National Healthy School status by 2009.

The themes of the initiative include:

- personal, social and health education
- physical activity
- healthy eating
- emotional health and well-being.

The initiative aims to help children and young people to:

- develop healthy behaviour
- reduce health inequalities
- raise their achievement
- promote social inclusion.

Active challenge

1 – In a group of four, choose one of the themes of the initiative each.

2 – Using the Internet, research your theme.

3 – Feedback the information to your group and discuss your findings.

Personal, Social and Health Education (PSHE)

Personal, Social and Health Education (PSHE) aims to give students knowledge about real life issues they may face as they grow up. Providing such knowledge and skills shows young people the choices they have in order to follow healthy and responsible lives and do so in a confident and worthwhile manner.

At Key Stage 3 and 4, PSHE is divided into two areas:

1. Economic well-being – links career education, work-related learning, enterprise and money management, including the value of saving.
2. Personal well-being – personal development, sex and relationship education, drug education, including ways to keep themselves safe when confronted with difficult situations, and how to deal with pressure.

3 — Healthy eating

A school's healthy eating policy should provide details of the balance of food available for both students and staff to buy. Having a well-proportioned diet helps keep a person healthy. Eating small amounts of fats and proteins, and larger amounts of carbohydrates, vitamins, minerals and fibre helps to keep the body in a good condition and its systems working efficiently.

Healthy eating has an important part to play in a person's healthy lifestyle. The **Whole School Food Policy (WSFP)** helps to guide each school to develop their own meaningful and appropriate food policy. It involves all those involved with the school including students, staff, parents, caterers, members of the community using the school and others associated with the school. As a result, it is hoped the policy will establish individual values and a school ethos based on food's part in health and well-being. The WSFP helps everyone in school have a shared view on food and can include:

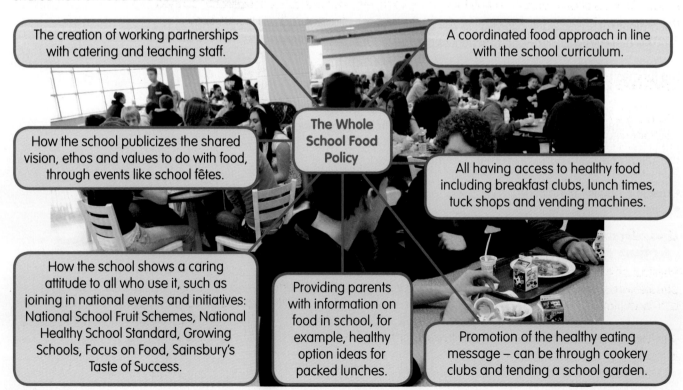

The creation of working partnerships with catering and teaching staff.

A coordinated food approach in line with the school curriculum.

The Whole School Food Policy

How the school publicizes the shared vision, ethos and values to do with food, through events like school fêtes.

All having access to healthy food including breakfast clubs, lunch times, tuck shops and vending machines.

How the school shows a caring attitude to all who use it, such as joining in national events and initiatives: National School Fruit Schemes, National Healthy School Standard, Growing Schools, Focus on Food, Sainsbury's Taste of Success.

Providing parents with information on food in school, for example, healthy option ideas for packed lunches.

Promotion of the healthy eating message – can be through cookery clubs and tending a school garden.

Active challenge

Using the Internet, find out more about one of these national events and initiatives:

- National School Fruit Schemes
- National Healthy School Standard
- Growing Schools
- Focus on Food
- Sainsbury's Taste of Success

Share your findings with four other people who have chosen different initiatives.

Standards and requirements for school lunch

The School Meal Review Panel (SMRP) has set out guidelines for standards at school lunchtimes. It is based on two sets of standards:

1. Food-based standards: types and frequency of food offered – maintain or boost the amounts of fruit, vegetables, meat and fish protein, starchy foods and milk and dairy products.
2. Nutrition-based standards: the proportion of nutrients students receive – including how much energy, protein, carbohydrates, fat, fibre, vitamins and minerals should be provided by school meals.

Food choices

Whether at breakfast club, lunch or break-time, healthy food choices should be made available in school. Lunches should provide a variety of healthy options including oily fish, meat protein and bread. Snacks brought in from home should be low fat and sugar free. Snacks such as nuts and seeds with no added salt or sugar should be made available from school. Schools should provide a fruit tuck shop, fresh vegetables (fresh, dried, frozen, canned or juiced), free fresh drinking water and drinks that consist of water, milk (skimmed, semi-skimmed), pure juices, yoghurt and milk drinks, low calorie chocolate, and tea and coffee.

Active challenge

Find out what the School Meal Review Panel require school meals to provide. Start your search off with:

- oily fish
- meat content in food available
- bread provision
- deep fat frying.

4 — Physical activity

Physical activity is seen to be a major way of improving the nation's health. Providing young people with daily opportunities for physical activity and an understanding of how physical activity contributes to good health helps to create the foundation for a lifelong active lifestyle.

A school's **Physical Activity Policy** is a strategy that sets out the ways in which physical activity is made available to school users.

The aims of the Physical Activity Policy are to:

• increase physical activity levels
• increase well-being
• increase understanding of the importance of a healthy active lifestyle and the part physical activity has to play in it.

The Physical Activity Policy can have a major impact on the health of all involved in the school and the community. Encouraging young people to take the opportunity to participate in a wide range of activities can impact on their lives in many ways. It can reduce weight, promote positive attitudes towards physical activity, instill healthy habits that could last a life time, enhance understanding of the curriculum and help students to learn to work with and respect the views of others.

To help schools achieve a high standard of physical activity, guidelines have been set out:

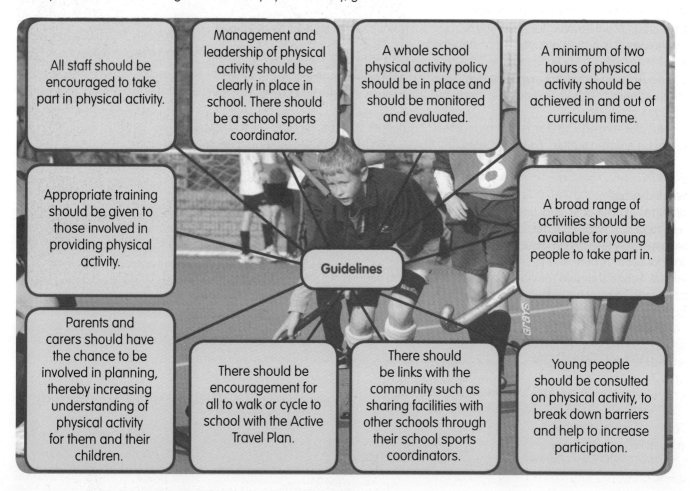

All staff should be encouraged to take part in physical activity.

Management and leadership of physical activity should be clearly in place in school. There should be a school sports coordinator.

A whole school physical activity policy should be in place and should be monitored and evaluated.

A minimum of two hours of physical activity should be achieved in and out of curriculum time.

Appropriate training should be given to those involved in providing physical activity.

Guidelines

A broad range of activities should be available for young people to take part in.

Parents and carers should have the chance to be involved in planning, thereby increasing understanding of physical activity for them and their children.

There should be encouragement for all to walk or cycle to school with the Active Travel Plan.

There should be links with the community such as sharing facilities with other schools through their school sports coordinators.

Young people should be consulted on physical activity, to break down barriers and help to increase participation.

5 — Extra-curricular opportunities and provision

As an extension to PE lessons many schools provide extra sessions after school, during lunch and at breakfast too. These are called extra-curricular activities and provide even more benefits to students because by taking part, students:

• become members of a team
• have a chance to be a captain or a leader of a team
• visit other schools and venues for matches

- may join organized trips to see top-class sports events
- become members of a club or society, taking part for the fun of the event and not for the competition
- develop links with clubs and providers. For example, local coaches may come into school to help or local clubs may offer their facilities
- improve their sports performance by joining after school clubs to increase skill and in some cases reach a standard for awards and proficiency tests
- have an opportunity to take part in a less traditional sport, for example, korfball (a passing game using skills similar to those in netball)
- could set up a general health club, involving aerobic or weight training for instance.

PE teachers have an opportunity to coach their specialist events in extra-curricular activities. At these sessions, coaching to a greater depth, competing against other schools and taking teams away to tournaments is a chance to develop students' skills to the highest level. The best equipment and facilities may also be put in place to support that activity.

Extent and quality of facilities

What facilities there are available in the school or the local area will have a bearing on the types of sports available. A school with large playing fields, all-weather surfaces, a gymnasium, halls and dance studios will have the chance to offer the widest range of activities. For those with more limited facilities, halls and outside areas can be adapted and shared, for example a hall could be used for badminton with six people sharing a court. Taking advantage of the local sports centre can be an alternative and make up for restricted facilities, but this may rely on the availability of regular, adequate transport.

Schools can create links to local clubs, such as health clubs and golf clubs. By using these providers, young people can experience and gain confidence in taking part in physical activity outside school. This familiarity can break down barriers, giving confidence to students to use the facilities independently and continue participation into adult life.

Outside visits give students the chance to participate in specialist activities such as ice-skating, ten-pin bowling or dry slope skiing. These provide an introduction to the activity and can lead to further pursuits outside of school.

Winning a final is the aim of all school teams, but playing at top-class venues can be a bonus.

Outside visits give students a chance to try something new.

Task 3

Your school may run extra-curricular clubs, teams, societies and visits linked with physical activity. Write down some or all of these activities to include the number of students involved, how often the clubs are run and if they have achieved successes, such as awards or trophys. You could use your school website to help you.

Key terms

National Healthy Schools Programme (NHSP) – an initiative promoting the link between good health, behaviour and achievement

Personal, Social and Health Education (PSHE) – a subject providing learning opportunities for students to develop the knowledge and skills to become a responsible member of society

Whole School Food Policy (WSFP) – a government initiative showing the importance of eating the correct food and how it has a bearing on health and well-being

Physical Activity Policy – an initiative for schools to promote physical activity

Summary

There is increasing importance put on physical activity, diet and personal, social and health education for the long-term good health of the nation. Schools can fully develop these areas by implementing the initiatives such as the National Healthy Schools Programme. Many schools have the opportunity to offer students a wide range of physical activities by using their own or other sport providers. Physical activity is encouraged in both curriculum and extra-curricular time to fulfil the National Curriculum requirements and provide additional physically active opportunities.

Exam questions

Multiple-choice questions

1. The initials NHSP stand for:

   ☐ **A** Nutrition and Healthy Schools Programme

   ☐ **B** National Healthy Social Programme

   ☐ **C** National Healthy Schools Performance

   ☐ **D** National Healthy Schools Programme

   (1 mark)

2. The National Curriculum has stated key concepts allowing for maximum learning. They include:

   ☐ **A** Competitiveness, performance, creativity and healthy, active lifestyle

   ☐ **B** Competence, performance, creativity and healthy, active lifestyle

   ☐ **C** Competence, performance, fairness and healthy, active lifestyle

   ☐ **D** Competence, application, creativity and healthy, active lifestyle

   (1 mark)

3. Which of the following best reflects the healthy food choices promoted by the National Healthy Schools Programme?

   ☐ **A** Roasted peanut snacks, fresh vegetables, fruit, oily fish, pure juices

   ☐ **B** Pure juices, nuts and seeds, fresh vegetables, chips, oily fish

   ☐ **C** Nuts and seeds, fresh vegetables, fruit, oily fish, pure juices

   ☐ **D** Oily fish, nuts and seeds, fresh vegetables, fruit, carbonated drinks

   (1 mark)

4. What do the initials WSFP stand for?

   ☐ **A** Whole School Food Policy

   ☐ **B** Whole School Food Procedure

   ☐ **C** Whole School Food Programme

   ☐ **D** Whole School Food Performance

   (1 mark)

Short answer question

5. What effect on children do the long-term aims of the NHSP hope to have?

   (2 marks)

Longer answer questions

6. In what ways can school affect a person taking part in sport?

   (6 marks)

7. The WSFP sets out guides for eating in school. What do the food-based standards and the nutrition-based standards involve?

   (4 marks)

8. What are the main aims of the Physical Activity Policy?

   (5 marks)

9. There are more ways of being involved in sport other than being a performer. Give **four** different ways a person can enjoy being involved in sport, stating why they might choose that pathway.

   (4 marks)

10. Teachers can positively influence participation in physical activity. If you were a PE teacher say how you would positively influence participation.

    (6 marks)

11. Extra-curricular activities help to promote a healthier lifestyle and involve people in physical activity. Describe different kinds of extra-curricular activities and their benefits that could be available to school students.

    (8 marks)

3.1.3 〜 Making informed decisions about getting involved in a lifetime of healthy physical activities that suit their needs

3.1.3b Further school influences

What you will learn in this topic:

1 — PESSCL
2 — PESSYP

1 — PESSCL

PESSCL (Physical Education, School Sport and Club Links) was a strategy funded by the government for working in partnership with the Youth Sport Trust. Sports colleges created links with PESSCL, giving a greater chance for people to participate in sport. The strategy operated between 2003 and 2008. Its aim was to increase the opportunities for sporting progression for 5 to 16 year olds. The target was to give 85 per cent of young people the chance to have a minimum of two hours PE and school sport a week. The target was met and then surpassed.

Specialist sports colleges

Sport is one of ten specializms in the specialist schools programme. Sports colleges act as flagships to show the way forward for sport. Schools apply to become a specialist school in order to raise the standard of achievement by linking with the community and local businesses. There is a network of over 400 sports colleges across the country who work with other schools and private sector sport providers (there are over 450 School Sport Partnerships), using government funding to raise the standard of sport and increase the opportunities for participation for young people.

Sports colleges share a vision of raising standards in PE for all students, leading to whole school improvement. In their efforts to promote excellence in PE they involve the whole community, sports bodies and local schools, sharing facilities, resources and good practice. By creating these links a structure is formed inspiring young people to pursue careers in sport and PE.

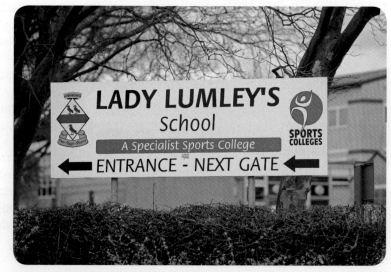

Sport is one of ten specialist subjects a school can focus on.

The Young Gifted and Talented programme

The Young Gifted and Talented programme is part of PESSCL and aims to improve the identification of and provision for gifted and talented students. It is supported by the Department for Children, Schools and Families, helping talented children to reach their potential. It includes four key areas:

1. Benchmarking excellence – how schools and local authorities can achieve standards of excellence with professional development for teachers to support young people in PE.

2. Talent identification in PE – Leeds Metropolitan University and Christ Church Canterbury created guidelines to help teachers identify talented students in their schools.

Gifted and talented programme

3. Provision for talented young athletes – Multi-skill Academies have been established to help young people to develop core skills used in all sports. National governing bodies support the scheme by providing over 30 performance camps so that elite athletes can experience aspects of elite sport.

4. Support for talented athletes – it can be difficult for talented athletes to balance school, home and sport commitments. Help is provided through the Junior Athlete Education Programme. The programme, put in place through School Sport Partnerships, trains and supports both teachers and talented young athletes. Gifted and talented students who are ahead of their year academically or excel in particular areas, such as in sport, are registered with the Young Gifted and Talented Learner Academy.

Step into Sport

The Step into Sport project is delivered by the Youth Sport Trust, Sport England and Sports Leaders UK and aims to help 14 to 19 year olds start, and keep involved in, sports leadership and volunteering. Experience and qualifications in leadership can begin in their own school, then move on to helping primary schools organize festivals of sport and then be involved in the community as a sports volunteer.

In 2006 there were 1.5 million volunteers in sport in roles including coaches, managers, administrators and officials. The Youth Sport Trust aims to increase the quality and quantity of these volunteers and has set up the following to help this happen:

Youth Sport Trust

Stage 1: Step on – Step into the sport pathway: Students are guided through the skills required to plan, manage and run sports sessions of their own as part of the PE programme. Students develop skills and gain experience of being a leader and are given opportunities to develop their leadership skills, giving them the chance to think for themselves.

Stage 2: Step in – TOP LINK programme: This involves schools giving young leaders a chance to put into operation their acquired skills from the Step into Sport stage. This provides the first step to active volunteering with school sport and inter-school competition, gaining experience in planning, managing and delivering festivals of sport and dance. Other possible involvement can include multi-skill clubs and TOP activity (run by Sainsbury's who organize pathways for students to lead a more active life through less traditional sports).

Stage 3: Step out – School and club links: Students move from school based volunteering and leadership to community based activities – students can then be placed in top-quality community clubs as a volunteer.

The TOP LINK programme supports young volunteers in organizing local competitions.

Swimming

Swimming forms part of the national PESSCL Strategy. The activity is recognized as not only a healthy activity but also an essential life-skill. Statutory guidelines are in place to ensure all Key Stage 2 students can swim a distance of at least 25 metres independently. Students have the chance to learn to swim in school via school swimming teachers or at an accredited club. Clubs should be accredited by the Aquamark learn to swim programme standards. Further swimming can be pursued at Swim 21 accredited swimming clubs.

Swim 21 clubs build partnerships with SSCo (School Sport Partnerships) so that:

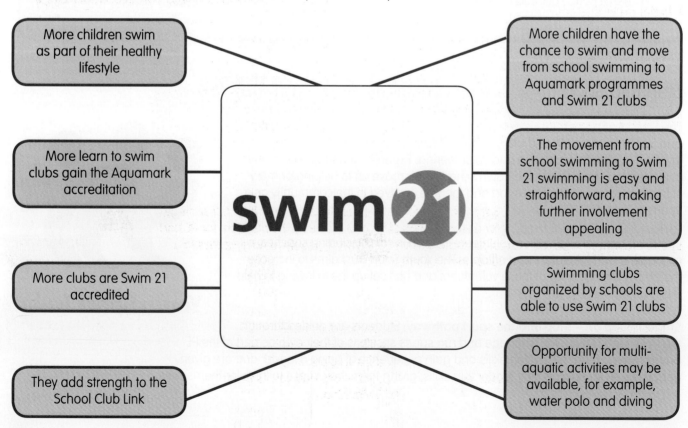

More children swim as part of their healthy lifestyle

More children have the chance to swim and move from school swimming to Aquamark programmes and Swim 21 clubs

More learn to swim clubs gain the Aquamark accreditation

The movement from school swimming to Swim 21 swimming is easy and straightforward, making further involvement appealing

More clubs are Swim 21 accredited

Swimming clubs organized by schools are able to use Swim 21 clubs

They add strength to the School Club Link

Opportunity for multi-aquatic activities may be available, for example, water polo and diving

Coaching

In order to deliver the commitment of two hours of PE per week to young people, extra coaches are needed. The Community Sports Coach Scheme helps this commitment by working with teachers to provide high-quality sport during and after school, on site. The government has recognized the importance of coaching and are aware of several areas to be addressed:

- shortage of coaches (professional and voluntary)
- recognition of coaching as a profession
- provision of accredited qualifications
- creation of a real career development structure.

The UK Coaching Framework was launched in 2008, setting out the government's 3–7–11 Action Plan. The plan runs to 2016 and is working towards coaching being a professionally regulated profession. The framework includes a vision that, through sound foundations, will:

- develop a coaching system that has skilled coaches supporting children at all stages of their development
- be the world number one for sports coaching.

This vision will be achieved through a structured action plan and a clear pathway for coaching in the UK. It is hoped that this will result in the quality of coaching at all stages being improved, leading to:

- greater participation in sport
- sustained participation in sport
- better performances.

The UK Coaching Framework aims to increase the quality and quantity of coaching at all levels.

Active challenge

Choose a sport with a pathway structure for coaching. Prepare a short presentation and deliver it to the rest of the class.

2 — PESSYP

PESSYP (Physical Education and Sport Strategy for Young People) is the new national strategy, replacing PESSCL. It is a strategy for all Key Stages aiming to create the best system for PE and sport for young people, and enabling more children and young people to have access to a wider range of sports for a greater amount of time.

The strategy has ten sections:

1. Club Links
2. Coaching
3. Competition
4. Continuing professional development
5. Disability
6. Extending activities
7. Gifted and talented
8. Infrastructure
9. Leadership and volunteering
10. Swimming.

The five hour offer

For schools in a School Sport Partnership (SSP) the aim is to build up the quality and quantity of coaching available to young people. This will contribute to the five hour offer and further advance local links and coaching programmes. The five hour offer means 5 to 16 year olds will have two hours of PE in school time plus have access to three hours PE outside of school time. This opportunity is created by the following bodies working together:

• Sports colleges
• School Sport Partnerships
• National governing bodies
• County sports partnerships
• Community providers.

Competition managers will be put in place in each of the 49 county areas in England linking together the School Sports Partnerships. Their job will be to help raise competition in quality and quantity throughout the network, working towards the fulfilment of the five hour offer. The following diagram shows the relationship between the managers, partnerships and schools and how they work together to provide the five hour offer.

The following diagram shows the relationship between the managers, partnerships and schools and how they work together to provide the five hour offer.

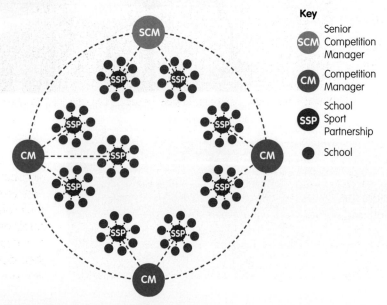

Key

SCM Senior Competition Manager

CM Competition Manager

SSP School Sport Partnership

• School

Increased coaching opportunities

Coaching grants will be awarded to schools to meet the increased demand for more coaches to deliver the five hour offer. The grants will provide 1000 hours of coaching. School Sport Partnerships will provide a coaching plan and the money will fund a small team of coaches delivering a minimum of 200 hours each. Coaching will be sustained over a period of time, hopefully leading to young people regularly engaging in clubs and competition.

School Sports Coaching Scholarships will be allocated at different levels:

• to level 1 coaches aiming towards **UKCC** (UK Coaching Certificate) level 2
• to UKCC level 2 coaches without experience of working with children
• higher level coaches.

Youth Sport Trust, Sport England and sports coach UK will together plan a recruiting strategy for volunteer coaches. They aim for 10,000 adult volunteers involved in coaching working towards the five hour offer.

National networks of school sport

The work of PESSYP has provided a national network of School Sport Partnerships linking maintained schools with specialist sports colleges. In England, over five million young people have had the chance to take part in two hours of sport per week. By creating partnership with schools, the community and sports colleges, increases in opportunities for young people to take part in sport have been created. On average, schools are offering 17 different sports, which shows an average increase in the range of sporting activities available.

Young Ambassadors

Young Ambassadors are young people who have been chosen to promote sport, PE and healthy living. They are 16 to 17 year olds who have shown outstanding talent, leadership or volunteering skills. Their presence will provide role models for other young people and promote the Olympic and Paralympic values, inspiring others to take up opportunities afforded by the 2012 Olympics. Their enthusiasm will help to spark a new generation of people in sport and possibly even Olympic medal winners.

Young Ambassadors are chosen to show the opportunities that the 2012 Olympics have to offer.

Active challenge

1 – Prepare five questions you would ask a Young Ambassador about their role.

2 – Swop your five questions with someone else and answer each others questions. Discuss your answers with each other.

Ask a Young Ambassador how they were chosen, their role and what qualities they have that help them in their duties.

National Talent Orientation Camp

The National Talent Orientation Camp aims to prepare talented 14 to 16 year olds for work beyond compulsory education through personal, academic and vocational challenges for their chosen sport. They will help talented athletes in several ways:

• Build up the young persons sporting knowledge
• Give insights into sport
• Give young people a chance to reflect on their own talent, ability, attitude and ambition
• Use role models in the sport to inspire others to do well
• Prepare young people for life from when they are aged 16 onwards, through further examinations or vocational education.

The camp deals with four areas:

1. Talent and ability: asks questions of the athlete about their ability and ambitions, their mental strength to succeed and their ability to perform when it matters.

2. Attitude and ambition: questions whether the young athlete aspires to be the best in the world, questions their attitude towards competition, asks if sport is where they want to be?

3. Knowledge and understanding: asks whether the athlete knows what top-class and Olympic champions look like, whether they realize what is required and expected in order to be the best, and whether they will study their sport and be professional.

4. Education and lifestyle support: asks whether the environment for training will match their ambition to reach the top. Will their family support them? What choices do they have with regards education?

The National School Sport Week

The National School Sport Week aims to motivate young people to take part in competitive sport. It provides a time for schools to celebrate their achievements in the past year, launch new initiatives, new school competitions and profile all that is good about sport in school. It provides a chance to raise the profile of sport in the community. Activities during the week include:

- Festivals of sport – Young Leaders, having followed the TOP Link programme, plan, organize and run events for primary school children
- Intra-school competitions – School Sport Coordinators lead these events with the support of the Young Leaders
- Inter-school competitions – arranged using the skills of Competition Managers
- New and creative ideas organized at a local level.

Key terms

PESSCL – Physical Education, School Sport and Club Links, a strategy by the government, managed by the Youth Sport Trust (2003 to 2008) to increase sporting opportunities for 5 to 16 year olds

PESSYP – Physical Education and Sport Strategy for Young People, the new name for PESSCL (from 2008)

UKCC – UK Coaching Certificate

Summary

The government strategies of PESSCL and now PESSYP, managed by the Youth Sport Trust, are increasing the opportunities for young people in sport. The aim is to create a structure that will give people the chance to be involved in sport and maintain a healthy lifestyle throughout their lives. The strategy deals with several areas including increased opportunities for sport for all, talented and gifted athletes, volunteers, swimming and coaching.

Exam questions

Multiple-choice questions

1. The initials PESSCL stand for:

   ☐ **A** Physical Education, School Sport and Club Links

   ☐ **B** Physical Exercise, School Sport and Club Links

   ☐ **C** Physical Education, School Sport and Competitive Links

   ☐ **D** Physical Education, School Sport and Club Liaisons

   (1 mark)

2. The initials PESSYP stand for:

   ☐ **A** Physical Education and Schools Strategy for Young People

   ☐ **B** Physical Education and Sport Strategy for Young Participants

   ☐ **C** Physical Exercise and Sport Strategy for Young People

   ☐ **D** Physical Education and Sport Strategy for Young People

   (1 mark)

3. Which of the following reflect reasons why young people are chosen to be Young Ambassadors?

   ☐ **A** Have outstanding talent, hog the play so they can score the most goals, are a role model to young people, have volunteering skills

   ☐ **B** Look good in their sports kit, show leadership skills, inspire others to take part, have outstanding talent

   ☐ **C** Show leadership skills, have volunteering skills, have outstanding talent, are a role model to young people

   ☐ **D** Inspire others to take part, show leadership skills, prefer to play computer games, are a role model to young people

   (1 mark)

Short answer questions

4. How are young people recognised as gifted and talented?

   (2 mark)

5. What is the title of the accreditation award that swimming clubs aim to gain as recognition for reaching particular standards in swimming teaching?

   (1 mark)

6. What is the scheme helping teachers to provide better coaching during and after school for students?

   (1 mark)

Longer answer questions

7. The Youth Sport Trust have set up stages to increase the quality and quantity of volunteers involved in sport with their 'Step on, Step in, Step out' strategy. What does this involve?

   (6 marks)

8. Swimming is both healthy and an essential life skill so has an important place in the government strategy for increased sporting opportunities.

   (a) What stages could a young person go through to learn to swim?

   (3 marks)

   (b) What aims do the government have for swimming?

   (3 marks)

9. The UK Coaching Framework was launched in 2008 setting out a 3–7–11 Action Plan. What is the vision for this plan?

   (8 marks)

10. The National Talent Orientation Camp aims to prepare talented athletes for possible challenges. How does it do this?

    (4 marks)

3.1.3 ~ Making informed decisions about getting involved in a lifetime of healthy physical activities that suit their needs

3.1.3c Emotional health and well-being

What you will learn about in this topic:

1 — Vulnerable individuals and groups
2 — Bullying policies
3 — Behaviour and rewards policies
4 — Confidential pastoral support systems

Emotional health and well-being is part of the National Healthy Schools Programme. To fulfil these criteria, schools should promote a positive attitude to emotional health and well-being to students. Students are encouraged to understand their feelings and feel confident to express them. By building confidence and emotional strength, students should be able to increase their capacity to learn.

1 — Vulnerable individuals and groups

No one should be **vulnerable** – exposed to the possibility of being attacked or harmed, either physically or emotionally – because of their ethnicity, gender, class, sexuality or disability. Helping vulnerable individuals or groups can help health and educational issues by enabling them to be more confident in themselves through the support provided. Appropriate strategies should be there for both the vulnerable and their families.

Schools can put in place pastoral support systems and care plans using guidelines and specialist input. Schools can seek the advice of the Child Protection Agency if necessary. Schools should identify individuals at risk from, or who are experiencing, behavioural, emotional and social difficulties. Those individuals should feel supported by having their own support plan, having a planned structure of intervention work to match their needs and having access to, and support from, other agencies.

2 — Bullying policies

Everyone in school should be aware of the school's anti-bullying policy. The policy should be available for discussion, inviting the views of students, parents, carers and staff. This gives ownership and credibility to the issue of bullying. The policy should reflect the anti-bullying charter and be agreed by all, with every person knowing their role within it. The policy should set out how to deal with bullying and staff should be confident that they are supported when identifying and managing this issue.

The key to an anti-bullying policy is for students to promptly report any concerns to parents, carers or teachers. A clear system of recording, following up and monitoring those involved gives the best chance of eliminating further bullying incidents. As a result of the policy young people should be able to feel safe in school.

3 — Behaviour and rewards policies

To support positive behaviour each school should develop their own individually designed behaviour and rewards policy. This should clearly explain how positive behaviour by students is rewarded and promoted so students know how to succeed.

Rewards can be in different forms. They may be general or specific to the individual, for example, merit stickers, food rewards, eligibility for trips, cinema ticket vouchers or an acknowledgement in special assemblies.

Students might enjoy trips to the cinema as a reward for good behaviour.

4 — Confidential pastoral support systems

Pastoral care aims to look after the social, emotional and medical needs of students in school.

Each school should have a clear plan set out for confidential pastoral care to which both students and staff have access. The systems should actively work against any discrimination or stigma and be in line with the child protection policy. All staff and students should be included in the system and be able to input ideas from time to time. They should understand the pastoral system and confidently identify the route for referral. The pastoral system should support all those in need, especially those experiencing major life changes or bereavement.

The theme of emotional health and well-being plays its part in all five outcomes of the national Every Child Matters agenda:

1. Be healthy.
2. Stay safe.
3. Enjoy and achieve.
4. Make a positive contribution.
5. Achieve economic well-being.

PE has an important part to play in growing students confidence and the feeling of achievement by providing opportunities to lead and coach with support and guidance.

Key terms

Vulnerable – being exposed to the possibility of being attacked or harmed, either physically or emotionally

Pastoral care – following policies and procedures in order to look after the welfare of young people

Summary

Schools now include their emotional health and well-being policy as part of their whole school policy following the National Healthy Schools Programme. Each school has the chance to design and implement the most appropriate systems for their circumstances. Staff and students should be fully aware of the policy and be able to have an input into its content.

The policy will help all vulnerable students who have emotional and behavioural difficulties.

Exam questions

Multiple-choice questions

1. Emotional health and well-being is part of which national programme?

   ☐ A National Happy Schools Programme

   ☐ B National Healthy Schools Programme

   ☐ C National Programme for Better Learning

   ☐ D National Schools Improvement Programme

   (1 mark)

2. Which of the following is not related to the behaviour and rewards policy?

   ☐ A Supports positive behaviour

   ☐ B Individually designed rewards are the most appropriate

   ☐ C Students should know how to succeed and gain rewards

   ☐ D Rewards should be targeted at emotional, social and medical needs

   (1 mark)

Short answer question

3. In what ways can vulnerable young people be helped in school?

   (3 marks)

Longer answer question

4. How can a policy on anti-bullying help schools deal with this issue?

   (4 marks)

3.1.3 ～ Making informed decisions about getting involved in a lifetime of healthy physical activities that suit their needs

3.1.3d Cultural and social factors

What you will learn about in this topic:

1 — Leisure time
2 — Fairness and personal and social responsibility
3 — Social groupings

1 — Leisure time

The amount of leisure time available to most people has increased due to a number of factors. The overall time spent in the workplace is less than it was a decade ago. There are several reasons for this. This extra leisure time has created a demand for more facilities and more opportunities to follow active leisure pursuits.

Opportunities available

Since technology has taken on a larger role in our lives there has been a gradual increase in leisure time. For example, machines have been built to do the jobs manual workers did years ago. New technology does the job more efficiently and in less time than manpower could, reducing the working hours of employees meaning some companies now employ part-time or temporary workers. This increases the time available for people working less hours to take part in leisure pursuits.

Improvements in technology has also provided people with labour-saving devices around the home such as washing machines and dishwashers, freeing up time previously needed to complete housework, giving greater opportunity for leisure pursuits.

An increasing number of people are taking advantage of working from home and are rearranging their day so that their time in the office is reduced. They can still be as efficient though due to computer technology and excellent communication systems such as mobile phones and the Internet, rearranging their working environment in this way provides more flexibility to pursue and take advantage of leisure activities.

With the increase in part-time work and flexi-time opportunities (flexible working hours), people have more time to pursue leisure activities. By law employers also have to provide their work force with paid holiday every year, therefore, people have more time and money to spend in the leisure industry.

People today are encouraged to plan for their retirement more carefully, with many taking early retirement. Although the retirement age will be between 60 and 65 for women from 2010 to 2020 and is 65 for men, most people aim to be financially secure at a much earlier age. By subscribing to pension plans early, people can stop working sooner, giving more time to pursue their leisure interests later in life.

By the year 2081, the population will have risen from 61 million to 108 million. As the population increases, there will be more demand for leisure facilities.

Retiring earlier and leading a healthier lifestyle allows more people to enjoy their leisure time.

Unemployed people also create a new group that need leisure provisions. In order to include this group in the community, concessions are made and reduced fees are available for them so they can still be involved in leisure pursuits.

All of these reasons put demand on the leisure industry to create more public and private facilities. The types of activities catered for range from the less-active pursuits to providing fully equipped sports centres. Local authorities take on board the task of making available the public amenities for a wide range of user groups. They aim to target these user groups and provide them with a window in the week where they have the opportunity to take advantage of the facility. For example, a sports centre may cater for mothers with young children during the week when it's quiet, offering access to nursery facilities, mother and baby groups and concessionary rates.

Task 1

Write two sentences for each of the headings below, giving reasons for their effect on the leisure industry.

- Working from home
- Early retirement
- Increased part-time work
- Technology
- Shorter working week
- The unemployed

Providers and users

Often, local authorities make provision for sport at the most convenient time of the day for a particular user-group, making the session available for the largest number of people as possible. Sports centres then make special time slots in the day available and charge a concessionary rate. The government aims to make sport and physical exercise available to everyone: research is carried out to highlight problem groups, a policy then sets out the plan to improve access for that particular user-group and finally, the implementation of initiatives removes barriers to participation so more people can become involved. It is then the job of the local authorities to ensure that each group is catered for. For example:

- parent and toddlers
- schools
- fitness sessions for the elderly
- novice performers.

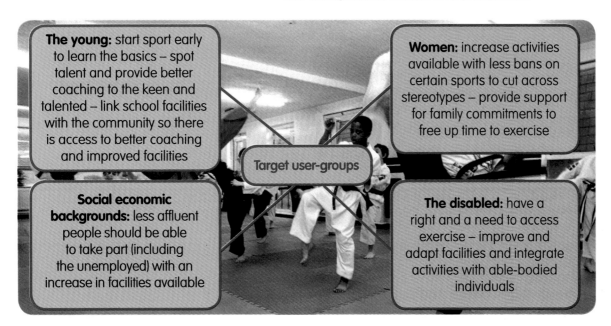

The young: start sport early to learn the basics – spot talent and provide better coaching to the keen and talented – link school facilities with the community so there is access to better coaching and improved facilities

Women: increase activities available with less bans on certain sports to cut across stereotypes – provide support for family commitments to free up time to exercise

Target user-groups

Social economic backgrounds: less affluent people should be able to take part (including the unemployed) with an increase in facilities available

The disabled: have a right and a need to access exercise – improve and adapt facilities and integrate activities with able-bodied individuals

2 — Fairness and personal and social responsibility

Participating in any event or activity requires a person to follow the rules or laws of the game. Often, good coaching and training will give the performer the correct understanding and knowledge of the activity and enable them to adhere to the relevant rules, conventions and codes of behaviour. By keeping to such rules a performer satisfies their own personal responsibilities in the activity and shows spectators the correct way of competing.

Etiquette in different sports

Etiquette is the unwritten code of behaviour a player stands by when competing. Each sport has its own code of behaviour. A general example of this is shaking hands before and after a game. It is a sign of good sportsmanship and fairness. Demonstrations of good etiquette can occur before, during and after a competition. For example, golf exhibits many unwritten codes of behaviour:

- Players are quiet when another is making a putt.
- The non-putting player stands out of the eyeline of the other player.
- The non-putting player is still when the shot is taking place.

The following photos all show examples of good etiquette:

Players shake hands at the beginning of a badminton match.

Tennis players shake hands after a tennis match.

169

Task 2

1 – Think of your own examples of etiquette that occur in a variety of sports and discuss them with a partner.

2 – Describe the effects that showing or not showing good etiquette can have on players and spectators.

Where etiquette is expected to take place

There are places in a game or competition where etiquette is expected to take place:

When an unfair advantage is seen to be had
If a line call in tennis is seen to be incorrect, there is no technology to back the call up. If the decision has not been overruled, a player may deliberately lose the next point to make amends for the mistake and maintain fairness.

After an injury in football
If the ball is kicked out in football after a player has gone down injured, the opposition may throw the ball back to their opponent.

A batter's honesty
In cricket, a batter may make contact with the ball as it goes through for a catch, but the contact may be so fine that the umpire did not detect it. Here the batter has the chance to 'walk' (when a batter declares themselves out without waiting for the umpire's decision), showing honesty and good etiquette in the game.

Respect in rugby
After a match both teams form a tunnel and applaud each other off the pitch. The battle on the pitch may have been hard fought but the teams have a chance to show mutual respect to the opposition for their efforts.

In the face of defeat
Players are expected to shake hands after losing a game despite feelings of abject misery. Congratulating the winner in this way can make you more determined not to be in that situation again.

In the face of success
Having won a game, controlling feelings of elation after the victory and shaking hands with the opposition, gives an opportunity to show them respect and commiserate with them in a sporting way.

Conduct of players and officials
Both the players and the officials should conduct themselves correctly during a match or event. Although the competition may be fierce, all players should control their behaviour for the good of the game. Areas to be controlled include:

- Language: words used and the way they are said
- Manner of play: avoiding time wasting, aggression, and not taking free hits and passes from the correct place
- Captains only addressing the referee.

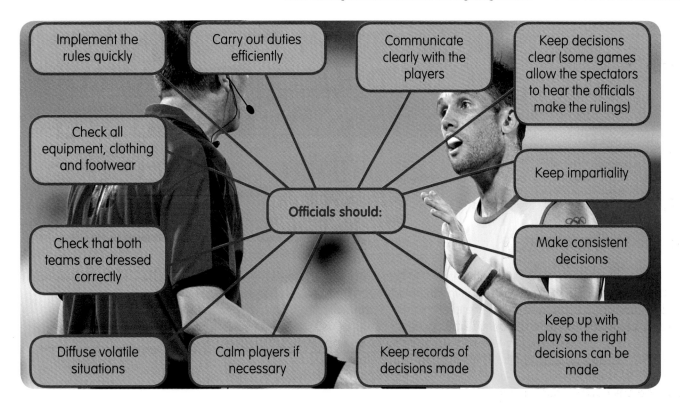

Implement the rules quickly

Carry out duties efficiently

Communicate clearly with the players

Keep decisions clear (some games allow the spectators to hear the officials make the rulings)

Check all equipment, clothing and footwear

Officials should:

Keep impartiality

Check that both teams are dressed correctly

Make consistent decisions

Diffuse volatile situations

Calm players if necessary

Keep records of decisions made

Keep up with play so the right decisions can be made

Active challenge

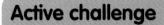

Discuss with a partner the difficulties of officiating. Use your own experience to give examples of incidents that have happened when you have been a player or official yourself.

You could think about decision making, speed of the game, weather conditions and the importance of the match.

Importance of rules keeping the spirit of the game

For a game to be fair for both sides all players should keep to the rules of the game and the officials should impartially stop any play that contravenes such rules. A referee should be seen to make decisions as they arise, correctly, efficiently and without fuss. The players have a responsibility to react to the whistle and the judgement of the referee and to resume the game as quickly as possible.

Some sports have rules in place so that if a player does not respond in the correct spirit of the game their team is further penalized. For example, a rugby player who questions a decision may find their team ten yards nearer to their own goal line as a punishment and when territory is hard-earned, giving away the yardage is a fitting punishment.

Some games have degrees of punishment which become more severe as the rules are contravened. There include:

• verbal warnings
• recorded warnings such as a yellow card in football
• the 'sin bin' where a player is excluded from the game for a period of time
• total bans from the game such as indicated by a red card in football.

In 2008, the Football Association (FA) introduced the Respect campaign in order to reduce the amount of arguing with the referee about decisions.

This campaign aimed to crackdown on bad behaviour in football both on the pitch and on the sidelines. Captains have been given more responsibility for behaviour on the pitch and before a match the referee gives a pre-match briefing to the captions and managers in order to focus them on showing good behaviour and responses to decisions made during the game.

The FA's Respect campaign shows that without respect there can be no game.

3 — Social groupings

A person can be influenced as to whether or not to take part in sport by different factors in society. The most influential cause can be the people around them, including peers and family. The availability of a sport may also depend on gender or **ethnicity**. Traditionally, an activity may involve a particular gender or be outside the accepted range of usual activities, so provision may not exist to attract all those interested. An awareness and appreciation of different cultures in society, and their relationships to sport, is therefore important.

Influence of peers on participation

Peers are people of a similar age. They can be in the same class, same year group or at a different school. Peers can sometimes have a great influence on their friends, also known as 'peer pressure'. If a peer group takes part in a physical activity or sport, they could influence others to join in too. There are positive and negative effects of peer pressure.

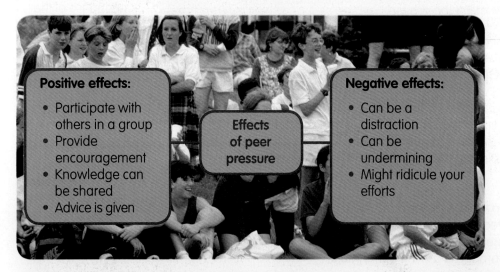

Positive effects:
- Participate with others in a group
- Provide encouragement
- Knowledge can be shared
- Advice is given

Effects of peer pressure

Negative effects:
- Can be a distraction
- Can be undermining
- Might ridicule your efforts

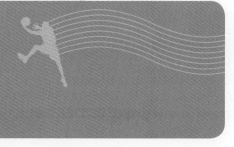

Active challenge

Consider how you would encourage a friend to join the same sports club as you. Share your ideas with a small group in order to build up a full picture of the ways people encourage others and whether this can be considered as encouragement or pressure.

Influence of family on participation

Parents have a great influence on their child's participation in sport. Youngsters who grow up in a family that has had good sporting experiences can be encouraged to follow the same interests. Their parents' enthusiasm, interest and enjoyment, experienced through the activity, can often be enough to start the appeal.

If a child is introduced to an activity at an early age and regularly participates in it, sport is seen as a usual part of life. It follows that the youngster could regard sport as part of their lifestyle and may keep taking part when they are older and are able to make their own decisions.

Families can have a major effect on participation in physical activity. There may be a family tradition of competing in a particular sport or relatives that want a young family member to do well. There are many ways that families can have both a negative and positive effect on participation in sport.

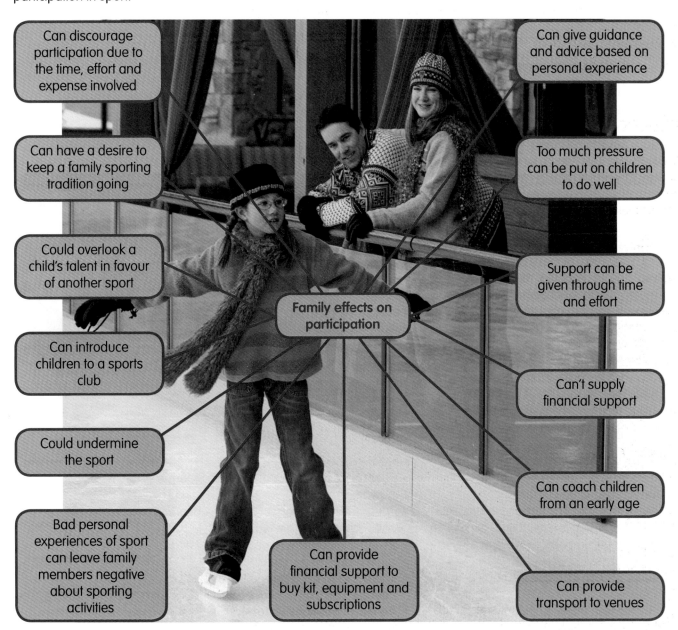

Can discourage participation due to the time, effort and expense involved

Can give guidance and advice based on personal experience

Can have a desire to keep a family sporting tradition going

Too much pressure can be put on children to do well

Could overlook a child's talent in favour of another sport

Family effects on participation

Support can be given through time and effort

Can introduce children to a sports club

Can't supply financial support

Could undermine the sport

Can coach children from an early age

Bad personal experiences of sport can leave family members negative about sporting activities

Can provide financial support to buy kit, equipment and subscriptions

Can provide transport to venues

Task 3

1 – Study the information on the ways family influence participation in sport.

2 – Divide the ideas into positive and negative influences.

3 – Record the lists in your workbook and add your own examples.

Active challenge

Using your own knowledge and experiences, compile examples of how a family you know has encouraged participation in sport.

> You could include ideas on help with transport, paying subs or buying kit for example.

Gender and participation

Gender can have a widespread influence on opportunities and involvement in sport. These can range from influences on performers to influences on managers and officials. When changes and progress occur then breaks with tradition often have to happen and difficult decisions have to be made. Frequently, change comes about because of the determination of individuals. This can be seen in the increase in the number of women referees in football, for example, an increase of women referees officiating in men's football games: Morag Pirie in Scotland, Nicole Petignat in Switzerland and Silvia Regina de Oliveira in Brazil, plus many more, have made the grade to take charge in football. The desire of these and other women to become involved was so great that the authorities created female referee courses to meet demand. There are no physical obstacles of strength and power in refereeing as there is in playing, so everyone has the opportunity to succeed. The European authorities running football are actively encouraging women's involvement in football, which will help increase the overall interest of women in the game.

Nicole Petignat was the first female to referee in a UEFA Cup match.

Increasing women's involvement in certain areas of sport has positive and negative features:

Positive:
- The tradition of women not playing certain sports is seen to be outdated.
- More women are encouraged to take part.
- More competition is available.
- The depth of competition is improved.
- Good coaches are available.
- New trends can increase the popularity of a sport.
- An increase in public popularity will mean more people will get involved.

Negative:
- There might be a lack of facilities aimed at women.
- There might be a lack of female coaches or coaches of female teams.
- In certain sports there might be few or no other teams to compete against.
- There might be barriers in the way of change.
- People in positions of power in certain sports might disagree with changes.

Active challenge

Add more of your own positive and negative ideas to the ideas on page 174. Discuss your ideas with a partner to build up your list.

Ethnicity

The development of a multicultural society increases the importance for an awareness and appreciation of traditional and new cultures in relation to PE.

Possible ethnicity factors that could impact on participation in sport may include:

- Dress codes – for example, not allowing women to wear certain items of sports kit could affect the safety of the activity.
- Codes of behaviour such as single sex rules regarding mixing with others may prevent participation. For instance, Muslim women are not permitted to take part in mixed sex sporting activities.
- Some cultures see a woman's role as in the home which limits their amount of leisure time.

Nature or nurture?

The Olympics provides a stage for most sports with some activities dominated by certain ethnic groups. In long-distance running events East Africans, such as Kenyans, dominate. Genetically they have bodies more suited to these events than others. They tend to be ectomorphs, with short and slender frames and large lung capacities. They also naturally have more slow twitch muscle fibres which are good for endurance events.

In sprinting events Afro-Caribbeans tend to dominate. Genetically they have bodies more suited to this event. They tend to be mesomorphs with small and efficient lungs and muscular lower bodies. They have a high proportion of fast twitch muscle fibres which are good for explosive speed.

To compete at the highest levels, athletes, wherever they are born, still require determination, drive and commitment to outplay the opposition. Coaches, psychologists and nutritionists are among the professionals who contribute to success, whatever the natural attributes of an athlete are.

Active challenge

Look at footage of a large sporting event such as the 2008 Olympics held in Beijing and see if there are patterns linking sports performers with different continents.

Historically, South Africa has segregated black people and white people. Sport is being seen as a way to break down these racial banners. Efforts are being made to provide equal representation for blacks and whites in their national cricket team. They aim to have teams made up of 50 per cent black and 50 per cent white players. This stems from the political history of **apartheid**. Sport is being used to bring members of the country back together and play its part in rectifying past mistakes.

Active challenge

With a partner, discuss the difficulties that people of various cultures might have when participating in sport.

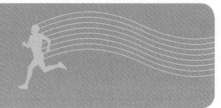

Key terms

Ethnicity – **particular attribute or affiliation resulting from racial or cultural ties**

Apartheid – **official policy of racial segregation**

Summary

Different types of people will influence others in participation. These people may readily encourage or discourage participation as a result of their own knowledge or experience of sport. Traditions, trends and culture will also have a bearing on whether a person participates in an activity. Currently there is a massive upward trend of girls playing football. The increase in numbers can be integrated into the current facilities to accommodate both males and females in the sport. An awareness of different traditions and cultures is required for everyone to be appreciated and when new sports are introduced then careful planning is required so that the sports can be sustainable.

Exam questions

Multiple-choice questions

1. Which of the following best describes good etiquette?

   ☐ **A** Having a good knowledge of the rules of the game

   ☐ **B** Responding quickly to the referee's whistle

   ☐ **C** Making sure the equipment meets the safety regulations

   ☐ **D** Keeping quiet when the opposition is putting in golf

   (1 mark)

2. The referee has many duties during a game. Which of the following is not one of them?

   ☐ **A** Keep a record of decisions made

   ☐ **B** Diffuse volatile situations

   ☐ **C** Make impartial decisions during the game

   ☐ **D** Feel sorry for the weaker team and be more lenient on them

   (1 mark)

3. The following describe effects that peers may have on a person's participation in physical activity. Which one is not a positive influence?

   ☐ **A** Joining in to be with friends

   ☐ **B** Receiving encouragement to take part

   ☐ **C** Distracting others so they do not take part

   ☐ **D** Advising friends to take part, based on personal experience

   (1 mark)

4. Which of the following best describes positive influences in football that encourage women to participate?

   ☐ **A** Participation is more acceptable, current trends encourage women, more competition, lack of coaches

   ☐ **B** Participation is more acceptable, lack of facilities, current trends encourage women, more competition

   ☐ **C** Participation is more acceptable, better coaches, current trends encourage women, more competition

   ☐ **D** Better coaches, current trends encourage women, more competition, participation frowned upon

   (1 mark)

Short answer questions

5. Fairness and personal and social responsibility should be taken seriously by all performers in sport. How can this responsibility be built up and kept to by a sports performer?

   (3 marks)

6. Give examples for **two** sports where etiquette is expected to take place.

   (3 marks)

Longer answer questions

7. Leisure time is increasing. Give reasons for such increases.

   (4 marks)

8. In order to make physical activity available to all, certain user groups are given special provisions. Describe **two** of these groups and say why such provision is important.

   (6 marks)

9. Our peers can often encourage participation in sports. Give examples of how they could do this.

   (4 marks)

10. Family influences can encourage participation. Give examples of such encouragement.

    (5 marks)

3.1.3 ～ Making informed decisions about getting involved in a lifetime of healthy physical activities that suit their needs

3.1.3e Opportunities and pathways available for becoming or remaining involved in physical activities

What you will learn in this topic:

1 — Roles: provision, choice and pathway opportunities
2 — Accredited courses and qualifications
3 — Cross-curricular possibilities

1 — Roles: provision, choice and pathway opportunities

The different roles school sport may offer can encourage all students to get involved. Some students may want to be individual performers or part of a team, others may be suited to the role of leader or coach, organizer, choreographer or official.

The classroom can be a place where information is given and skills to perform the activity are practised and put into operation. The opportunity to learn a wider range of skills and have the chance to develop and apply new practical knowledge is available too. For example:

- Planning skills are needed for gymnastics and dance routines or strategies in a game.
- Problem solving skills are needed to work out how to beat the opposition.
- Observing skills are needed in order to learn correct techniques and to identify them in performances.
- Communication skills are needed when discussing instructions or coaching points with others.
- Leadership skills are needed when coaching or organizing others.
- Coaching skills are needed to help others develop an understanding of good technique and goal setting.
- Organizing skills are needed when arranging an event or tournament.
- Official skills are needed to judge a performance and check rules are followed.
- Choreographer skills are needed in dance and gymnastics.
- ICT skills give the opportunity to use the latest technology and link it with sport, such as finding information on the Internet and recording sporting results.

Active challenge

Think of a sporting example where you have a role or job to do. Discuss with a partner what you do and what skills you have developed as a result. Try to think of three skill examples.

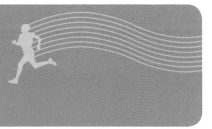

There are increasingly more opportunities to become regularly involved in PE, sport, dance and healthy physical activity. Schools can organize internal competitions, teams to play other schools in the area and join in local community sport and dance activities.

Links with junior schools in the local area can also be encouraged. Young students may be invited into secondary schools to take part in an activity or groups of older students may go into junior schools to encourage active participation.

Active challenge

List all of the internal and external sports activities and events that your school has been involved in. Share your ideas with a partner to increase your list.

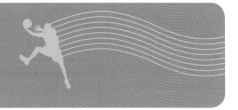

When taking part in physical activity, the level of involvement can be complex and challenging. Planning, communicating, problem solving (independently or in a group) are all necessary skills to complete the tasks successfully. Experiencing, learning and meeting challenges can lead to further involvement on a lifelong basis, for example, a person may become involved in sport as a career opportunity or as a volunteer.

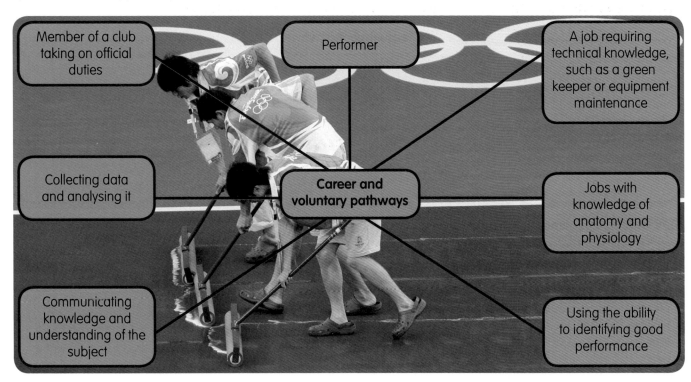

- Member of a club taking on official duties
- Performer
- A job requiring technical knowledge, such as a green keeper or equipment maintenance
- Collecting data and analysing it
- Career and voluntary pathways
- Jobs with knowledge of anatomy and physiology
- Communicating knowledge and understanding of the subject
- Using the ability to identifying good performance

Active challenge

Make a list of specific career and voluntary roles linked with PE. Share your ideas with a partner.

2 — Accredited courses and qualifications

Accredited courses and qualifications are recognized nationally as proof of understanding and competence in a particular area. There are many accredited courses available for people who are interested in sport. The nature of the courses differ greatly, with each one having its own aim. Aims can include:

- Giving an opportunity to enjoying participation as a player.
- Teaching understanding and developing performance, such as the GCSE course you are studying now.
- Skills based courses, such as the BCU (British Canoe Union) Certificate in Coaching Paddle sports course.
- Qualifications for those employed in sport such as the VTCT (Vocational Training Charitable Trust) Level 2 NVQ (**National Vocational Qualification**) Sport, Recreation and Allied Occupations: Activity Leadership.

Active challenge

Choose a sport and search the Internet to find more examples of skill-based courses supported by the associated governing body.

There are also a number of different exam-based courses:

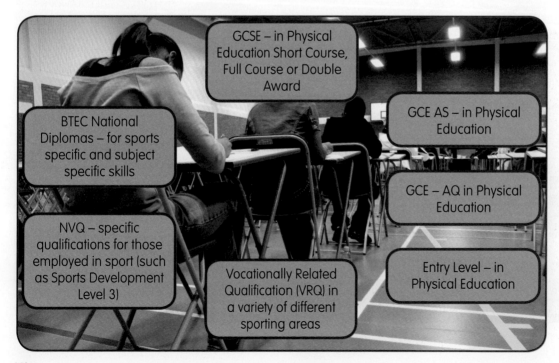

GCSE – in Physical Education Short Course, Full Course or Double Award

BTEC National Diplomas – for sports specific and subject specific skills

GCE AS – in Physical Education

GCE – AQ in Physical Education

NVQ – specific qualifications for those employed in sport (such as Sports Development Level 3)

Vocationally Related Qualification (VRQ) in a variety of different sporting areas

Entry Level – in Physical Education

Courses can be flexible, have a credit value and build up experience, allowing learning to be structured to suit the individual. Courses can:

- have a grading level: 1 = entry, 2 = higher, 3 = advanced
- have credit values: credits can build up until the student has the desired number
- have a different number of learning hours
- be geared towards different ages
- involve different components so the course can be tailor-made to suit the needs of the individual.

The range of job opportunities these courses cover can include:

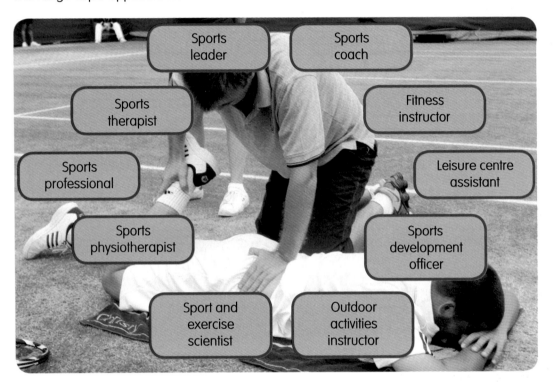

Sports leader

Sports coach

Sports therapist

Fitness instructor

Sports professional

Leisure centre assistant

Sports physiotherapist

Sports development officer

Sport and exercise scientist

Outdoor activities instructor

Active challenge

With a partner, make a list of other job occupations linked with sport. Think what qualifications you would need to be able to do these jobs.

Task 1

1 – Study the information about accredited courses on page 180.

2 – Look on the Internet and find courses and qualifications for the following:

- Coaching rugby
- Nutrition for healthier foods and special diets
- Being a grounds person or green keeper
- Certificate in coaching athletics.

Some activities have personal achievement awards that young people can work towards. Swimming is a good example of a sport that has a variety of different performance and proficiency awards to achieve. These awards encourage involvement, give a focus to the activity and reward success and achievement. Such opportunities often occur in extra-curricular clubs.

Gymnastics run by the governing body British Gymnastics.

Swimming sponsored by Kellogg's, in association with the Amateur Swimming Association.

Duke of Edinburgh Award: flexible, non-competitive programme which includes cultural and adventurous activities.

The organizers of these schemes provide information and activity packs, pointing out the skills of the game or activity to the teacher and performer. These supply a base of skills to learn, practice and hopefully apply to competition. Working towards an award gives performers a goal to aim for and can often keep them focused, interested and motivated to do well.

There is often a structure to an award scheme, involving several levels of achievement. Having different levels makes success attainable for all and the grade reached allows the individual to experience feedback in that activity. The chance to progress from one stage to another can provide motivation and interest to the performer in a particular season or from year to year.

The presentation of a certificate or badge is tangible feedback of the skills achieved. The award reached shows a competency and can give the incentive to build on that success and earn a higher award in the future.

Active challenge

Use the Internet to research the awards that swimming offers. The following website could help you: www.britishswimming.org/.

Research into other sports that offer similar performance awards for young people.

Task 2

1 – List the ways your school promotes PE.

2 – Find out about other companies and products that put their name to sports awards.

Think about the following: staff, clubs, teams and visits.

3 — Cross-curricular possibilities

There are many opportunities for cross-curricular links with physical education. Some subjects relate directly to the human body: how it functions and its care and development. Other subjects support and enhance the collection of information, images and communication of PE.

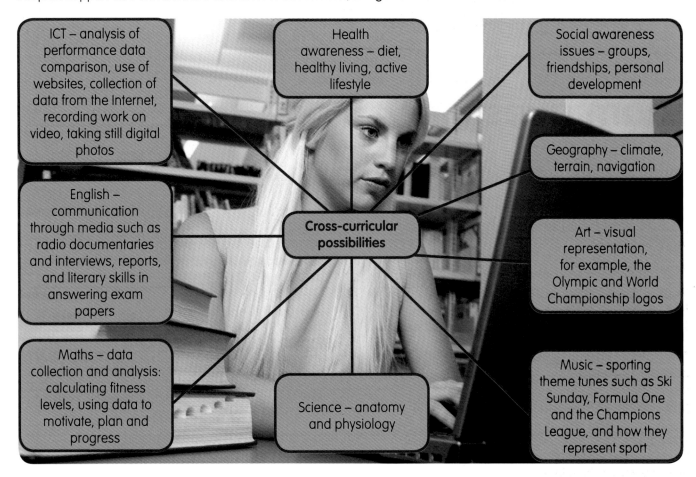

ICT – analysis of performance data comparison, use of websites, collection of data from the Internet, recording work on video, taking still digital photos

Health awareness – diet, healthy living, active lifestyle

Social awareness issues – groups, friendships, personal development

English – communication through media such as radio documentaries and interviews, reports, and literary skills in answering exam papers

Cross-curricular possibilities

Geography – climate, terrain, navigation

Art – visual representation, for example, the Olympic and World Championship logos

Maths – data collection and analysis: calculating fitness levels, using data to motivate, plan and progress

Science – anatomy and physiology

Music – sporting theme tunes such as Ski Sunday, Formula One and the Champions League, and how they represent sport

Task 3

1 – List other ways PE links with other subjects.

2 – Give examples of how PE subjects can cross with other subjects, for example, learning about the pulse and sport links with circulation in science.

Key terms

National Vocational Qualification (NVQ) – qualifications based on competence and that test a candidate's ability to adapt learning to the workplace

Summary

There is a wide range of roles linked with physical activities, each requiring the application of skills and personal qualities in order to be successful. Experiencing these roles gives a young person skills to use throughout their life. Career or voluntary pathways are structured and in place for those who seek further involvement. The complex nature of PE can link itself with other subjects, helping to create continuity throughout the school and reinforce knowledge.

Exam questions

Multiple-choice question

1. There are many roles a person can take up which are directly associated with sport. Which of the following best describes these?

    ☐ **A** Coach, volunteer, official, grounds person, treasurer

    ☐ **B** Player, fixtures secretary, manager, coach, painter, official

    ☐ **C** Leader, coach, administrator, spectator, farmer

    ☐ **D** Volunteer, official, coach, lawyer, player
    (1 mark)

Short answer questions

2. As well as a performer, what other roles and skills can be experienced in classroom activities?
    (3 marks)

3. What personal skills can physical activity provide and be useful for in life?
    (1 mark)

4. Many sports have personal achievement awards. How does a young person benefit by gaining an award?
    (3 marks)

Longer answer questions

5. PE has many opportunities for cross-curricular links. Give examples of these links and how they could be recognized in school.
    (4 marks)

6. There are many skill-based courses run and supported by the governing bodies of different sports. Give the name of such a course, the associated governing body and the skills it covers.
    (4 marks)

3.1.3 ∼ Making informed decisions about getting involved in a lifetime of healthy physical activities that suit their needs

3.1.3f Vocational opportunities for becoming or remaining involved in physical activities

What you will learn about in this topic:

1 — Sports performer
2 — Careers

1 — Sports performer

Anyone can choose to take part in sport, especially a person who has the desire and ability to make the grade as a professional player and earn their living from sport.

A professional and an amateur performer.

Professionals

To the professional player, sport is their job. They receive financial reward for participating and this is how they make their living. In top-class sport, the rewards can be enormous, providing a luxurious lifestyle to the sportsperson. The greater the success, the bigger the financial rewards. Professionals train on a full-time basis and are usually controlled by the club they play for, as is the case with footballers. Each player signs a contract, not only to play for the club, but also to be engaged in other events to do with the club.

How professionals earn their money
- Wages – many performers have agents who negotiate contracts for them before they sign to a club or sponsor. The agent's job is to get the best wage deal for the player.
- Bonuses – these are negotiated at the contract-signing stage and rely on the success of the player or the team.
- Appearance money – some of the top athletes are such a public draw that they are paid to enter an event or make an appearance, boosting the crowd numbers and making the event more popular.
- Winnings – players winning tournaments, such as in tennis, golf and snooker, win prize money.
- Transfer fees – when players are bought by other clubs they can receive a percentage of the transfer fee.
- Media work – television appearances, radio work and magazine articles generally have a fee attached for the performer, negotiated by their agent.
- Sponsorship – a company may pay money to an athlete or team to wear their company logo on their clothing.
- Endorsements – a player may receive money by putting their name to a product and showing the positive advantages of the product.

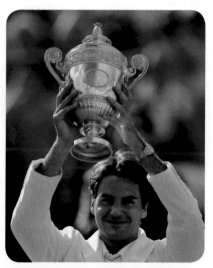

The financial rewards for being a top-class performer are enormous. Roger Federer has won many major titles and earned millions. His focus is now on winning more major competitions and breaking tennis records.

Amateurs

Amateur sportspeople participate in sport as a leisure activity, which takes place in their own time and is totally separate from their work. There is no payment for their involvement. In fact with annual subscription and match fees, it usually costs the amateur to participate. As their livelihood does not depend on playing sport it is their choice to take part. Sport provides an enjoyable interest outside of the workplace, relieving stress, keeping the body healthy and providing an opportunity to socialize. Many amateurs will train to improve their skill, but not to the same extent as a professional. In any competition, they will have to keep to a set of rules laid down by the governing body just like professional players.

How amateurs can make a living
Some amateur sportspeople gain money indirectly for participating. Although payment to amateurs is illegal, 'loopholes' are found so they can still receive payments for their services.

- Expenses – often paid out in relation to travel and personal expenses, the money an amateur receives can exceed the actual cost of the travel and other personal expenses.
- Gifts – presented to the performer for taking part or winning an event. Some gifts could be cashed in and so, indirectly, act as a payment for performing.
- Scholarships – the athlete can be accepted, free of charge, into a university and receive expert training as part of the course at no expense.
- Trust funds – money is deposited in a fund, usually by a relative, for use by the athlete.

- Occupation – a token job is taken by the athlete for which they are paid. This allows them to be financially secure so they are able to take part in their chosen sport. Often, in foreign countries, a job in the armed forces covers this kind of payment to a talented sportsperson.
- Sponsorship – a company supplies an amateur team with money or equipment in return for their company logo on the sports kit.
- Illegal payments – some performers receive illegal payments for participating in an event. This used to be common in amateur football, where money was placed in the boots of a player on completion of the game, known as 'boot money', after they were bribed to throw a match.

Athletics was traditionally viewed as an amateur sport. The International Amateur Athletic Federation (IAAF) was founded in 1912. In recent years the International Olympic Committee (IOC) has relaxed their rules about payment to performers in order to keep the standards high. This means that athletes are able to train and compete on a full-time basis. This move towards a more professional sport was particularly recognized in 2001, when the IAAF Congress voted unanimously for the organization's name to be changed to the International Association of Athletics Federations.

Task 1

Make a list of the differences between professional and amateur sport.

Open competitions

Open competitions invite all performers to compete irrespective of gender or amateur or professional status. This brings together sportspeople from all backgrounds and with all levels of experience. In golf, the British Open is a good example. The prize money given to the professional winner is enormous. If an amateur were to win, they would receive a medal as best amateur, but no prize money for their efforts. In this sport there is a clear distinction between the two levels of player.

Improved sports facilities and an increase in leisure time mean that amateurs can commit more time to their sport. They can have time to increase their fitness and skill levels. As the golfing example shows, a dedicated amateur can compete on an equal footing with a professional (even if they don't reap the same rewards).

As an amateur, Melissa Reid helped Britain win the Commonwealth Tournament in South Africa in 2007.

Some amateur competitors see these open events as a way of gaining money (through expenses or appearance money for example) and ignore the recommendations of the governing bodies of the sport. In some cases turning professional is more appealing than remaining an amateur but if the player had been a member of their national amateur squad and then decides to leave to become a professional, it could weaken the country's amateur team. As players make progress in their sport, small clubs may be unable to make it financially viable for them to remain there: this could be because an athlete is drawn to another team that offers them more money, for example.

For some amateur performers, as they become more successful, their desire to win at all costs grows too. As they progress, they form an elite group of amateur performers, which can make amateur competitions predictable and less appealing. Open competitions can end up undermining the amateur ideal of playing for the love of the game.

2 — Careers

There are a vast number of careers with a sporting link. Recognized pathways for jobs directly linked to sport are now better established, so more people can make a living in this way. For example, a person wanting to be a coach can now follow a well-structured pathway to achieve their goal.

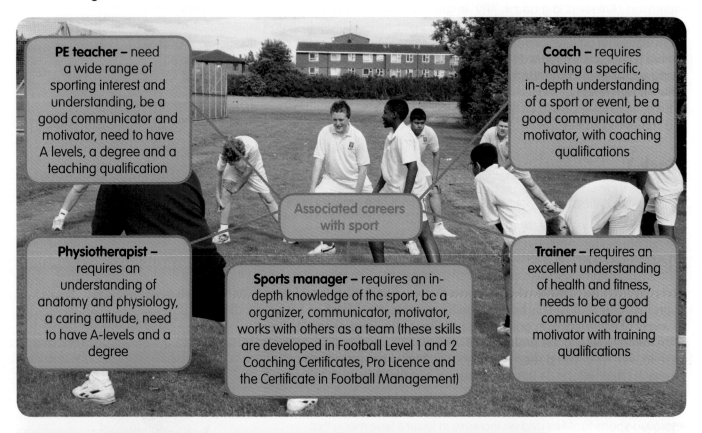

PE teacher – need a wide range of sporting interest and understanding, be a good communicator and motivator, need to have A levels, a degree and a teaching qualification

Coach – requires having a specific, in-depth understanding of a sport or event, be a good communicator and motivator, with coaching qualifications

Associated careers with sport

Physiotherapist – requires an understanding of anatomy and physiology, a caring attitude, need to have A-levels and a degree

Sports manager – requires an in-depth knowledge of the sport, be a organizer, communicator, motivator, works with others as a team (these skills are developed in Football Level 1 and 2 Coaching Certificates, Pro Licence and the Certificate in Football Management)

Trainer – requires an excellent understanding of health and fitness, needs to be a good communicator and motivator with training qualifications

Active challenge

Make a list of other careers that are associated with physical activity. Compare your list with a partner and combine your ideas together.

Key terms

Open competition – a competition inviting both professional and amateur performers to participate without restrictions

Summary

The reasons for taking part in sport are wide and varied. Those who choose to pursue careers in sports performance have to be at the top of their game and be able to deal with sporting pressures on a daily basis. Barriers for amateurs and professionals competing together are diminishing as different ways of financing participation are offered other than those of professional salaries. For the top-class performers there is a good living to be made from sport. The best athletes can be paid appearance money for their ability to draw in more spectators whilst premiership footballers can become millionaires! The Olympics shows how barriers can be eliminated by attracting both amateurs and professionals to compete at the same event. Jobs associated with sport, other than as a sports performer, are plenty, with many people having successful careers in these linked areas.

Exam questions

Multiple-choice questions

1. Which of the following describes an amateur performer's reason for participating?

   ☐ A Plays for enjoyment, sport is a leisure activity, means of socializing, interest outside of work

   ☐ B Plays for enjoyment, sport is a leisure activity, means of earning money, interest outside of work

   ☐ C Plays for enjoyment, it is their job, means of socializing, interest outside of work

   ☐ D Plays for enjoyment, sport is a leisure activity, means of socializing, to earn a living

   (1 mark)

2. Which of the following best describes open competition?

   ☐ A An event where the entry is free

   ☐ B An event inviting all performers to play, whether amateur or professional

   ☐ C An event available to members of a club

   ☐ D An event open to all sports

   (1 mark)

3. Which of the following best describes the qualities needed to be a good sports manager?

   ☐ A Understands anatomy and physiology, good communication skills, a motivator, works well in a team

   ☐ B Good organization skills, good communication skills, a motivator, works well in a team

   ☐ C Works well in a team, good organization skills, has coaching qualifications, a motivator

   ☐ D Good organization skills, good communication skills, has a degree in human biology, works well in a team

   (1 mark)

Short answer question

4. Amateur athletes can still gain money to help their progress and participation in sport. Describe the different ways this can happen.

   (3 marks)

Longer answer questions

5. How does a professional sportsperson earn their money?

   (6 marks)

6. What helps to make a good coach?

   (8 marks)

3.1.3 ～ Making informed decisions about getting involved in a lifetime of healthy physical activities that suit their needs

3.1.3g The media

What you will learn about in this topic:

1 — The media
2 — How the media helps to give an understanding of performance and participation
3 — Different types of output
4 — Director's and writer's influence

Sport uses all the different forms of media to bring itself to the widest audience. For example, each newspaper has a sports column and pull-out supplements. Magazines and specialist publications focus on all aspects of sport. There are programmes and whole channels on television and radio devoted to sport, and the Internet provides access to many websites committed to a particular sport, team performer or sporting issues.

Task 1

1 – Copy the spider diagram shown above.

2 – Add the names of television channels, newspapers, magazines and websites that have connections with sport to each category.

1 — The media

The press

The back pages of most newspapers are devoted to current sporting news. Each newspaper employs journalists and photographers to gather up-to-the-minute information about matches and events for publication in the morning press. With this form of media the reader sees the match through the eyes of the journalists, who are able to put their opinions forward and influence the reader.

Sports magazines devoted to the specialized reader are an expanding market, the most popular subjects being football and golf. These publications contain entertaining, instructive and informative articles on events and players.

The following table highlights the growing number of readers of specialized magazines:

Title	Sport	Issues actively purchased	Total average net circulation per issue
Match	Football	110,779	113,049
Runner's World	Running	87,029	88,567
Angling Times	Fishing	50,947	51,006
Rugby World	Rugby	45,377	48,381
Shoot	Football	30,885	35,830
Cycling Weekly	Cycling	26,786	27,609

Source: ABC, data between January 2007 and December 2007.

Television

The impact of television coverage on sport has been both positive and negative. Terrestrial television has had the share of sport it can broadcast reduced by cable and satellite channels, as it cannot pay the same amount of money to buy the rights to broadcast particular events.

Terrestrial television
Terrestrial television includes BBC1, BBC2, ITV, Channel 4 and Channel 5. All televisions can receive these channels providing they have an aerial to pick up the signal. If you own and use a television you must have a television licence. BBC programmes are financed by revenue from television licence sales, whilst the independent channels pay their way by advertisements during and at the end of programmes shown. Certain programmes may even be sponsored by particular products, which are seen at the beginning, during breaks and at the end of the programme.

The competition between terrestrial and **satellite television** companies is such that the Independent Television Commission (ITC) has to organize the allocation of sporting broadcasts between them as they feel that some sporting events are of major importance and should be available to everybody. This prevents the wealthier satellite companies buying up all the best sporting events. As a result, there are some sporting events that are protected by the ITC so that terrestrial television can broadcast them. These sporting events make up two groups, group A and group B. Events on the group A list are legally bound to have the rights of their live coverage shown on the free television channels. Those on the group B list can be shown on satellite or digital television as long as provision is made for highlights and delayed coverage to be shown on terrestrial television. There are strict regulations for group B list events in relation to the length of the highlight coverage and how long after the live event it can be transmitted. Protecting sports events in this way guarantees the traditional channels, which the majority of the population still only have access to, broadcasting rights to some top-quality sport.

The following is a revised list of sports events protected under part IV of the Broadcasting Act, 1996:

Group A events (full live coverage protected)	Group B events (secondary coverage protected)
The Olympic Games	Cricket Test Matches played in England
The FIFA World Cup Finals Tournament	Non-finals matches at Wimbledon
The European Football Championship Finals Tournament	All other matches in the Rugby World Cup Finals Tournament
The FA Cup Final	Six Nations Rugby Tournament Matches involving home countries
The Scottish FA Cup Final	The Commonwealth Games
The Grand National	The World Athletics Championship
The Epsom Derby	The Cricket World Cup (limited to the final, semi-finals and matches involving UK teams)
The Wimbledon Tennis Finals	The Ryder Cup
The Rugby League Challenge Cup Final	The Open Golf Championship
The Rugby World Cup Final	

Positive effects of sports coverage on terrestrial television:

• Keeps people informed of new trends and current players.
• Particular sports get exposure on television with improved quality of coverage.
• Better technology aids decision making such as playbacks and ProZone.
• Pundits can help increase people's appreciation of sport through their professional opinion.
• The BBC licence fee helps to fund more channels and therefore extend their sports coverage.
• New events can be seen.
• Enhances development of sport.
• Seeing sport on television may encourage participation.
• The more a sport is seen on television the more supporters it may attract.
• The more coverage there is of a sport in the media, the easier it may be to attract sponsors, making more money available to that sport.
• People become familiar with sports personalities who can become positive role models.
• Money from broadcast bids goes direct to the sport.
• Coverage of disabled sportspeople in events such as the Paralympics brings about an awareness of the needs of others and how sport can be undertaken by all.

Negative effects of sports coverage on terrestrial television:

- Major sports have most of the coverage to the detriment of minority sports.
- Can discourage watching sport live as it's more convenient to sit in comfort at home.
- Small incidents on the field of play can often be exaggerated and sensationalized.
- The director of viewing controls what is watched.
- A channel can put its own slant on a subject for its own benefit.
- Excessive coverage can affect interest.
- Subtle rule changes to sports may occur to increase the appeal to television spectators, such as the tiebreak rule in tennis.
- Replays can undermine the officials and umpires.
- Puts extra pressure on sports stars on both performance and demands for interviews.
- Demand to see a performer can affect their privacy.

Task 2

Choose six of the positive effects of sports coverage on terrestrial television and put them into full sentences with examples.

Cable and satellite television
Cable and satellite broadcasts have had a major influence on watching sport. Although there is greater airtime and a wider variety of sports, they are only available to those who can pay a monthly subscription.

Positive effects of sports coverage by cable and satellite television:

- There is a greater coverage of minority sports (Sky's Extreme Sports Channel broadcasts an average of 18 minority sports per week, including the World Motocross Championships, mountain biking and drag racing).
- Makes a wide variety of sports more accessible.
- Helps increase the funding for sport.
- Heightens the profile of sport and so can attract interest and sponsorship.
- Increased depth of coverage for major sports; some football clubs have their own channels such as Manchester United and Celtic FC.
- Can encourage greater participation by stimulating interest, thereby encouraging people to take part in sport themselves.
- More live sport can be viewed by more people.

Cable and satellite have similar negative effects as terrestrial television, for example, it discourages live watching, sensationalizes incidents in play and the viewing is controlled by the director, but there are also specific negative effects associated with this coverage.

Negative effects of sports coverage by cable and satellite television:

- Some networks may have the traditional gender pundits and presenters matched with a sport, although more women are now making a positive impact in these areas.
- Reinforcing stereotypes in this way may give the impression that the sport is unavailable to certain groups of people and therefore doesn't encourage participation.
- Matches can be rescheduled due to the best broadcast day for the network; this often happens to premiership football coverage.

- American Football rules have changed to suit advert breaks; the referees of the game will receive a signal if the adverts are still running and will delay the restart accordingly.
- The Rugby Super League season has changed to summer to suit the media so it is broadcast at peak viewing times.
- The start time of a match can change so it goes out at the optimum time for the network.
- Some traditional events have gone to Sky, for example, only subscribers can see Welsh football and live test cricket matches from 2006.
- Sport can suffer from overexposure as people tire of the coverage saturation.

Sometimes the influence of television coverage is not so black and white. A person may see an event on television and as a result be so motivated that they go to see it live; on the other hand, they may not bother to leave home when television gives them the best view in the comfort of their own surroundings.

Pay-per-view

If a person subscribes to a particular satellite channel such as Sky they are eligible to watch **pay-per-view** events, (which would otherwise not be shown on terrestrial or normal satellite channels) whereby the customer pays a certain amount of money to receive the event. Boxing is one of the main sports that is broadcast in this way. Here the companies feel that there will be such a demand to see some events that they can make money by showing it in this way.

Task 3

Write a paragraph on how terrestrial and subscription television differ.

The Internet

The Internet is the newest and quickest-developing form of media. The Internet provides a way to access up-to-date information about sports, events and personalities in sport for those with access to an online computer. (It is worth remembering that some websites remain unchanged for a long time, so they may not be that current, but generally there is a note at the end of the website saying when it was last updated.) Many sports governing bodies, major clubs and smaller teams provide a website for those interested to learn more about them. The Internet also provides an advertising vehicle for retailers. Goods can be bought and sold quickly and easily using this service. Games and programmes can be re-watched and accessed online, for example, through the BBC's online iPlayer service, and highlights can now be sent straight to mobile phones.

Up-to-the-minute club news is available on club websites.

Radio

Radio regularly broadcasts specialist sports programmes. These include coverage of live matches, discussion programmes and informative programmes. There is little rivalry between radio and television, as television regards itself as far more popular. Radio is therefore allowed to broadcast all sporting events live. There are several channels devoted solely to sport and news, including Five Live, Talksport and BBC Radio 4's coverage of the cricket test matches. Cricket enthusiasts take their radios to the matches so that they can hear a commentary whilst they are watching the match live. Some people watch an event on television with the sound down whilst listening to the radio commentary.

2 — How the media helps to give an understanding of performance and participation

The media helps improve people's understanding of sport and current affairs, popularizes personalities and provides sports' entertainment. Each form of media employs a series of experts (past players, pundits, presenters and journalists) to give their judgements, opinions and views on the sport in question.

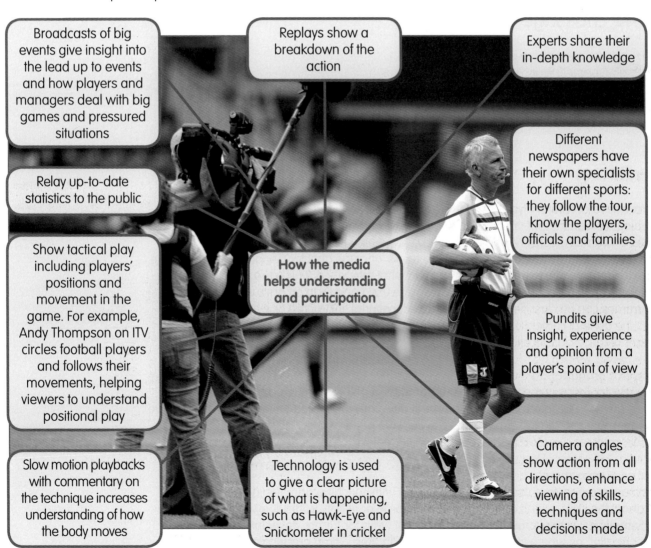

Broadcasts of big events give insight into the lead up to events and how players and managers deal with big games and pressured situations

Replays show a breakdown of the action

Experts share their in-depth knowledge

Relay up-to-date statistics to the public

Different newspapers have their own specialists for different sports: they follow the tour, know the players, officials and families

Show tactical play including players' positions and movement in the game. For example, Andy Thompson on ITV circles football players and follows their movements, helping viewers to understand positional play

How the media helps understanding and participation

Pundits give insight, experience and opinion from a player's point of view

Slow motion playbacks with commentary on the technique increases understanding of how the body moves

Technology is used to give a clear picture of what is happening, such as Hawk-Eye and Snickometer in cricket

Camera angles show action from all directions, enhance viewing of skills, techniques and decisions made

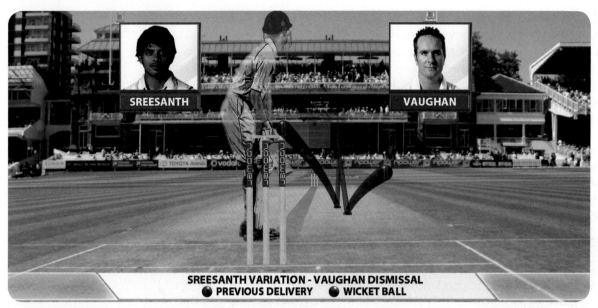

Hawk-Eye cameras around the ground record the action and a computer generates the potential outcome.

Active challenge

With a partner, add your own ideas to the spider diagram on page 195, and discuss how media helps understanding and participation in physical activity. Include examples of how media has influenced you.

3 — Different types of output

There are several different types of sporting output, each with a different way of presenting the subject. For each event the director of the sports programme has an influence on how the information comes across: what is shown, how something is said and which particular points are discussed. Therefore, the public sees and hears what the director decides they should see and hear. Presenters may put their own slant on what they say during a broadcast, as long as it is within stated boundaries, or a script may be used and read off an autocue. Television programmes can be classified as informative, educational, instructive or entertaining. This reflects the general content and aims of the programme. Many programmes contain different elements of these classifications.

Informative programmes
News, news bulletins and sport update programmes, together with Ceefax and Teletext services, are all in the informative programme group. They are based on facts, intending to give the viewer more information about a sport, event, club or performer. They are designed to give the public updates on results, future events and current issues regarding a sport or activity.

Educational programmes
Educational programmes are productions dealing with coaching and helping people learn about the skills, tactics and strategies of a game or activity particularly at grassroots level. Sometimes, school programmes will suggest ways for further development and give information on where to take up an activity in an area. Some broadcasts are

documentary-based and so are concerned with the facts about an event or activity, like the history of a sport, for example. For some people, knowing more about a sport is interesting and increases their understanding of the game.

The BBC produces both radio and television programmes for schools as an aid to learning. In addition to television there are many websites offering information for different sports to help with skills and tactics.

- **Documentaries** – on players, teams and current issues in sport
- **School programmes** – focusing on health and leisure
- **Media and education**
- **Coaching series** – for specific sports
- **Skill development** – skills such as leadership and coaching

Instructive programmes

This type of coverage is closely linked with educational programmes, but is mainly interested in teaching the viewer about a specific sport. They appeal to a specialist market interested in a particular activity. Some programmes mix the type of coverage shown and include an entertainment and instructive element. The cricket test match broadcasts largely come under the heading of entertainment, and have a 'master or super class' section in the lunch break, where experts and coaches relay coaching points, instructing young players on how to improve their techniques.

Entertaining programmes

These programmes are designed for enjoyment, such as highlight programmes and celebrity quiz shows. They can also include coverage of live matches and special events. For some, the drama of a game can be entertainment enough, but the addition of the commentary gives greater information and insight,

On-the-spot interviews after a race capture the emotion of the moment making the sports coverage entertaining.

and can enhance the appeal even more. To add to the entertainment, a series of presenters, pundits and experts are employed to give their opinion on the event. Expert commentators, who have often competed at the highest level themselves, give in-depth views which aim to be accurate and factual. Those currently involved in the sport can give up-to-date information on the issues relevant at the time. Live coverage matches are cheap to produce and attract large audiences even when broadcast off-peak.

Sports quiz shows have high ratings on television. This is due to the popular personalities on the show attracting the audiences: the quiz seems secondary to the antics of the personalities. The appeal to the public may be that they see respected sportspeople having fun and making people laugh. Guest appearances of current, popular sportspeople can attract a bigger audience, as people want to know more about, and have greater access to, their sporting role models.

Some large football teams, such as Manchester United, have such a following that they produce their own club dedicated TV programmes. These channels give their fans up-to-date information on players, the club and fixtures.

Task 4

1 – Study the information on the types of television output.

2 – Prepare a presentation on the different types that you can deliver to a Key Stage 3 class.

4 — Director's and writer's influence

Highlight programmes, which show the events of the day, pick out the best of the action in the time they have available. Here the audience sees exactly what the director wants them to see. This is usually the best of the action and any contentious moments too (particularly in football). However, these isolated incidents can be over-sensationalized by the panel of experts, becoming more talked about than the play itself.

Audiences view what the director wants them to see.

Active challenge

Search the Internet and find sites that help your understanding of two sports of your choice. Discuss with a partner the different ways in which they help performance. For example, do they show the tactics of the game?

Key terms

Terrestrial television – **programmes available to everyone with a television set and a television licence**

Satellite television – **programmes available to those who purchase a receiver and pay a subscription**

Pay-per-view – **extra sporting events, bought individually by the viewer and available only via subscription**

Summary

Sport is such a popular and marketable commodity that all forms of media devote time and money to it. There are several successful television channels specifically devoted to sport. The influence of the director of the programme or columnist of the newspaper is massive on the viewer or reader, enough to persuade them to think in a certain way. Although there are many advantages of the media's involvement in sport, there are also disadvantages as well; for the benefit of sport, getting the right balance is important.

Exam questions

Multiple-choice questions

1. Different types of sporting television broadcast include:

   ☐ **A** Educational, drama, entertaining, informative

   ☐ **B** Informative, current affairs, instructive, entertaining

   ☐ **C** Instructive, informative, educational, political affairs

   ☐ **D** Informative, educational, instructive, entertaining

   (1 mark)

2. Different forms of media include:

   ☐ **A** Magazines, television, coaching, Internet

   ☐ **B** Magazines, television, Internet, radio, newspapers

   ☐ **C** Internet, radio, newspapers, exam qualifications, newspaper supplements

   ☐ **D** Television, Internet, radio, newspapers, sponsorship

   (1 mark)

3. Examples of terrestrial television channels include:

   ☐ **A** ITV, Channel 5, BBC 4, Channel 4, BBC 2

   ☐ **B** ITV, Channel 5, BBC 1, Channel 4, Sky Sports 1

   ☐ **C** ITV, Channel 5, BBC 1, Channel 4, BBC 2

   ☐ **D** ITV, Channel 5, BBC 1, E4, BBC 2

   (1 mark)

Short answer question

4. What effects does the editor of television programmes have on the viewing public?

   (2 marks)

Longer answer questions

5. The many forms of media can help the viewer understand performance better. Give examples of how this is achieved.

   (5 marks)

6. What are the positive effects of terrestrial television coverage?

   (5 marks)

7. Cable and satellite television channels can have negative effects on sport. What could these include?

   (4 marks)

3.1.3 ～ Making informed decisions about getting involved in a lifetime of healthy physical activities that suit their needs

3.1.3h Sponsorship

What you will learn about in this topic:

1 — The range, scope and the effects of sponsorship
2 — Advantages and disadvantages to the sponsor
3 — Advantages and disadvantages to the performer
4 — Advantages and disadvantage to the sport or activity
5 — Ease of obtaining sponsorship at various levels
6 — Acceptable and unacceptable types of sponsorship

Any sportsperson or team, irrespective of amateur or professional status, can benefit from **sponsorship**, whilst the sponsor will always want a return for their financial input and often, the bigger the deal, the greater the demands from the sponsor.

1 — The range, scope and the effects of sponsorship

Companies can choose to sponsor sport in different ways. Some prefer to put their name to leagues, events or sports facilities whilst others choose to sponsor a particular individual or team. Within a team, players may also have personal deals with their own sponsor and be used to endorse a particular brand or company. The **Institute of Sports Sponsorship (ISS)** predicts that the worldwide market for sports sponsorship will rise to $50 billion by 2010. This increase will be due to more attractive spectator and corporate facilities, but mostly from televised coverage and sponsorship deals.

The impact of sponsorship can be seen in many ways:

- Sponsorship of the London 2012 Olympics is predicted to be in the region of £625 million.
- A third of all sponsorship deals go to football players or teams because it is the largest generator of revenue from sponsorship.

Sponsorship is involved at all levels of sport.

- Major sports that have sponsorship deals include: Formula One racing, rugby union, athletics, cricket and horse racing.
- The government's drive to improve the fitness of the population is leading to greater sponsorship of grassroots sport.
- Successful bids for major events have a massive, positive effect on sponsorship in general.
- Viewing of sport is increased as a result of sponsorship deals. Without the backing of sponsors, some events could not take place.
- Prime-time coverage of sport provides the maximum exposure of the sponsor and its product.
- Sales of replica kits and other clothing advertise the sponsor and its products.

Year	Value (£m)	% change (of value)	Number of sponsors	% change (of sponsors)
1991	238	–	759	–
1992	238	+0.4	659	–13.2
1993	250	+4.6	745	+13.1
1994	265	+6	818	+9.8
1995	285	+7	939	+14.8
1996	302	+6	977	+4
1997	322	+6.6	995	+1.8
1998	357	+9.6	969	–2.6
1999	377	+6.8	1172	+20.9
2000	400	+6.1	1200	+2.4

Trends in professional sports sponsorship expenditure.

For example, in 2008 the Football Champions League's official sponsors where Heineken, Sony, MasterCard, Vodafone, PlayStation and Ford.

Task 1

1 – Choose five major sporting events and list the sponsors associated with each event.

2 — Advantages and disadvantages to the sponsor

Advantages

Although football and motor sport dominate the market for sports sponsorship in the UK, other sports such as rugby, cricket, athletics, golf, tennis, equestrian sports, swimming and snooker enjoy significant support from sponsors.

There are several reasons why companies sponsor sport. The most important is for financial gain. Before a sponsor puts their name to a sport, individual or team they work out the financial benefit of linking their product to a particular person or team. This is usually estimated in the form of increased sales of their product. In competition, which can range from local events to worldwide exposure with television coverage, the sponsor's logo is clearly seen. **Advertising** the brand name in this way can save companies money in comparison with the expense of creating adverts for various forms of other media.

Linking the brand name with a certain sport can develop a healthy image, making it more popular in the public's eyes. Sports can also benefit from being linked to a company with a good image, as they can be regarded as being successful in the same way.

To promote a caring image the sponsors can help promote minority sports. In schools, a company may provide sports equipment or put their name to an award scheme to help the interest and participation in a particular activity. This can be seen as a gesture of **goodwill** to help get people involved in sport, whilst at the same time advertising their product.

The money sponsors make available to a sport can improve its standards by helping to provide better coaches, facilities, training and administration. Companies can become more popular and well respected because of their positive and loyal involvement with sport. Many companies finance a showcase event, such as a league or major competition. This can increase the size and standard of the competition, attracting the best performers in the world. The sponsors not only finance the organization, but the prizes and prize money too.

A company may also gain financially through tax relief if they sponsor a sport. The amount they sponsor can be claimed against the tax that they pay and so save them money over the year. In certain cases a sports equipment manufacturer may be researching and developing a new product. They will back a performer in return for the performer using the new product and giving feedback on its effectiveness. In this way, improvements are made in the sport and the performer is supported in their training and competition. For example, golf manufacturers often give a professional their newest club to try out.

In some cases, a company may sponsor a person or sport with no thought of financial return. Goodwill gestures such as these are a sign of a company's passion for the sport and its commitment to maintaining its standards and further progress. A company who sponsors an event can usually take advantage of corporate hospitality for their employees. They will be allotted good seats and sometimes meals at the events.

The Rugby Six Nations tournament benefits financially from sponsorship from the Royal Bank of Scotland.

In 2008, McCain signed a five-year deal to sponsor UK Athletics.

Task 2

Create a spider diagram of the ways sponsors benefit from advertising in sport.

Disadvantages

However, sponsorship does not automatically guarantee success; the sponsor can take a risk if backing new talent. The sponsor speculates on the performer reaching the top of their chosen field. Another risk with sportspeople is injury, which may stall, shorten or even finish a career. The sponsor takes on these risks knowing that there may be a limited return on their investment if an athlete is out of action.

Investing large amounts of money in a national team relies on that team qualifying for showcase events and tournaments. If a team fails to qualify then the global advertising for the product fails to come about, together with the impact of the failure image on their product. The behaviour of individual performers can also have a negative effect on sponsorship. For instance, athletes who use banned drugs to enhance their performances bring the sport, and by implication the sponsor, into disrepute.

3 — Advantages and disadvantages to the performer

Taking part and competing at the highest level in sport is expensive. To reach the necessary standard an individual performer needs sponsorship so that they do not have financial worries, leaving them to concentrate on training and competing. The obvious way sponsorship helps is by supplying the equipment, clothing and training for the event. Sponsorship deals are good while they last but they can be imposing on an athlete's life too.

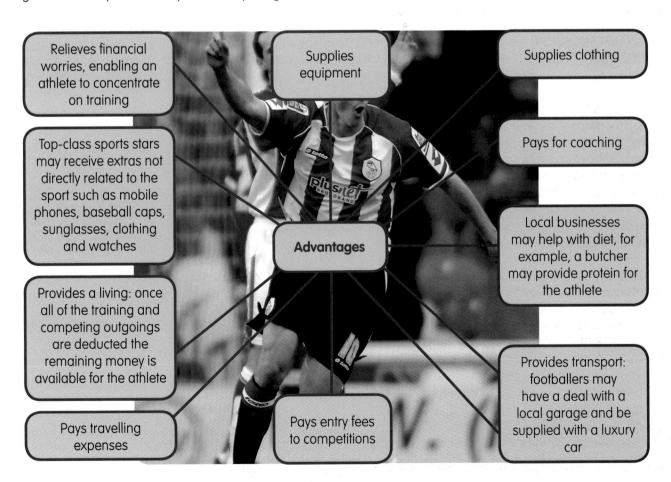

Relieves financial worries, enabling an athlete to concentrate on training

Supplies equipment

Supplies clothing

Top-class sports stars may receive extras not directly related to the sport such as mobile phones, baseball caps, sunglasses, clothing and watches

Pays for coaching

Advantages

Local businesses may help with diet, for example, a butcher may provide protein for the athlete

Provides a living: once all of the training and competing outgoings are deducted the remaining money is available for the athlete

Pays travelling expenses

Pays entry fees to competitions

Provides transport: footballers may have a deal with a local garage and be supplied with a luxury car

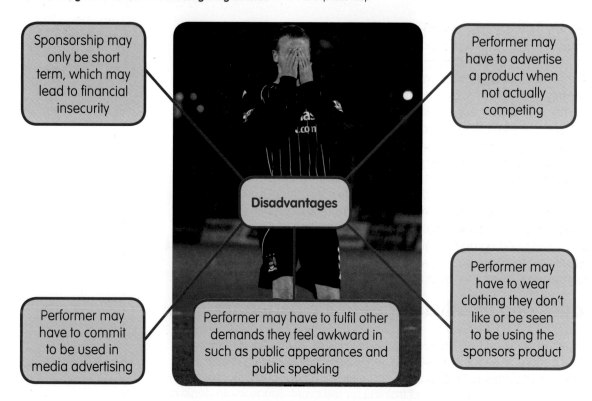

Sponsorship may only be short term, which may lead to financial insecurity

Performer may have to advertise a product when not actually competing

Disadvantages

Performer may have to commit to be used in media advertising

Performer may have to fulfil other demands they feel awkward in such as public appearances and public speaking

Performer may have to wear clothing they don't like or be seen to be using the sponsors product

4 — Advantages and disadvantages to the sport or activity

Advantages

Some sports are seen to be so popular and an excellent advertising medium, both nationally and internationally, that larger companies will sponsor the whole sport – football is a prime example of this. This gives the sport or event financial security for the future so that improvements can be made to its facilities and administration processes. The increase of money attracts the best performers, which in turn improves the standard and appeal of the sport or event. In return for a sponsoring company having exclusive rights on advertising, the organizers, clubs and players benefit from the financial input.

Disadvantages

If the sponsors get too much control over the sport then they may begin to take the management of events away from specialized sports bodies. To make a game more marketable the rules of the sport can change due to the sponsor's demands. This has happened in cricket. For example, rather than follow the traditional rules of the game and wear whites as their kit, each county team wears a different coloured kit for one-day games. In some cricket competitions the number of overs in the game has changed (20/20 matches for example) and night games have been introduced in order to make it more appealing to the television audience as they provide an opportunity for families and workers to see the game.

Sponsors can also control the timing of the events. Traditionally, football matches used to start at 3pm on Saturday afternoons. After Sky made an exclusive deal to broadcast live Premiership football, it influenced a change so that matches are played on Sundays, have various starting times and there are later kick-offs for midweek matches. The sponsors have demanded the changes in order to capture prime-time viewing slots for television coverage. For international matches similar changes to starting times have been made to suit viewing audiences. Although the changes are good for the audiences they are not always in the best interests of the performers.

In extreme cases, the sports become reliant on the sponsors for a major part of their financial existence. After ITV Digital bought the rights to broadcast Nationwide League football games the company collapsed. This caused financial concerns for clubs with some, such as Bradford City, being forced into administration.

Sponsors are attracted to the major sports and the most successful performers, as they want their product to be linked with success. This creates an imbalance not only in sports coverage in the media but also in competition, where the best-financed performers have more resources to compete and win at the highest level. It is difficult for less popular sports to get sponsorship, despite the sports being worthy in their own right.

In an attempt to promote minority sports the government has set up the 'Sportsmatch Scheme', targeting under-funded, amateur and minority sports. Any money given by a company to sponsor such a sport will be matched pound for pound by the government. The minimum award is £1000 (£500 for schools) and the maximum is £50,000. In England, Sport England is responsible for the scheme. In Scotland, Wales and Northern Ireland it is administered by their own sports councils.

Many sponsors will only put money into a high-profile sport, as this is the easiest way of getting the best return. Ten years ago, many athletes found it difficult to get sufficient sponsorship to compete at the highest level. It is only recently, now that the image of athletics has risen, due to the personalities in the sport and increased television coverage creating an international appeal, that sponsors are more willing to direct money towards athletics. For some involved in sport, the importance of making money for the sponsor spoils the enjoyment of the sport.

Active challenge

Research into your school's PE department for the names of companies helping them. Look into award schemes, adverts for sports events, books and any local sponsors linked to your school.

5 — Ease of obtaining sponsorship at various levels

In order to keep a team running efficiently, sponsorship may be necessary. If a local youth side needs some financial help then often contacting local businesses is the first step. Local businesses may agree to sponsor a local team in order to help them and as a result build up good relations in the community. Finding local sponsors is often a case of using personal contacts via a team member, a parent or coach. A telephone call describing the team, what success they have had and their aims for the future may be enough to have a business supply a team with funding for sports equipment. Usually, shirts, showing the business logo, practice and match balls are bought with sponsorship money.

With high-profile sponsorship hoping to attract a more corporate response, greater depth of preparation is required. Finding a sponsor with the right image and a willingness to invest large sums of money will need careful preparation:

The following stages will help prepare a team for sponsorship:

1. What company would suit being linked with you and your sport? Look at companies that give the same message as you.
2. Set out your plan for success, for example, tournaments, league, and so on.
3. Set out on paper a presentation of information about you and your aims for the future, how the team and the company are suited, what you need from the sponsor, how the sponsor will benefit, and so on.
4. Contact the company and request a face-to-face meeting.
5. Present your information to the company.
6. After the meeting make a follow-up call to find out their decision. If sponsorship is agreed, check any conditions of the deal and make sure you both agree to them.
7. Work hard to be successful and relate any success to the sponsor in order to build their confidence in you.

6 — Acceptable and unacceptable types of sponsorship

When sports seek sponsorship they generally do so from companies that have an appropriately healthy, positive and wholesome image. For example, Steven Gerrard has advertised Persil and a selection of sports stars are linked with Gillette. These products are considered to be reliable, household names with good reputations.

However, there are some products that have been traditionally linked with sports which in today's society are losing their credibility. Two prime examples are alcohol and tobacco. These products, although continuing to have a link with sport, have restrictions on them so that they can only have a link with adult events. Tobacco companies were major sponsors of Formula One racing and had been for many years. The link with cigarettes was so controversial, as smoking is increasingly associated with poor health conditions, that the sponsorship stopped in 2006. Cricket led the way by breaking their links with tobacco sponsorship in 2002, whilst snooker broke their ties in 2006.

BE YOUR BEST TODAY WITH GILLETTE FUSION POWER.

Start today with the confidence you get from Gillette's closest, most comfortable shave. Turn it on — soothing micro-pulses help you reduce friction. You'll barely feel the blades.

Gillette
The Best a Man Can Get™

Gillette
Fusion
gillettechampions.co.uk

Roger Federer, Thierry Henry and Tiger Woods all advertise Gillette razors.

Task 3

1 – Make a list of the advantages and disadvantages of sponsorship. Note down points from both the individual sport or activity and the sponsor's viewpoints.

2 – From what you have read in this section, note down your opinions on why some sponsorship is seen to be unacceptable and some acceptable.

Key terms

Sponsorship – backing performers financially in return for advertising a product

Institute of Sports Sponsorship (ISS) – promotes best practice in sponsorship, working closely with sports bodies, government and the media

Advertising – displaying a product, name or logo in public

Goodwill – supporting a performer or sport financially without any monetary return

Summary

In most sponsorship deals, both the company and the performer gain from the partnership. For the performer, having financial backing relieves the stress of how a training and competitive programme is funded. This gives the performer freedom to choose the best methods in order to challenge the top sportspeople in the world. For the company, they are seen to support a particular sport, putting them in a favourable light with the public whilst advertising their product nationally or internationally.

The sponsor may feel that the more money they provide, the greater their influence in the running of the sport. At times, this has a detrimental effect on the performer and can change the traditions of the sport itself. Some sponsors who care about the sport they are involved with can ensure the standards of the sport are maintained and developed in the future.

Exam questions

Multiple-choice questions

1. Which of the following best describes advantages of sports sponsorship to the sponsor?

   ☐ **A** Pay entry fee of athlete, wide range of advertising, linked with healthy image, increased popularity

   ☐ **B** Linked with healthy image, increased popularity, wide range of advertising, traditional games adapted

   ☐ **C** Financial gain, wide range of advertising, linked with healthy image, increased popularity

   ☐ **D** Increased popularity, financial gain, poor performance of team reflected on sponsor, linked with healthy image

   (1 mark)

2. Which of the following group of products best reflects acceptable types of sponsorship?

   ☐ **A** Flora, Rolex, Marlborough cigarettes, Gillette, Royal Bank of Scotland

   ☐ **B** Persil, Flora, Rolex, Sainsbury's, Gillette, Royal Bank of Scotland

   ☐ **C** Rolex, Sainsbury's, Gillette, Embassy cigarettes, Royal Bank of Scotland, Persil

   ☐ **D** Flora, Bell's whiskey, Rolex, Sainsbury's, Gillette, Royal Bank of Scotland

   (1 mark)

3. Which of the following give examples of advantages of sponsorship?

   ☐ **A** Achieve financial security, improved facilities, attracts best performers, raises the standard of the sport

   ☐ **B** Improved facilities, be controlled by outside agencies, attracts best performers, raises the standard of the sport

   ☐ **C** Attracts best performers, start times changed to fit television schedules, achieve financial security, improved administration

   ☐ **D** Raises the standard of the sport, achieve financial security, improved facilities, be financially dependent

   (1 mark)

4. Which of the following best describes the advantages of sponsorship for the performer?

   ☐ **A** Equipment supplied, coaching paid for, relieves financial worries, contracted to take part in public appearances

   ☐ **B** Coaching paid for, may still have to advertise product when not competing, equipment supplied, travel expenses paid

   ☐ **C** Entry fees paid for, pays for cost of living, sponsorship may be a short-term deal, travel expenses paid

   ☐ **D** Relieves financial worries, equipment supplied, coaching paid for, travel expenses paid

   (1 mark)

5. Teams can prepare in stages for sponsorship. Which of the following is not one of these stages?

   ☐ **A** Choosing a company suitable for the sport

   ☐ **B** Setting out a plan for success in tournaments or leagues

   ☐ **C** Check that all players like the company's product

   ☐ **D** Presenting your information to the company

   (1 mark)

Short answer question

6. What does ISS stand for?

   (1 mark)

Longer answer questions

7. What are the disadvantages of sponsorship to the sportsperson?

   (4 marks)

8. What are the advantages of sponsorship to the sponsor?

   (4 marks)

9. What are the advantages of sponsorship to the sportsperson?

   (4 marks)

3.1.3 ～ Making informed decisions about getting involved in a lifetime of healthy physical activities that suit their needs

3.1.3i Competitions

What you will learn about in this topic:

1 — Types of competition used in sport

There are different types of competition used in sport. Knock-out competitions exist in games such as football and racket sports like Wimbledon. Ladder competitions are better suited to individual sports such as squash. Often, a sport can be adapted to several types of competition irrespective of the ability level of the performers. The choice of competition entered into can depend on:

- the time allowed (such as the hiring of facilities)
- the numbers involved (team or individual event)
- the age of the competitors
- the standard of the competitors
- facilities available.

1 — Types of competition used in sport

Different sports can use a variety of formats such as **knock-out tournaments**, **ladder** and **combination events** to run their competitions. Some formats better suit some sports.

For some events, teams or individuals will have to qualify for the event. For example, in athletics, a competition may require a qualifying distance or time from the athlete in order for them to enter the event. In the FIFA World Cup there are a series of World Cup qualifying rounds that teams must win in order to be involved in the final.

Active challenge

From your own experiences, recall any competitions you have been involved in or know of. Think of examples from both inside and outside of school. Share your knowledge of how each competition worked, with a partner.

Ladder – in squash, competitors' names are drawn and placed vertically in a ladder formation. Players are able to challenge other competitors above them in order to move up the ladder. If they win they can swop places on the ladder with the player they played. There is often a limit to how many places above on the ladder a challenge can be made (usually two or three depending on the number of people in the ladder). The aim is to keep challenging until you are at the top of the ladder and then maintain your position throughout the season.

Competition formats in sport

Knock-out tournaments – in tennis, the players that keep winning tournaments stay in the competition until there are two players remaining and they play a final match to find the winner – the losing opponents will have been knocked out along the way. The numbers involved at the initial round stages is crucial so that there are eight players left at the quarter-final stage.

Combination events – in modern pentathlon and decathlon events, each is made up of a series of different disciplines. The result in each discipline earns points for the competitor. The points are accumulated throughout the competition and the athlete with the highest number of points at the end is deemed the winner. This format allows the performers to gain points in their strongest events to make up for any points lost in their less strong events.

Key terms

Knock-out tournament – competitions where progress is dependant on winning each game played

Ladder – a competition where participants are allowed to challenge those ranked higher, in order to move up in rank

Combination events – an event where different activities make up the whole sport

Summary

There are different kinds of competition format. Some activities suit a particular format. The number of competitors entered in an event can bring about the need for preliminary rounds in order to run smoothly. With knock-out competitions like tennis, depending on the number of entries, multiples of eight at the round stages is vital in order to reach the quarter-final stage with eight remaining competitors.

Exam questions

Multiple-choice questions

1. Which of the following best describes a ladder competition?

   ☐ **A** A competition played in rounds with only the winning teams playing again

   ☐ **B** A qualifying score must be attained in order to take part in the competition, then success in each round keeps a performer in the competition

   ☐ **C** A competition where players organize their own matches against higher placed opponents and move above them if they win

   ☐ **D** Competition starts with qualifying rounds and then the finalists compete

   (1 mark)

2. Which competition format does the Wimbledon Championships follow?

   ☐ **A** League format

   ☐ **B** Knock-out tournament

   ☐ **C** Qualifying tournament

   ☐ **D** Round robin

   (1 mark)

Short answer question

3. There are many different ways a competition can be organized. What affects the choice of competition used?

   (3 marks)

Longer answer question

4. Describe how a combination event works.

   (4 marks)

3.1.3 ～ Making informed decisions about getting involved in a lifetime of healthy physical activities that suit their needs

3.1.3j   International and other factors

What you will learn about in this topic:

1 — Competitions
2 — International sport and events
3 — The link with role models
4 — Health, safety and the well-being of others
5 — Rules relating to sport and equipment
6 — Science and ICT

1 — Competitions

There are many different levels of competition. These levels can depend on the age or experience of the participant. An athlete may progress via school to area, county, national and international competitions. In the initial stages, winning qualifies the athlete for the next stage, but in high-level events, the only way to compete is by achieving qualifying times and distances set for the competition.

Grassroots

Grassroots competitions are for those young beginners learning the sport and developing their skills. The competitions involve games that have been adapted from the full game, using modified rules and equipment. Competitions can follow the format of the full event. Types of modified games include: mini tennis, touch rugby, high five netball and non-stop cricket.

Active challenge

Choose one of the modified games listed and either, from your own experience or by searching the Internet, list facts about the modified game. Report your findings back to the class.

Using gymnastics as a model, there are clearly defined steps and recommendations to follow when introducing young people to competitive school gymnastics: they follow the National School Competition Framework.

- Five to seven year olds – fun and friendly mixed competition between the local primary schools in a cluster, taking place at one of the primary schools. This level uses Key Steps gymnastics for Key Stage 1.
- Seven to nine year olds – fun and friendly mixed competition between the primary schools in a cluster, held at a central site, such as a primary school, secondary school, local leisure centre or gymnastics club. This level of competition uses the Key Steps gymnastics for Key Stage 2.
- Nine to 11 year olds – 11 week coaching leading to a Key Steps competition in week 12 for those working towards Key Step Level 3. Winners then move on to a round two competition held at a local sports college or gymnastics club. Competitions lead to a centrally located county final with representatives from each School Sport Partnership.
- 11 to 12 year olds – Key Steps competition with the groups working at Level 3 between secondary schools, based at a local leisure centre or secondary school. Competitions lead to a county final held at the same time and place as the 9 to 11 finals.
- 12 to 16 year olds – compete in year groups against other schools in inter-school leagues. Held at school or leisure centre venues.

Active challenge

Search the Internet to find the National School Competition Framework for a sport of your choice. Make an account of the age groups, level of competition and venues involved, and report back to the class.

Novice competitions

Novice competitions can be adapted to many sports including fencing, triathlon and trampolining. The City of Leeds Diving Club holds annual novice diving competitions for four age groups ranging from eight or nine through to 14 to 16 year olds. Novice competitions generally use the official equipment and rules of the sport and can be used as a way of easing the participant into full competition.

Each sport and competition has its own format. A particular sport may use several different formats for different competitions depending on tradition or the organizer's needs, making each one an individual event.

League games

Local amateur leagues can be adapted to most sports such as bowls, cricket, netball and hockey. Sunday league football exists for those who work full-time and enjoy competing in football at an amateur level at the weekend. Each team usually plays all the other teams in the league on a home and away basis, usually for promotion and relegation depending on the number of leagues in the area. Professional leagues include the Premiership (football), the English Super League (rugby league) and the Guinness Premiership (rugby union).

Each team in a league has set fixtures between all the other teams in a league, and accumulate points for wins and draws. The Guinness Premiership awards four points for a win, two points for a draw, one point for losing by seven points or less, and one point for scoring four tries in a match. The teams with the four highest point tallies at the end of the 22 rounds (12 teams play each other home and away, which equals 22 matches) play a semi-final and a final to find the champion team for that season.

Active challenge

In football, what is the difference in the final top four placed teams in the Premiership and the Championship? Write an account of your findings that would clearly explain the differences to a person who knows nothing about football.

> Think about answering the following: do they play again? Do they qualify for other competitions?

Round robin

Round robin competitions involve each team playing all the other competitors. The team winning the most games wins the competition. In some cases where there are too many teams, two round robin competitions run side-by-side with the top teams having a play-off for the overall winning place.

The Six Nations Championship in rugby is a straightforward competition with each of the same six teams (England, Italy, Scotland, Wales, France and Ireland) playing each other once, with the home advantage alternating each year. Teams earn two points for a win and one point for a draw. The team with the most points wins the Championship. There are other honours to be achieved during the competition too. If a team wins all their games they are 'Grand Slam' winners. Teams beating all the other home nations (only between England, Ireland, Scotland and Wales) are 'Triple Crown' winners. England and Scotland play for the Calcutta Cup and England and Ireland play for the Millennium Trophy.

In the rugby Six Nations Championships, teams only play each other once, so the home advantage changes each year.

The ATP (Association of Tennis Professionals) World Tour Finals are played on a round robin basis, but with a twist. Firstly, the players have to qualify for the competition. The top seven players in the ATP Race automatically qualify. The eighth place goes to either a Grand Slam Champion of that year, who is not in the top eight in the ATP Race, but is in the top 20, or the eighth player in the ATP Race.

The players are divided into two sections based on rankings. Players are ranked according to their position in the ATP Race with players one, four, five, and seven in one group and players two, three, six, and eight in the other. The winners of each group play the second place of the other group in the semi-finals. The winners of those games play each other in a final to find the Champion.

At times, in round robin competitions, teams tie on points. If this happens the organizers can pre-state in their rules how they will determine the positions. For example:

- shots, points or goal differences. In rugby for example, the points for are subtracted from the points against to give a plus or minus figure
- the most shots, points or goals wins
- the least shots, points or goals wins.

Tournaments

The FIFA World Cup is an example of a tournament. Teams need to qualify for the competition. These qualifying games are held in the six FIFA continental zones (Africa, Asia, North and Central America and the Caribbean (CONCACAF), South America, Oceania and Europe). The qualifying period takes place in the three preceding years leading up to the finals. There are 32 teams in the final competition and they are drawn into eight groups. Each team plays the others on a round robin basis. Winning a match is worth three points and drawing one point. The top two teams, those with the most points, from each group go through to the knockout stages and only the winning teams move on to the next round. The competition rounds off with quarter-finals, semi-finals, the third place match (between the losing semi-finalists) and ultimately, the final.

The winning finalist will have played six matches to win the trophy over the two weeks of the competition.

Qualifying rounds

The Women's British Open golf tournament involves **qualifying rounds**. The top players are automatically included in the competition with further places settled in a qualifying competition (in 2008 there were 18 further places to be played for) making the total entries 150. The Women's British Open competition takes place over four days. For the first two days players are trying to make scores so they finish as one of the top 80 players. This allows them to stay in the competition for the two final days and ultimately play for the championship.

Active challenge

Choose one of the following:

- The Champions League
- The UEFA Cup
- The Davis Cup
- The Ryder Cup
- The Olympics.

For your chosen competition, research how teams or individuals qualify and progress to the final stages of the event.

Key terms

Round robin – a competition where all teams in a group play each other

Qualifying rounds – a competition where a standard must be reached to allow the performer to go to the next stage of the competition

Summary

Often, the reason people take part in sport is to compete. A young performer can gradually increase their experience in such competitions through grassroots, novice and school competitions. Each event has its own format making it both individual and challenging.

2 — International sport and events

It is always a triumph for the country that succeeds in their bid to host a major showcase event as the UK did to secure the 2012 Olympic Games. The task of putting on such an event is mammoth, so there needs to be good management, detailed planning, discipline and organization to meet deadlines. The Olympics differs from other events as it brings together a wide variety of sports, each with its own governing body, with their own needs and requirements.

There are many advantages and disadvantages of hosting a major event:

Advantages	Disadvantages
• Home teams receive greater support. • Home teams are motivated by the country's support. • Home performers are used to the diet, culture, country's day to day running, language, altitude and temperatures. • More family members around to provide support. • People of the nation are inspired to take up sport by seeing top-class performers. • Can improve the health of a nation. • Host city gains prestige. • Infrastructure improved – road, amenities, housing, stadiums, and so on. • Increase in jobs. • Increase in tourism. • Increase in local business trade. • Increased assets of the country and city. • Wasteland utilized. • Chance to demonstrate environmental innovations used in new buildings. • Poorer areas improved.	• Magnet for protest groups. • Possibility of the threat of terrorism. • Political loss of credibility for poorly organized events. • Possible increase in taxes for the local area to help pay for event if the costs spiral. • New facilities are expensive. • Homes and businesses may have to move out of the community. • Aerobic long-distance activities can take longer to complete in areas with pollution problems. • Increased pollution and congestion with greater numbers of people needing transport. • Increased pollution and congestion from new construction work. • Natural wildlife habitats may be lost when venues are built.

The Olympic Games

Hosting the Olympic Games is an honour and a measure of the manger's and coordinator's planning and organizing abilities. The correct facilities need to be in place in the lead up to the event. All Olympic sports' governing bodies are involved and correctly qualified and experienced officials and volunteers need to be in place. As well as making sure that the needs of each sport are met. Plans must be in place to look after dignitaries from each country.

The 2012 Olympics

In 2012, the Olympics will be hosted by Great Britain in London. Hopefully, the spectators will see the final Olympics as a well-organized, entertaining and memorable event. Before reaching that final product, political, financial and environmental considerations have been carefully considered.

POLITICAL ISSUES The Department of Culture, Media and Sport (DCMS) set out five high-level legacy promises for after the Olympic games in their 'Legacy action plan'. It sets out the long-term benefits that should come about from hosting the 2012 Olympics:

1. To make the UK a world-leading sporting nation.
2. To transform the heart of East London.
3. To inspire a generation of young people.
4. To make the Olympic Park a blueprint for sustainable living.
5. To demonstrate that the UK is a creative, inclusive and welcoming place to live in, visit and for businesses.

Active challenge

Research on the Internet to find details of one of the points from the DCMS document. Share your findings in a small group.

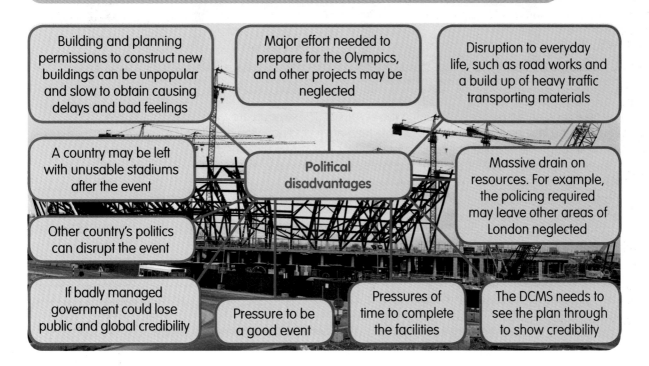

Building and planning permissions to construct new buildings can be unpopular and slow to obtain causing delays and bad feelings

Major effort needed to prepare for the Olympics, and other projects may be neglected

Disruption to everyday life, such as road works and a build up of heavy traffic transporting materials

A country may be left with unusable stadiums after the event

Political disadvantages

Massive drain on resources. For example, the policing required may leave other areas of London neglected

Other country's politics can disrupt the event

If badly managed government could lose public and global credibility

Pressure to be a good event

Pressures of time to complete the facilities

The DCMS needs to see the plan through to show credibility

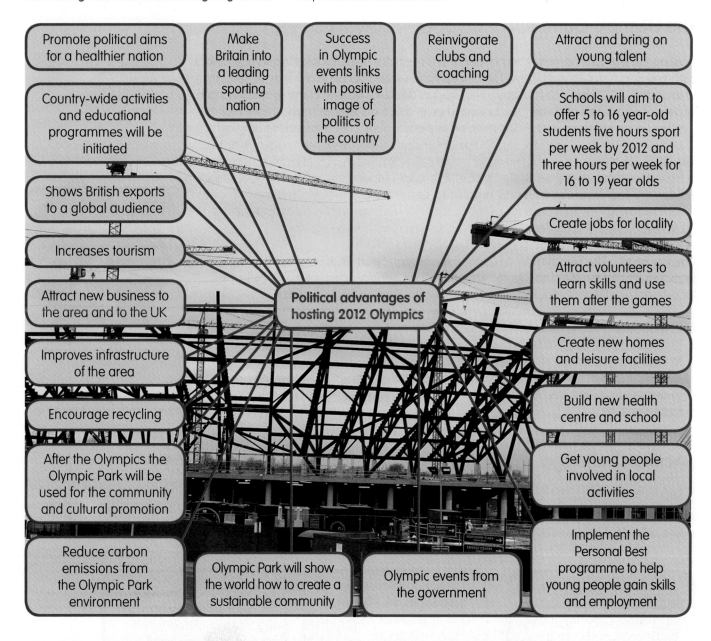

Promote political aims for a healthier nation

Make Britain into a leading sporting nation

Success in Olympic events links with positive image of politics of the country

Reinvigorate clubs and coaching

Attract and bring on young talent

Country-wide activities and educational programmes will be initiated

Schools will aim to offer 5 to 16 year-old students five hours sport per week by 2012 and three hours per week for 16 to 19 year olds

Shows British exports to a global audience

Create jobs for locality

Increases tourism

Attract volunteers to learn skills and use them after the games

Attract new business to the area and to the UK

Political advantages of hosting 2012 Olympics

Improves infrastructure of the area

Create new homes and leisure facilities

Encourage recycling

Build new health centre and school

After the Olympics the Olympic Park will be used for the community and cultural promotion

Get young people involved in local activities

Reduce carbon emissions from the Olympic Park environment

Olympic Park will show the world how to create a sustainable community

Olympic events from the government

Implement the Personal Best programme to help young people gain skills and employment

FINANCIAL ISSUES There is an enormous cost to staging the Olympics. These costs are met from different sources and include both public and private funding, including lottery funding. The National Lottery, through the Olympic Lottery Distributor (OLD), has made a major grant to the Olympic Delivery Authority (ODA) for constructing facilities and improving the building infrastructures for the Olympic and Paralympic Games. Private funding often comes in the form of construction firms providing buildings, for the Olympic Village for instance, and then retaining the buildings after the Games. Some costs are met after the Olympics by assets, such as land and buildings, being sold off for housing and for private enterprise use.

Major companies will contribute to the costs of hosting the games by paying to have their product on show or used throughout the competition. This will show their product as a global one, having the integrity to be linked with such an event. Sponsorship deals include Coca-Cola, Samsung and VISA.

Funding for the 2012 Olympics	
National public funding	£9,325 billion
Exchequer	£5,975 billion
National Lottery	£2,175 billion
Greater London Authority	£925 billion
London Development Agency	£250 billion
Total	£18,650 billion

Massive incomes are generated from the television rights of the Olympics.

Local businesses outside the Olympic Park are expected to see an increased trade for the duration of the games. Public money will provide a major contribution to the funding of the Olympics. Public taxes have risen to help finance the Olympics, although sponsors may have a monopoly in the Olympic Park, cutting out local businesses.

ENVIRONMENTAL ISSUES   When changes occur in an area, especially if new buildings are put up, there is often an impact on the environment. The 2012 Olympics aims to be the 'greenest Games in history'. Contaminated land in East London will be reclaimed and the Olympics will implement environmentally friendly policies to do with minimizing:

- waste
- pollution
- impact on wildlife habitats.

The Olympics will also promote sustainable practices and aims to be a car-free event, only allowing disabled drivers access to venues. Only **brownfield sites** will be built on.

During the event, there will be a greater volume of traffic which will increase noise pollution and reduce air quality. The increase in tourism will mean an increase of people visiting the area which can cause social problems and increase the amount of rubbish produced.

There are however some environmental disadvantages such as noise, dust and pollution from construction work. Some wildlife habitats, including woodlands, will also be destroyed to make way for the Olympic Park.

Political issues –
making a bid, having the right facilities, accommodating the teams and officials, segregating the fans, policing the event

Features of hosting major World Cups and Championships

Environmental issues –
increased population for duration of the event so an increase in pollution

Financial issues –
television rights, sponsorship, local business benefit, tourism increased

Task 1

Create a table of advantages and disadvantages of hosting the Olympics.

Major World Cups and Championships

Major World Cups and Championships can be the pinnacle of a sportsperson's career. They attract and involve the best performers worldwide and so potentially show off the event at the highest level. Popular events include the Football World Cup, the Rugby World Cup and the Snooker World Championships. Some features of these events are as follows:

- They concentrate on one sporting area.
- An increase in interest and participation in a new sport.
- If it is a one-off chance to host the event, organizers only have one chance to get their bid right.
- Attract spectators who are interested in that particular sport.

Task 2

1 – Study the information on hosting a major international event. Divide the information into advantages and disadvantages.

2 – Add your own suggestions to your lists.

High-profile events

High-profile events attract competitors from all over the world. These events are a draw for spectators both at the events and on television so can be broadcast worldwide.

High-profile events include Wimbledon, the Super Bowl, Test Matches and Premier League Football games.

Advantages	Disadvantages
• Keeps with tradition.	• Monopolies trade at the event making purchases expensive.
• Focal point for that sport.	• Television rights may be bought up by satellite companies which can exclude some viewers.
• Established event in the sporting year.	• Events with leagues may find teams suffer the 'yo-yo' effect of being promoted and relegated each year.
• Organizers can continue to improve the event year on year.	• Rich clubs may dominate as they can afford the top players.
• Performers can train to play on the event's particular surface.	
• Fans and players look forward to the event.	
• Television broadcasts takes sport to new countries, creating interest.	

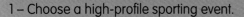

Task 3

1 – Choose a high-profile sporting event.

2 – List any advantages and disadvantages the event may experience and share your views with a partner.

Key terms

Infrastructure – basic facilities and services for the functioning of a community or country, for example, roads, schools, and amenities

Brownfield sites – underdeveloped, derelict, contaminated or vacant areas

Summary

Hosting a major sporting event will have a significant affect on the host city and country. Some events are awarded to a city after several bids from other areas have been considered. Other events are traditional and find themselves on the sporting calendar year after year in the same place. Sport can motivate and influence its audience, none more so than when the event is taking place on home territory. The prestige, excitement and inspiration of hosting an event can have advantages on a political, financial and environmental level. The disadvantages should be considered, planned for and guarded against as much as possible.

3 — The link with role models

Sportspeople who are regularly seen in the public eye can often set trends. Their fans can be influenced to change their attitudes about a sport, making it grow or decline in popularity as a result of the ability, behaviour and success of their hero. For example, Michael Schumacher had a massive following in Formula One racing and, as a result of his retirement, some of his fans have lost interest in the sport.

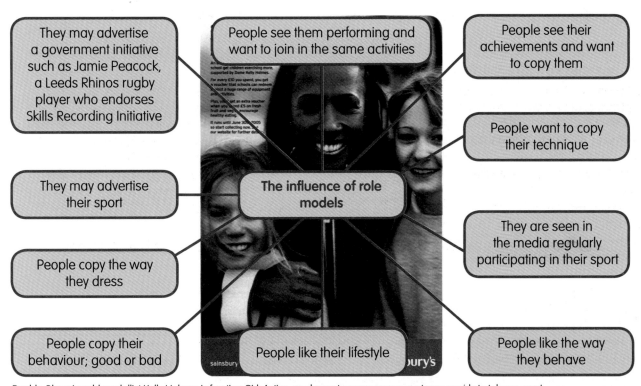

They may advertise a government initiative such as Jamie Peacock, a Leeds Rhinos rugby player who endorses Skills Recording Initiative

People see them performing and want to join in the same activities

People see their achievements and want to copy them

They may advertise their sport

The influence of role models

People want to copy their technique

People copy the way they dress

They are seen in the media regularly participating in their sport

People copy their behaviour; good or bad

People like their lifestyle

People like the way they behave

Double Olympic gold medallist Kelly Holmes is fronting GirlsActive, a scheme to encourage more teenage girls to take up sport.

The popularity of an activity can change quickly as particular **trends** in sport fall in and out of fashion. For example, during Wimbledon week, more people can be seen using local tennis facilities, inspired by what they are seeing on the television. A more long-term effect can come about by a national side doing well in a major tournament, which causes an increase in popularity in that sport, which may in turn encourage local authorities to fund new facilities. For instance, when the England rugby team won the Rugby World Cup in 2003 there was a surge in the popularity of the game.

If a **minority sport** begins to receive greater coverage on the television, this can lead to an increase in its popularity. In recent years, snooker has gained in popularity, perhaps due to the coverage of top personalities within the sport, thereby inspiring and attracting young people to the game. Often, a major televised event, like the Olympics, can give greater coverage to minority events and inspire people to join in and try a new activity. A sport can also decline in popularity with fewer people taking part. In recent years, squash has taken such a downturn. However, squash courts in local sports centres, rather than remaining unused, are being adapted for more popular activities such as aerobics and yoga.

Active challenge

Discuss with a partner events in the media that may affect the popularity of sporting activities.

4 — Health, safety and the well-being of others

Any involvement in sport carries possible risks. Following correct guidelines for the event, employing the correct techniques in a skill and using the appropriate footwear and clothing can help prevent these risks.

Play safe and health and safety legislations and guidance

UK Sport produces a 'Safety in Sport' document setting out guidelines for safe play. It recognizes that the responsibility for safety in sport falls in four directions where each has their own part to play in safeguarding the participants and reducing the risk to health and safety:

1. The National Governing Bodies for sports
2. Affiliated clubs and societies
3. Officials
4. Participants

Safety in sport can be jeopardized as a result of actions falling in four categories:

1. Unpredictability of the sport – playing surface and conditions may become difficult to adapt to.
2. Attitude of the participants – can be overly aggressive or competitive.
3. Officials – not implementing the rules and keeping order adequately.
4. Poor equipment and inadequate facilities – equipment and facilities old or faulty.

Provide liability insurance

Create a health and safety philosophy within the sport

Provide laws and rules for competition and practice

Provide liability insurance for club activities and events

Prepare and implement risk assessments

Provide and maintain approved equipment and facilities

Record matters of health and safety in the sport

Give guidance to clubs and societies on risk assessment

Record health and safety incidents

2. Affiliated clubs and societies

Provide competent instructors

1. The national governing bodies for sports

Implement discipline within the sport

Ensure club members comply with laws and rules of the sport

Provide competent officials

Give guidance on procedures for health and safety of participants and spectators

Identify and develop training programmes for participants and officials

Provide first aid equipment and emergency services at events

Provide personal protective equipment

Provide own personal liability insurance

Fit and capable to officiate

Provide own personal liability insurance

Fit and capable for the activity

Knowledge of rules and laws

3. Officials

4. Participants

Protect participants from injury caused by unsafe equipment and other participants

Comply and administer rules and laws during event

Provide personal protective equipment

Comply with laws and rules

Active challenge

Research a sport of your choice on the Internet and find out what safety guidelines the governing body for that sport has set out.

Correct technique when performing a skill

All sports have their dangers. These dangers can be greatly reduced if the correct techniques are adopted when performing the relevant skills. Practice is vital so that the techniques can be repeated. Good coaching will build up the technique of an activity, keep the action close to the recognized action and correct deviations as soon as they occur.

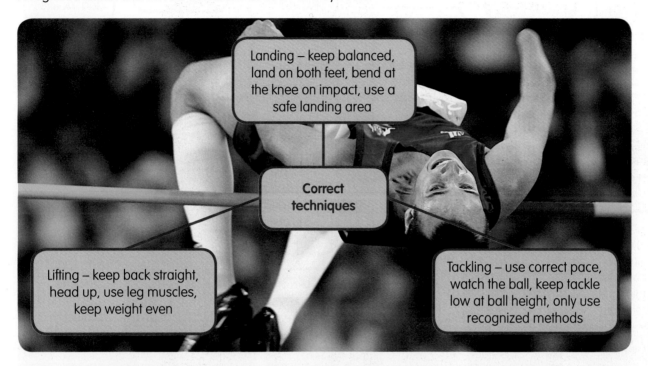

Landing – keep balanced, land on both feet, bend at the knee on impact, use a safe landing area

Correct techniques

Lifting – keep back straight, head up, use leg muscles, keep weight even

Tackling – use correct pace, watch the ball, keep tackle low at ball height, only use recognized methods

Active challenge

With a partner, choose a sport and discuss the skills that are important to avoid injury.

Appropriate footwear

Footwear is a specialized part of sports gear; each sport has its own design. Some sports have several different technical designs to suit a variety of conditions. The correct footwear helps in many ways: it gives support, protection, grip, greatest or least amount of movement and is an aid to performance and streamlining. For example, for each athletic event there is different specialized types of footwear providing the best support, grip and stability for the athlete.

Active challenge

Research on the Internet and find various footwear suited to different athletic events. Look at the strapping, sole and support and discuss with a partner why each item is best suited for the event.

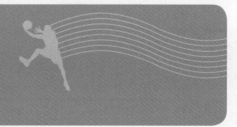

The condition of studded footwear should be smooth so that studs do not cut into another player. Checking studs is the job of a referee at the beginning of the game and referee's assistants can be seen checking the studs of football substitutes. There are specific rules set out in certain sports in which some footwear may be seen as dangerous. It is therefore essential to keep footwear in good order.

Sport A.

Sport B.

Sport C.

Sport D.

Task 4

1 – Study the footwear photos A to D. Notice that each sport has a different kind of footwear.

2 – Say which sport is shown in each picture.

3 – Give a reason why the footwear has been developed in that way for each sport.

Look at the differences in the sole, strapping and materials.

Appropriate clothing

The clothing for team events not only gives a feeling of unity to the group but it can also play a part in safety. Each sport has a unique type of clothing, which has been developed due to the nature of the game. It may allow protective guards underneath or be close fitting so it does not catch on equipment. Importantly, it provides free movement so the full range of skills can be performed in each sport.

Some activities require clothing, not to protect the body, but to keep out of the way and not hinder performance. In trampolining for instance, tighter fitting clothing that will not catch is important for safety, as is the wearing of socks to protect the toes from being caught in the webbing.

Clothing should:

• be in good order
• fit appropriately
• not catch on equipment
• ensure the performer can keep a clear view ahead
• not flap in the opposition's face and hinder their performance
• allow free movement to perform the skills of the game.

Sports equipment and clothing should be checked regularly. Repairs should be made so that there is nothing to act as a hindrance or danger to anyone. The correct design of equipment should be used for the job.

Carrying, lifting and lowering

When carrying, lifting and lowering equipment, care should be taken to make the action safe: always keep your back straight, have a firm grip of the equipment, keep the head up and lift the item by extending at the knees, using the leg muscles.

Keep your back straight and firmly grip the item.   Lift by extending at the knees.   Keep your head up.

Key terms

Trends – current fad or fashion

Minority sport – a sport with few participants or followers

UK Sport – a body responsible for managing and distributing public investment and proceeds from the National Lottery, aiming to lead UK sport to world-class success

Summary

For many activities large and small apparatus need to be positioned and set up prior to any action taking place. All involved should be well-trained in the lifting and lowering of such equipment and have a full understanding of their role in the team. All people taking part in an activity should be familiar with the relevant protective equipment. It is important that everyone understands that it should be worn in practice and competition and kept in good order. Guidelines from the relevant governing body on safety should be strictly adhered to.

5 — Rules relating to sport and equipment

The link to safety

Each practical activity has its own safety considerations. There will be rules within each sport to make the game safe. With any physical movement there is always a possibility of injury so care should be taken to minimize this threat. The nature of the activity, standard of opponent and level of competition are some factors that influence the need for safety measures to be in place. The surface performed on, the lighting used and the clothes worn can all have a bearing on safety.

Rules have a major role to play in making participation as safe as possible. Some activities have a need for more safety rules than others. Over the net games require teamwork and control of the equipment whereas invasion games require close competition with an opposition that can involve physical contact. Specific rules exist to make the rules of contact clear. For individual events performers are required to:

- look after themselves
- wear the correct supports and strapping
- use appropriate knee, shin and elbow pads
- use the correct techniques
- make sure their equipment is in good order
- have trained sufficiently for the event
- have warmed-up enough for the event
- wear the correct clothing.

Task 5

1 – Study the safety considerations for an individual event.

2 – Add your own suggestions to the list given.

3 – Choose an individual event such as javelin throwing, and link the safety considerations to that event.

Rules for the condition of equipment

The equipment for an activity should be kept in good condition, helping the player perform and protecting the safety of all concerned. Rules and recommendations exist, where necessary, to ensure the condition of the equipment is kept at a high standard. For example:

- Studs should be smooth with no sharp surfaces.
- Hockey sticks should have a smooth surface.
- Goal posts should be sturdy and intact, have protectors if necessary, netting should be secured down.
- Corner flags should be an appropriate height.
- Climbing ropes should not be frayed and should be within the recommended age limit for use.

Sometimes it is difficult to know whether equipment is wearing out.

Active challenge

With a partner, discuss other items of equipment that need regular checks and that could be unsafe if neglected. Find the rules governing the condition of equipment for a variety of sports.

You could use the Internet, rulebooks and safety manuals to help you.

Performer's actions within the rules

Each game or activity has its own rules to make the game fair and safe. It is the player's responsibility to keep within the rules or laws of the game in competitive situations. Abiding by the rules is especially important in invasion games where tackling, physical contact and equipment can be dangerous such as in hockey.

In the game of basketball, players are expected to foul the opposition during the course of play. Within the rules of the game they are allowed a number of personal fouls (usually five) to be used for the benefit of their team.

The rules of hockey allow only safe stick play in a game.

Active challenge

Pick three games activities and think of rules that are aimed at making those games safe. Share your ideas within a small group to build up your knowledge and awareness of such rules.

Rules are designed to control potentially dangerous play in games situations. These can include the following subjects:

- Tackling – the following tackles are not permitted: two-footed, from behind the player and high (to guard against neck and head injuries in rugby).
- Tripping – for example, in football and rugby. Most games do not allow deliberate tripping of a player whether in possession of the ball or not.
- Controlling equipment in a safe way – for example, raising the stick above head height in hockey is not permitted.
- Dressing safely – loose clothing gets in the way. For example, a trampolinist wearing loose clothing is in danger of becoming unsighted and losing orientation, this can lead to them falling or jumping off the trampoline.
- Performer not being a hazard – length of nails, wearing of jewellery and hair tied back. For example, in netball, having short nails reduces the risk of catching someone's face whilst attempting an interception.

Rules and using correct technique

Some rules of an activity are clearly there to make the competition or performance safe. These rules often have a direct bearing on the technique permissible. The nature of some activities result in them having danger elements.

The form of danger can be due to the equipment. A hockey ball or stick can be hazardous to others if not controlled. Therefore, within the rules of hockey there are clear restrictions on lifting the ball and stick – a ball may be lifted in the air in a pass, but if evasive action is required to avoid the ball then the pass is deemed to be dangerous.

Certain footwear can allow the performer to maintain steady footing and change direction efficiently. Studs on football boots can also be dangerous to others. The laws of football are clear on dangerous play to do with raised boots and two footed tackles, infringements of this kind attract severe penalties. For example, a player may not go into a tackle with their studs showing.

The physicality of rugby makes it a joy to watch and play. Tackling can be spectacular to watch, but if incorrectly performed, it can be dangerous so the rules protect the person being tackled and the tackler. The rules on 'high tackles' protect the runner from being unfairly and dangerously brought to the ground – the rules state that a player may not tackle an opponent above the line of the shoulders.

Each activity has its own rules affecting technique and skills. It is important to know and understand the rules of your chosen activities. It is the responsibility of students to learn the rules of the game they are playing, for safety purposes.

In dance, using the correct lifting techniques are essential for safety:

• flexing the legs
• keeping the back straight
• keeping the weight close to the body.

Combining safety with the message of the dance takes practise and understanding.

Working out new techniques and practicing lifts until they can be performed expertly is important for safety in dance.

Summary

Rules are specific to the activity and some are especially related to safety. The nature of the activity can require more rules and sterner penalties in order to reduce the dangers. Such rules can control the behaviour and actions of the players and the equipment used.

6 — Science and ICT

The developments in ICT and the links with science and sport have brought about many useful applications. These devices can be used to improve performance and prevent injury. Various products can analyse individual and/or team performance. By using different packages, students can learn to develop their analytical skills to help their own understanding of physical activity.

For planning and improvement and involvement in physical activity

ICT helps the participant, performer and coach in many ways in the improvement of performance. Various products analyse individual and team performances. They:

- Give instant feedback on tactics and team and individual performances.
- Make it easier to understand the main ways an action needs to improve.
- Use visual support to help understanding.
- Record performances which helps comparisons to be made between previous performances and other performers.
- Can be applied to different sports.
- Replays are controllable for more complex analysis.

Performance analysis software and hardware

There are many sports-related **software** and **hardware** products available, which serve as an aid to performance improvement. Each package has a different set of tools and devices and can help in different ways.

Heart rate monitors, which stand alone or can be linked to a computer show:

- speed
- effort
- work rate.

Foot pods attached to the laces of an athlete record:
- speed
- distance
- pace
- level of performance.

Visual recording and analysis software:

- improves understanding of skills involved
- shows the correct technique to follow
- can give an understanding of how the human body moves.

Data management software allows athletes to display performance statistics. This means they can track their own development and compare themselves with other performers and performances. Motion measurement systems measure and analyse movements using sensors.

ICT to record and analyse performance – track involvement and improvement

There are many software packages designed to help a performer or coach to record and analyse performance. Each package has a different set of tools and devices and can help in the following ways.

Time linking action to show different levels of performance throughout the game

Preventing injury from repetitive use: results of a performance can be loaded onto a programme and any new results can be compared with previous ones

Synchronizing performance for working in pairs, for example, in diving, skating and dancing

Linking images with text to explain actions and improvements

Monitoring performance, recording data and using for further progress

Flipping the image over to coach both left- and right-handed players

Analysing basic mechanical movements, for example, angle of release and take-off

Freeze-frame to show position of the player at different stages of the action

Tracking a player's involvement in a game

Uses of software packages

Time-lapsed photography showing shape and action

Recording matches to show positional and tactical play to analyse after the game

Showing two performances overlaid to compare shape, action, speed, and so on

Showing work rate of a performer

Helping with the biomechanics of an action

Showing key techniques and positions to replicate

Showing measurements and angles of an action, highlighting adjustments to be made

Supplying information on the speed of a performance in action and at different stages

Using previous measurements and information against new performance to show improvement and further adjustments required

Showing actions as simplified drawings to help with understanding

Task 6

Research on the Internet to find the different packages available that are linked with performance analysis.

Use the following headings to help guide your answer:
• Training software
• Visual recording and analysis software
• Data management
• Motion measurement systems.

Team training computers

Some products are geared towards teams. Each player wears a transmitter belt, which wirelessly feeds back heart rate data to a computer. This builds up a record of each individual's condition and overall performance. It can be adapted to a variety of sports such as running, cycling, team games, outdoor sports and fitness. These sorts of systems can be used to:

• store past results for comparison
• control intensity of training sessions
• create and analyse individual training plans
• download data
• view results and use to plan for the future.

Interactive tool and devices, including games consoles

Interactive tools and devices simulate involvement in the chosen activity. Some are designed purely for entertainment whilst others have a more technical application. Games software can focus on sport and can be handheld, free standing or linked with televisions and personal computers using accessories such as driving wheels and dance mats. When such devices are technically accurate, they can show how to improve the different components of the performance and work towards overall success.

Such tools and devices include the Wii, PlayStation® (PS2), skiing machines, golf driving machines and computers, which simulate where the ball goes and the accuracy of the swing, and target sport simulators.

Technological innovations

Technological innovations can help with enforcing the rules of the game. In modern stadiums, video screens play an important part in understanding for the spectators. A replay of an incident can be seen by all, which puts pressure on an official to get the call right. This increases the entertainment for the spectators but puts the officials under pressure as they have to make their decision immediately and are expected to be correct 100 per cent of the time. With such developments, rules increasingly incorporate the new technology as well, for example, the third umpire in cricket and the fourth official in football help the officials on the pitch in their decision making with the use of video playbacks. Video officials are away from the play so have no influence and are impartial judges.

The following rules have technology backing them up:

• Cyclops is an electronic line judge in tennis. It beeps if a ball is out. It needs careful setting up and adjusting.
• Hawk-Eye is used in cricket. Six cameras around the ground record action at different angles. These images are turned into 3D, tracking spin, bounce, swing and seam. This technology is used by pundits to show the accuracy of the decisions.
• Hawk-Eye is also used in tennis. Cameras track the trajectory of the ball in the same way as cricket, this is then transferred to a computer to create a television replay image. The technology is used in the Centre and Number One courts at Wimbledon. Challenges have been introduced to major tennis events; a player is allowed three challenges to a line call

per set. Hawk-Eye is used for this. On the other courts at Wimbledon, the old technology of cyclops is still used to help with line calls. In various other tennis venues, sensors below the surface of the court and covering the lines and areas around the lines are in place, making line calls more accurate.

Hawk-Eye in action at the All England Lawn Tennis Championship at Wimbledon.

Active challenge

Discuss with a partner other sports that use technology to help with rules and decision-making.

Key terms

Software – **programmes and applications that run on a computer**

Hardware – **devices and equipment that make up a computer system**

Summary

Science and ICT can play an important part in aiding progress in performance. The types of packages available are wide and varied. Software packages include data collection, visual recording and statistical analysis. Hardware can consists of heart rate monitors, computers and cameras. The information gathered only works when it is analysed, shared and acted upon. The feedback can help motivate a coach and performer to change and adapt the training to continue progress.

Exam questions

Multiple-choice questions

1. Footwear should fit the sport. What makes a type of footwear suitable for a particular event?

   ☐ **A** Protection, support, appropriate sole for stability, colour

   ☐ **B** Cost, protection, colour, support

   ☐ **C** Support, protection, stability, designed for the event

   ☐ **D** Make, colour, style, cost

   (1 mark)

2. Rules can prevent dangerous play in a game. Types of dangerous play include:

   ☐ **A** Tripping, two-footed tackling, pushing, not warming-up properly

   ☐ **B** Two-footed tackling, not playing the right tactics, pushing, obstruction

   ☐ **C** High tackle, tripping, two-footed tackling, pushing

   ☐ **D** Pushing, marking a player closely, tripping, two-footed tackling

   (1 mark)

3. In a competition or match, performers should keep their actions within the rules. Which of the following best describes these actions?

   ☐ **A** Play fair, keep to the rules when the referee is watching, respond quickly to decisions made

   ☐ **B** Contest decisions, play fair, respond quickly to decisions made

   ☐ **C** Keep to the rules, respond quickly to decisions made, take advantage of a weak referee

   ☐ **D** Play fair, keep to the rules, respond quickly to decisions made

   (1 mark)

4. Which of the following group of comments best describes the advantages of competing in the home country?

   ☐ **A** Motivated by a greater number of home supporters, no cultural barriers to overcome, used to the environment

   ☐ **B** Motivated by a greater number of home supporters, save money on travelling, used to the environment

   ☐ **C** Motivated by a greater number of home supporters, no cultural barriers to overcome, used to the environment

   ☐ **D** Greater numbers of home supporters can become frustrated with poor play, no cultural barriers to overcome, used to the environment

   (1 mark)

Short answer questions

5. What are the political disadvantages of hosting the Olympics?

   (3 marks)

6. There are environmental issues that come about due to hosting the Olympics. What are they?

   (3 marks)

7. Hosting a high-profile game year after year has many positive effects. What are they?

   (3 marks)

Longer answer questions

8. What are the advantages of being the host country for an international event?

   (8 marks)

9. What influence can role models have on attitudes towards and participation in sports?

   (8 marks)

10. a) There are four bodies responsible for safety in sport. The participant is one, what are the other **three**?

    b) How is the participant responsible for their own safety?

    (Total 7 marks)

3.4.1 ～ Skills for effective performance

What you will learn about in this topic:
1 — Administrative and management skills
2 — Communication and interpersonal skills

There are many skills and personal qualities that a person needs in order to be effective in their chosen role. Whichever role is chosen, be it player or performer, organizer, leader or coach, choreographer or official, each requires the development of skills which will produce an effective performance.

1 — Administrative and management skills

Administrative and management skills include the controlling and planning of paperwork, people and facilities. These skills are in operation before, during and after a performance or event. For maximum success, all areas of administration and management should be developed to a high standard.

Planning and showing initiative and innovation

Planning is vital to all roles in sport. It involves an understanding of the current situation, the direction and pathway for the future and the desired outcome.

This area of skill can involve:

Some roles lend themselves to a more creative approach such as choreographing a dance routine.

- Looking at the whole performance or event.
- Putting a working team in place to help with the event.
- Setting short, medium and long-term targets.
- Relaying all information accurately to those involved.
- Keeping to timetabled dates.
- Bringing in new ideas, making the event different, fun and workable.
- Inviting local dignitaries to events to encourage participation or more spectators.

Monitoring and evaluating

Once work has started in your chosen role, constant monitoring is required to make sure the job is being done in the right way. Regular checks against targets, results and performances help to focus on your current performance and goals for the future. Evaluating performances highlights successes and identifies areas where improvements are necessary.

This area of skill can involve:

- Monitoring the progress of skill acquisition, the adaptation of the body to a training programme and identifying changes to be made.
- Keeping to a specific timeframe.
- Meeting targets such as entry into an event or competition.
- Keeping good results records.
- Comparing results and working out where differences have occurred by deciding on what has worked and what has not.

Attending to detail

The main aim when planning a performance, training session or event is that everything will run smoothly. By attending to detail there is a better chance of success in your chosen role. These details may include having the right equipment available, making preliminary telephone calls to the right people, advertising the event correctly and working within specific timeframes.

This area of skill can involve:

- Having all of the sporting equipment for the event, for example, sports kit, correct footwear, and so on.
- Organizing all of the additional equipment such as bibs, scorecards, scoreboard, results table, technicians, music, lighting, props, seating, and so on.
- Keeping events running on time. For example, preliminary rounds to be completed on schedule, in one day.
- Organizing 'runners' (messengers linked with officials to relay information to other officials).

Commitment to high standards of care

Each role requires a duty of care to all of those involved in performing, including the spectators. Measures should be taken to ensure the personal safety of people, the equipment and areas used.

This area of skill can involve:

- Making sure changing areas, seating, refreshments and stewards are provided.
- Making sure equipment is safely stored and that there is additional equipment for emergencies.
- Providing first aiders.
- Ensuring the safety of all involved in the event.
- Making sure everyone involved is wearing appropriate clothing.
- Keeping to the rules of the game to make it safe.
- Training volunteers in their role to ensure they work well within their team.
- Knowing what to do in the event of an emergency, including a fire drill.
- Making sure everyone involved gets enough rest breaks.

It is the duty of the organizer to plan for the safety of everyone at an event.

Organizing, arranging, coordinating and supervising events, facilities, personnel and time

Bringing a performance or event to a conclusion requires the ability to orchestrate all of the components involved such as people, facilities, scheduling, and so on, so that they reach a peak or are carried out at the appropriate time.

This area of skill can involve:

- Working out what equipment is needed and arranging the transportation and storage of extra equipment that might be required.
- Coordinating people, equipment, facilities, recording of results, and so on.
- Checking that all of the areas of an event are running smoothly on the day.
- Listening to feedback from volunteers and performers and responding where appropriate.
- Choosing the right people as volunteers, training them, making sure they know what to do, building a team spirit, keeping all informed before, during and after the event of matters that may arise.
- Keeping the event to the correct running time; if the event does go too slowly or is running overtime, being able to adapt and manage the event is important.

Active challenge

Think of three additional ideas for each of the items you have just read. Go round the class and swap one idea at a time with other class members, until you have ten new ideas to add to your own.

2 — Communication and interpersonal skills

Developing a range of communication and interpersonal skills will help a person to relate to everyone involved in an activity, whether volunteers, performers or spectators. It is important to develop these skills to the highest level possible in order to put ideas across with enthusiasm and certainty.

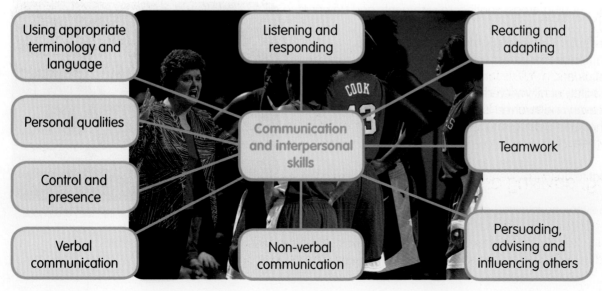

Using appropriate terminology and language

Listening and responding

Reacting and adapting

Personal qualities

Communication and interpersonal skills

Teamwork

Control and presence

Verbal communication

Non-verbal communication

Persuading, advising and influencing others

Use of appropriate terminology and language

When taking part in a particular activity, it is important to learn and use the specialized terms associated with it to show knowledge, understanding and professionalism. The terms used for skills or infringements differ from sport to sport, even though they are usually referring to the same thing. For example, in basketball, an illegal movement with the ball is called travelling, yet a similar violation in netball is called footwork. After a simultaneous infringement, basketball players will compete in a jump ball whereas netballers will compete in a toss up. It is important to use the correct terminology in a game to not only show understanding, but to ensure everyone understands the actions, infringements and resulting decisions.

Listening and responding to users

A major part of communication is listening. Feedback from others based on knowledge and experience should be taken onboard and responded to so that further improvements can be made in future activities, performances or events. This feedback may involve guidance on skills, tactics, timing of events, the number of competitors involved, and so on.

Reacting and adapting to trends and changing situations

Observing and adapting to new trends in activities may help to make an event or performance more appealing. This may involve such things as clothing, tactics or adapting training methods to an exercise programme. For example, winter sports have changed dramatically over recent times. Traditionally, skiing was the main winter sport, now, snowboarding has become more popular with younger people due to its image as an extreme sport and its associated fashion trends.

Situations may also change when preparing or carrying out an activity. For example, personnel may be unavailable such as coaches or stewards, changes in the weather, access to facilities, and so on. To help prepare for any unforeseen changes, a contingency plan is required. Being able to adapt to last-minute issues is important and is helped if potential problems are identified in the planning and preparation stage of an event.

An event may have to continue indoors or be postponed due to bad weather.

Teamwork, including cooperation, adaptability and delegation

In order for events and activities to run smoothly, everyone should be encouraged to work as a team, be supportive of others and help out in different roles when required. If organizing the event, you should be able to oversee all of the proceedings, delegate jobs to other team members and monitor how tasks are being completed.

Persuading, advising and influencing colleagues and customers

In your role it might be necessary to have to encourage people around to your way of thinking. This can be done through having knowledge of and enthusiasm for the subject. For example, a coach will advise others from a position of strength, based on experience, knowledge and having researched the subject thoroughly. It might be necessary to talk to and relate to all involved in an event, including volunteers, participants and other key people, for example, when asking to borrow equipment or use facilities to host an event.

Non-verbal communication

Non-verbal communication includes demonstrations, signals and gestures, using body language. Being able to give accurate demonstrations of skills is useful, although may need to be accompanied by a verbal explanation before or afterwards to break down the action into smaller sections for clarity. When officiating, a referee or umpire will need to give clear, recognized and appropriate hand signals to relay decisions to everyone involved in play. A dancer or rhythmic gymnast will include appropriate gestures when performing their routine to put across the emotion, message and feeling of the piece.

Verbal communication

The signals given by a cricket umpire need to be clear so that everyone understands what is happening.

Communicating through speech is a powerful tool when used correctly. Projecting the voice so it is at an appropriate volume and speech is clear, is vital for effective communication, especially when addressing others in a large area such as an auditorium or outside. Taking deep breaths and speaking from the diaphragm area can help when projecting your voice. Changing the intonation (how the voice rises and falls in a sentence) makes what is being said more interesting and keeps the attention of the listener. All of these aspects of public speaking require practice and so every opportunity should be taken to improve this skill.

Control and presence

When addressing an individual or a group it is important to keep their attention. Verbal skills will come into play here, but there are also other ways to gain and maintain a listener's interest. For example, having good posture by standing well, with the head up and shoulders back, looking relaxed, making eye contact with different members of the group from time to time and speaking with conviction and enthusiasm will help.

Personal qualities

To see a performance or event through to its conclusion will take the application of many qualities such as determination, conviction, organization and enthusiasm. These qualities are built up over time through experience and knowledge, accumulated by carrying out the role. Every opportunity should be taken to experience challenging situations so personal qualities have more of a chance to develop: from creating the initial plan of the activity to orchestrating the final programme of events.

Summary

Whichever role is chosen in which to specialize it will require care and detailed planning in order to maximize the success. Most administration and management activities take place prior to the day of the activity so the thoroughness and thought given at this stage will have a major bearing on the outcome of the event – successful or otherwise. This preparation is a chance to apply communication and interpersonal skills in order to reach the best possible results for everyone involved.

3.4.2 ~ Testing, training and lifestyle choices to assess and improve performance

What you will learn about in this topic:

1 — Methods of testing aspects of fitness
2 — Training and preparation
3 — Lifestyle choices

1 — Methods of testing aspects of fitness

Completing a variety of physical tests helps to build up a person's fitness profile. The tests should relate to the reasons for testing. There is little point in recording someone's cardiovascular endurance and stamina results if the person is training for a throwing event in athletics. The first test will show the starting point of the athlete's abilities and fitness. After training, the next test will show the effectiveness of the training programme and highlight changes for the future. Each test measures one particular aspect of fitness.

Testing is useful when assessing games players as they will need many different skills to play their game properly. The tests can be designed to include all of these aspects of fitness.

When a performer or coach plans and prepares an exercise programme, they need to gear it towards the individual needs of the exerciser. Assessing their current level of fitness and forming a fitness profile is essential to make the programme safe and relevant to the athlete. These tests can give a general understanding of the heart and lung capacity and can focus on particular aspects of fitness.

Below is a recap of why evaluating and testing is important:

Why test?

- To have an idea of the next performance results
- To highlight weaknesses
- To show improvements
- To show how successful a training programme has been
- To motivate the performer.

How to test:

- Each test should concentrate on one fitness component only
- The test should be straightforward to complete
- The performer should completely understand the test
- The test should be carried out in the same way every time.

How to evaluate the test results:

- Choose the fitness component to measure
- Choose a way of measuring it
- Carry out the test and record the results
- Work out what the results imply
- Decide on the best exercises to do based on the results
- Put the exercises into a training programme.

Methods of testing

The methods of testing each of the following tests are described in detail in section 3.1.2b
Aspects of training an pages 97 to 107.

- **Flexibility and suppleness:** sit and reach test
- **Cardiovascular endurance and stamina:** Cooper 12-minute run and multi-stage fitness test
- **Strength:** hand grip dynamometer

Task 1

1 – Write a sentence on how you would recognize good strength.

2 – Choose a sport and give two examples of how good strength improves the performance of the activity.

- **Agility:** Illinois agility test
- **Coordination:** alternate hand ball throw
- **Balance:** stork stand test

Task 2

1 – Write a sentence on how you would recognize good balance.

2 – Choose a sport and give two examples of how good balance improves the performance of the activity.

- **Power or strength:** vertical jump test and standing board jump test

Task 3

1 – Write a sentence on how you would recognize good power or strength.

2 – Choose a sport and give two examples of how good power or strength improves the performance of the activity.

- **Reaction time:** ruler drop test

Task 4

1 – Write a sentence on how you would recognize good reaction time.

2 – Choose a sport and give two examples of how good reaction time improves the performance of the activity.

Summary

People who decide to train need to think carefully about the type and intensity of the exercises they are to do. Age, ability, gender and experience will all influence the type of programme that is suitable. A clear awareness of the reason for training will influence the type of activities in the programme. The more serious the athlete, the greater intensity the exercise will be. Any part of the body exercised will develop, if done so at the correct intensity. When increasing strength, the shape and size of the muscles change. It is important that an athlete develops the type of strength needed for the activity and exercises both sides of their body equally so that their shape stays as symmetrical as possible.

2 — Training and preparation

In order to improve performance generally or to improve a particular aspect of performance, knowledge and understanding of exercise or training programmes needs to be applied.

FIT: applying this principle

The FIT principle stands for:

- **F**requency
- **I**ntensity
- **T**ime

By using the FIT principles (also known as FID – frequency, intensity and duration) as a guide for exercising, a person can reach the minimum level of fitness or train to a top-level performance.

Frequency

Frequency is the number of times exercise is undertaken per week. The more times a person exercises the more often their body is put under stress. Three to five times a week is the recommended number of times exercise should be repeated, to reach the minimum level of fitness. However, top-class sportspeople have to train a lot more frequently than this if they are to achieve results good enough for their aspirations.

Intensity

This is the level of difficulty of the exercise. For instance, when considering cardiovascular fitness your pulse rate can show you how intensely you are working.

Working in a target zone of 60 to 80 per cent of the maximum heart rate is the level where fitness will usually increase. When training for strength the intensity is calculated in the same way. For instance by finding the maximum weight they can lift and working to 60 to 80 per cent of that weight. As the amount of weight lifted increases with training, this adds to the intensity.

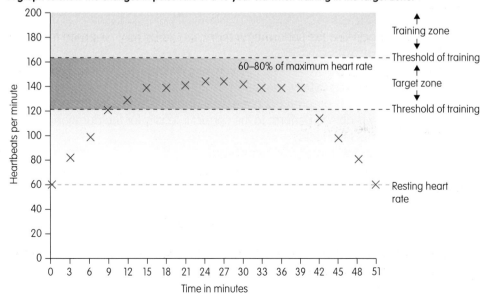

A graph to show the changes in pulse rate of a 16 year old when training in the target zone.

But remember, the body also needs time to recover from training. Training very hard, every day, may be harmful even for a top-class athlete.

Time (duration)
Time relates to how long the exercise session lasts. During the session, keeping your pulse at 60 to 80 per cent of its maximum for 20 minutes is the target. Warming-up is not included in the 20 minutes. The time begins when the pulse is at 60 per cent of its maximum.

Preparing a performer in skill acquisition

When a performer is being trained to acquire a skill they should be shown the correct technique to follow, in order to be able to adopt the proper physical and mental states.

Correct technique
Learning the correct technique gives a performer the best chance to acquire skills. Listening to instructions, watching coaching DVDs and clips of top-class performers in action all help to understand the way to perform an action. By replaying action slowing and pausing it, a performer can be guided as to what is required of them in their performance.

Comparing two techniques can draw attention to areas for improvement. The image on the left shows a professional and the image on the right shows a novice.

Correct physical state
Before all physical activities the performer or team should be fully prepared for the action to come. They should:

- warm-up for the event or activity
- practise, so their body is prepared with the skills and techniques for the activity
- train so their body is able to perform to the correct intensity for the duration of the activity
- be able to implement the tactics
- effectively fufil their designated role in the team
- be equipped for the level of competition, through experience of competing at different ages and stages of competitions.

Correct mental state
Not only do competitors have to be physically fit, they also have to have mental strength too. Sport puts a number of pressures on the performer and the way these are handled can have a big influence on the outcome of the game or event. By using the following mental preparation techniques the performer can have a better chance of completing the task successfully.

Relaxation – Different strategies can be used to keep players relaxed; deep breathing to help clear mental tensions or anger arising from previous play; shake tension from arms to relax the muscles so that skills can be performed properly.

Mental rehearsal – The performer will go through a mental rehearsal of the routine in their head before and on the day of the event, giving them a familiar order to their day. During the competition, the performer will visualize the successful action or shot to be completed. Players taking a penalty kick in rugby run through the shot they want to perform in their head before taking the actual kick so they 'see the shot' before playing it. This method is also used to great effect in athletics and golf.

Focusing – Here, an attempt is made to clear the mind of other thoughts so they do not interfere with the successful outcome of an action. The crowd may be chanting, other players may be making comments or personal doubts may be in the performer's head. Focusing helps to shut all of these interferences out. The aim is to think only of the job in hand and to concentrate on the technique to be used.

All members of the team should be physically prepared for the challenges to come.

Before a race, American athlete Marion Jones visualizes her successful outcome.

Key terms

Mental rehearsal – going through an activity in the mind

Visualize – create positive mental pictures of the successful attempt prior to actual execution

Focusing – blocking out other thoughts and concentrating on the performance only

Summary

For a performer to do their best, both body and mind should be trained to compete. The stress of an important competition, spectators or the opposition may all play a part in making the challenge more difficult. By controlling thoughts before and during the event the player can use certain techniques that help keep their physical performance at a peak.

How skills are acquired and developed

Acquiring skill can be difficult for some people, as it depends on the individual and the complexity of the skill. An element of natural ability will help a person to accomplish skills. All physical activities come with their specific mix of skills so to be good at that activity, mastering these is important. In invasion games for instance, there may be a different set of skills required for players in specific positions: those for a defender are not the same as those for an attacker. All performers will need to learn skills and be able to apply them to the game in order to play well.

The definition of skill

Skill is learnt through coaching and practice. The standard definition of skill is 'a learnt ability to bring about the result you want, with maximum certainty and efficiency'. When a performer is seen to be skilful they can perform a task successfully.

Some skills are more complex. They may require more than one action in order to complete them correctly. Complex actions, such as the butterfly stroke in swimming, need all the parts of the stroke to work in harmony so the skills are successful – arm pull, breathing and leg kick all need to be coordinated.

A complex skill such as the butterfly stroke needs all the parts of the stroke to work in synchronization.

Characteristics of a skilful performance

The following are examples of characteristics of a skilful sporting performance:

- Shots that make the target – this shows that the skill is being performed with accuracy when a kick, serve, stroke or pitch of the ball goes where the player intended. A good cricketer, specializing in bowling, can place the ball on a chosen target by pitching the ball consistently around a chosen spot.
- Actions that often have a successful outcome – this shows consistency. Hitting a target or completing a pass regularly requires skill. Regularly making a pass in netball from the Centre to the Goal Attack gives the team a goal shooting opportunity.
- All parts of the body work in unison to affect the skill – this relies on coordination.
- When executing skills, a performer maintains a smoothness to the technique even when responding to different and difficult situations.
- The correct weight or strength is put on a pass or hit, which requires control. A tennis player can still play a winning shot despite having been defending, running across the baseline for the ball and being late in the game.
- The action performed looks good and is aesthetically pleasing.
- The specific physical components appropriate to the skill are applied: power, strength, agility, reaction time, balance and speed for example.
- The technique used to perform the skill follows the correct technical model.
- The skill is performed with the maximum output, but with minimum outlay of energy and time – this shows timing and coordination. A golfer may strike the ball with ease, but if it travels further than usual, this can make the next shot much easier.
- A skilled performer can easily adapt to changing circumstances and be successful. An attacking footballer may need to run back to make a tackle and then dribble out of trouble in a deeper position on the pitch.
- A player is confident that their play will be successful and plays as such.

Task 5

1 – Give six examples where you have witnessed a skilled performance.

2 – Develop four of these examples into sentences.

Characteristics of an unskilled performer

Just as there are characteristics of a good performance, there are features which identify a poor performance too. When analysing a performance it is important to be able to recognize both types of performance in order to give accurate feedback to improve future play.

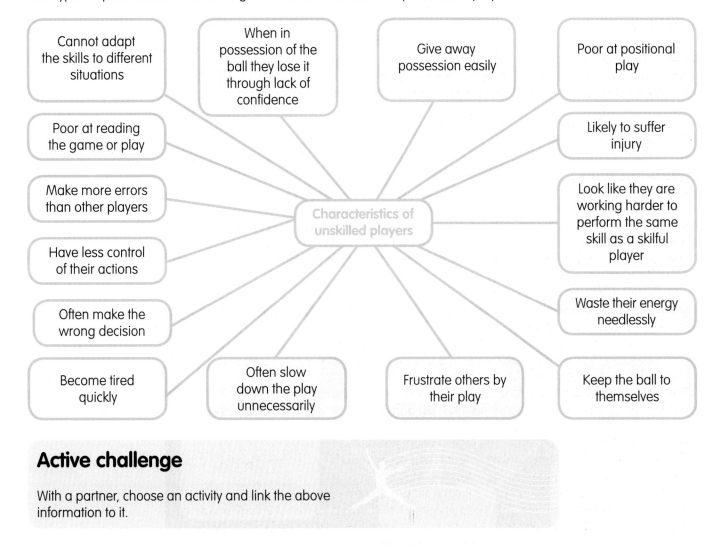

Active challenge

With a partner, choose an activity and link the above information to it.

How skills are learnt

Skills can be learnt in a variety of ways. Usually a person will use a combination of the following ways in their attempt to master the skills of their chosen game.

PRACTICE   This can be achieved by repeating an action many times, using the correct technique. It can begin with a person working individually on basic skills. This leads to working with other teammates on group skills. As the skills become accomplished, an opposition may be added, in order to apply the skills in a competitive situation. The opposition may start as just obstacles to negotiate round; this is known as static opposition. As progress is made, real opponents become more involved – this is known as active opposition, demanding more effort and refined skills from the performer. Throughout his career David Beckham has spent hours after full training on his free kick technique. He attempts to kick a dead ball through a tyre hanging from the crossbar in the corner of the goal. He uses this target to fine-tune his skills to apply to the game.

COPYING In the initial stages of learning a skill it may be easier to watch and copy the coach or teacher. This relies on good observational skills and tends to have good initial results. After a short time further instructions can be given to the performer to help them refine the action.

TRIAL AND ERROR Attempting the skill until successful without any instruction is called 'trial and error'. Although the action may become successful, the correct technique may not be used and further instruction will be needed to make the skill technically accurate. The performer using this method is often highly motivated and has a strong desire to achieve their goal.

ROLE MODELS Watching the best performers execute skills can inspire people to copy their technique. We can see these performers on the television in current or archive footage or at live matches. We all have different role models and they earn their status for different reasons.

Active challenge

Decide on other skills that can be improved with trial and error practice. Use your own experiences in sport to help you.

There are many ways a role model can inspire a person to take part in sport and develop their skills to the best of their ability.

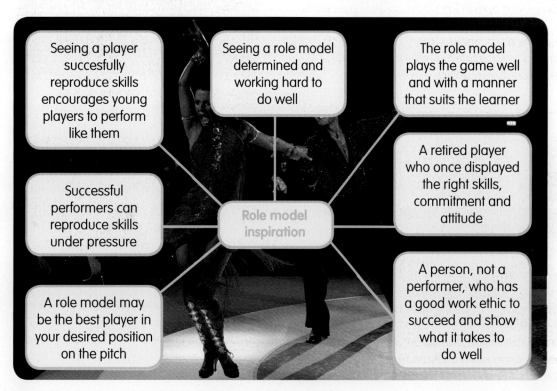

Seeing a player succesfully reproduce skills encourages young players to perform like them

Seeing a role model determined and working hard to do well

The role model plays the game well and with a manner that suits the learner

Successful performers can reproduce skills under pressure

Role model inspiration

A retired player who once displayed the right skills, commitment and attitude

A role model may be the best player in your desired position on the pitch

A person, not a performer, who has a good work ethic to succeed and show what it takes to do well

Types of skill

Skills can be divided into those that have only one outcome and those where the outcome is unpredictable. Games generally use open skills but there are times when closed skills are necessary for success.

CLOSED SKILLS   Closed skills are basic skills performed in situations that remain the same with no variations. The skills are unaffected by environment and are habitual in nature. Few decisions need to be made to perform them so they are relatively straightforward to complete. The performer can control the pace of how the skill is executed. For example, swimming can be classed as a closed skill. It is not affected by the environment, other performers or pool conditions. The action to perform the stroke follows a prescribed pattern of movement, which is repeated habitually with little variation.

OPEN SKILLS   Open skills are performed in an environment that is constantly changing. They are affected by the sports environment, such as:

- other players' movements
- the angle at which the ball is approaching
- the pace of the ball
- the distance the ball must reach
- the height of the approaching ball.

Open skills require adaptability from the performer: although the skill is mastered it must be quickly modified to change with the needs of the environment. In order to complete the skill successfully, decisions need to be made prior to its execution. The speed of play is often decided by others or by the situation.

THE OPEN/CLOSED CONTINUUM   The open/closed continuum represents the degree to which a skill is open or closed. A skill placed to the left of the continuum shows that it is open and therefore complex, if placed to the right then it is closed and basic. Each skill will find its own place according to its habitual nature or variability.

Open skill _____ Closed skill

A free throw in basketball is an example of a closed skill as the distance from the basket is always the same and the shot is unchallenged.

A rugby player avoiding an oncoming tackle is an example of an open skill.

These sports will sit on the open/closed continuum in a different place.

These sports will sit on the open/closed continuum in a different place.

For example, in tennis although the distance of the baseline, height of the net and the service box make the skill of serving seemingly a closed one, there are factors that take this skill more towards the open end of the continuum:

• Where the opponent is standing will influence where the ball is to be placed, as the angle of the ball's flight will have to be changed.
• The opponent may have strengths to avoid and weaknesses to exploit, needing variations of the service action.
• If playing outdoors, the weather may have a bearing on the service – the wind may cause the ball to be blown in a certain direction so to compensate, the performer will have to adapt the ball toss to hit the ball in a different way or direction.
• There may be a need to vary the type of service as the opponent may be getting used to the usual one. Putting spin on a serve, to take the opponent by surprise, gives them a new set of problems, but also creates variation.
• The pressure of the stage of the game may influence the serve. It may be important to make sure the service goes 'in', caution is applied rather than a usual shot played.
• The crowd may also be a variable as they become noisier. A crowd cheering for one side or another evokes an emotional response that may affect the execution of the skill. The pressure of the occasion may cause the performer to tighten up or rise to the challenge.

Task 6

1 – Choose a sport and list skills used in that sport.

2 – Draw an open/closed continuum line. Place the named skills on that line for your chosen sport. For each skill say why you have made that decision.

Types of guidance: visual, verbal and manual

When learning a new skill guidance is required. The coach or teacher gives this guidance. A mixture of different methods are often used to teach skills successfully. These can include visual, verbal and manual methods of guidance.

Visual guidance

Visual guidance is often the first method used, especially when someone is learning a new skill. It shows the whole, overall skill, enabling the learner to see a complete image of the skill and where it fits in with other actions.

This method is also appropriate when evaluating performance and giving feedback. The action can be repeated and variation from the correct technique can be commented on.

Visual guidance can take several forms:

- A demonstration from a teacher or skilled performer
- A playback of a clip of top-class performers in action
- A playback from a special training DVD
- Looking and observing the body position from a poster or chart.

Watching a coach explaining strategy gives learners a visual image of what is required.

Verbal guidance

Giving verbal guidance to performers can also be helpful. The terminology, phrases and sentences used must be clear, simple and straightforward. The language used should be appropriate to the skill and the level of understanding of the performer.

The language for instructing a skill can change and there may be several ways to express the same guidance. This gives the best chance for the performer to understand.

The same or similar instructions can be repeated over again if necessary. Often this form is best used with other types of guidance. It is an especially good support to the visual guidance method by linking verbal and visual images together.

The difficulty with this form of instruction is that the performer must be able to:

- Understand the terminology used
- Remember the instructions that have been given
- Translate the words given into actions.

Manual or mechanical guidance

This method is used when the skills or movements being learnt are potentially dangerous and complex. The teacher, coach or equipment handler applies a 'hands on' approach, acting as a support or safety measure to the performer. This method gives freedom to the performer to attempt the actions without fear of injury, overbalancing or landing awkwardly.

Mechanical aids can also help the performer. These include armbands for swimming or an overhead rig for trampoline, gymnastics or diving. The presence of these safety measures gives confidence to the performer and it often affords the performer a one-to-one situation with the coach.

Armbands are an example of mechanical aids.

Active challenge

With a partner, discuss the three methods of guidance. Give each other examples of when you have personally learnt from these methods.

Types of feedback: intrinsic feedback and extrinsic feedback

Intrinsic feedback

Intrinsic feedback happens internally to the performer. They either know that the skill they performed was not quite right or that it was the best it could be. Intrinsic feedback is assessed by the senses: did the shot feel good? When cricketers middle the ball, they hit the ball forcibly, with what seems like little effort. When the ball is hit on the 'sweet spot' in this way, the sound of the contact is different too. If, in addition to the feeling of the shot, it is placed in a gap in a scoring position, the batter forms the intrinsic feedback in his brain. The resulting positive feelings are those of satisfaction, pleasure and confidence about their play.

Task 7

Refer back to a competition or match you have been involved in. List the examples of intrinsic feedback you experienced during the event.

Extrinsic feedback

Every player or athlete needs feedback on their performance in order to improve. Extrinsic feedback comes externally to the performer. Any information can go towards helping develop future attempts, training or play:

- Watching a recording of their own performance
- Listening to a coach remarking on the skill
- Having a professional instruct on skill technique – this often happens in golf when a professional tells the player about the grip, stance and address of the ball
- The final score of a game
- Studying the match analysis.

Knowledge of performance (KP), of both its good and bad points, helps the learning process and will shape the future actions and refine the skills of the performer. Feedback reinforces the correct actions and tells the player what they should do next time in order to improve that skill.

During the game statistics may be kept of different aspects of the activity. These may be recorded and analysed at a later date and training adapted according to the needs of the performer. Having knowledge of results (KR) provides evidence of the successful and unsuccessful aspects of the performance.

Therefore there are two lines of feedback given to the performer:

1. Knowledge of results (KR) – the outcome of the performance.
2. Knowledge of performance (KP) – how well the player performed, rather than the results.

Giving feedback to the performer

Comments made should refer to both the strengths and weaknesses of a performance and should serve to motivate the player. Highlighted points will indicate the need for changes and aspects to work hard on during training.

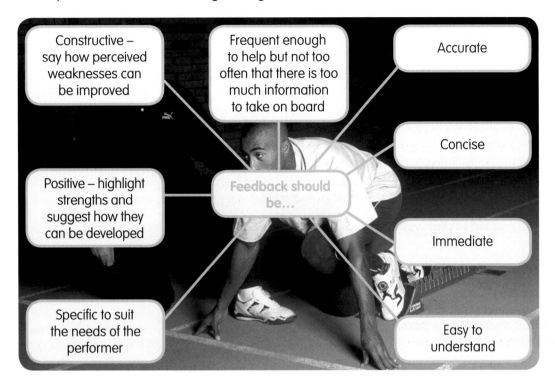

Constructive – say how perceived weaknesses can be improved

Frequent enough to help but not too often that there is too much information to take on board

Accurate

Positive – highlight strengths and suggest how they can be developed

Feedback should be...

Concise

Immediate

Specific to suit the needs of the performer

Easy to understand

Active challenge

With a partner, discuss the examples of extrinsic feedback given to you about your performances in sport over the past two weeks. How are you going to use it to help you improve your play?

Key terms

Closed skills – basic skills unaffected by the sporting environment

Open skills – complex skills performed in constantly changing conditions

Guidance – help and instruction given to complete a task

Intrinsic feedback – internal information gathered by the performer at the time of the action about how they feel the performance is going

Extrinsic feedback – external information gathered by the performer based on what is seen or heard at the time of the action

Types of practice

The type of practice chosen depends on the skills to be improved. There are a series of different practice methods that suit particular complexities of skills. These include whole, part, fixed and variable. The aim of practice is to help the performer learn how to complete the skills successfully, so not only is it important to choose the correct method for the action, but also a way to deliver the instructions to suit the personality of the athlete too.

Whole practice

The whole practice method suits practising simple skills and involves repeating the whole of the action at once. These skills are unlikely to confuse the performer due to their simplicity and so can be practised in this way in order to get the feel of the action. Gymnastic skills such as simple pin, star or tuck jumps from a box, can be practised in this way.

Games skills that are difficult to split into parts also suit this method. Dribbling in football and basketball or catching in netball or rugby are skills that lend themselves to being taught in this way. As the action is simple and quick to carry out, the performer can repeat it over and over again, each time having listened to the feedback of the coach and modifying their performance according to the instructions.

Part practice

Part practice is best suited to skills of a more complex nature, which have several different parts making the whole. The triple jump is a good example of a skill that would complement this type of practice.

In many cases, it helps if the performer attempts the whole skill first. By doing this they see and understand the need to break down the skill into its component parts, learn them separately and gradually build up to the whole action.

Whole practice is used to learn simple skills.

For this method to work the key parts of the skill need to be identified. As the different parts are rehearsed the performer receives feedback accordingly. When a stage is performed well a new stage is practised. A tennis serve is a skill that can be broken down into several parts. These include:

• Ball toss
• Transfer of weight
• Racket preparation
• Throw action
• Contact
• Follow through.

Task 8

1 – Study the following complex skills:
- Breaststroke in swimming
- Lay-up shot in basketball
- Triple jump
- Gym routine.

2 – Choose one of these complex skills and break it down into the component parts a performer would practise.

WHOLE-PART-WHOLE PRACTICE This method is also usually used for complex skills. It involves a combination of the whole and part practice approaches.

The whole action is attempted, which allows the performer to experience the action and get a feel of the skill. The action is then broken down into parts, practised section by section and then reassembled into the whole action again.

This method is complicated in itself as it can be technically difficult to reassemble the whole action. As a result of its complexity this type of practice is often suited to already skilled or experienced performers. This method suits long and triple jumps in athletics.

Fixed practice
Fixed practice is suitable for closed skills, where the environment for performance stays the same and for those actions that can be performed in the same way on each repetition. These conditions for practice always remain the same, rarely varying. The skill is continually repeated, feedback is given to the performer and necessary adaptations are made. Examples of skills that benefit from this type of practice include gymnastic skills, such as forward and backward rolls, penalty kick taking in football and tumble turning in swimming.

Variable practice
Open skills adapt to variable practice as the sporting conditions change during the execution of the skill. When training for invasion games, such as netball, hockey and basketball, variable practices are often used. These exercises aim to simulate the changing situations that might occur in a game. By presenting the player with these problems they may be better prepared for competition conditions. During practice time, feedback is given on the performance, indicating further changes necessary for improvement.

Netball can be used as an example to show some ways of how variable practice can work. Once a potential netball goal attack has reached a suitable level of success and is able to dodge an opponent, and can regularly score goals from different places in the circle unopposed, variable practices will demand that these skills are adapted to cope with competitive conditions.

Practising the same skills in different pressured situations is an example of variable practice.

The goal attack will be faced with increasingly more difficult conditions, simulating those likely to be met in a game. These may include finding a way to score against:

- one marker stopping the shot
- two markers; one blocking the pathway to the circle and one marking the shot
- three markers; two blocking and one marking in the circle.

Each time, the goal attack will have to adapt the skills learnt to overcome the new problems.

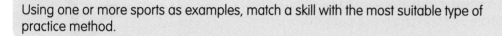

Task 9

Using one or more sports as examples, match a skill with the most suitable type of practice method.

Key terms

Whole practice – repeating the complete action in training

Part practice – completing part of a complex action in training

Fixed practice – repeating closed skills in the same conditions in training

Variable practice – performing whole skills in changing conditions in training

Summary

In training, applying the FIT (or FID) principle allows the performer to increase the intensity of the training according to the desired outcomes of the session. For the best performance the correct skills training should be followed. For games players, correct skills training can include starting with basic individual skills, moving on to team play and then practicing with the opposition. The top performers need to be able to adapt their skills to the situation at hand. Most team game sports involve open skills where this adaptability is vital, although there are times in a game where a closed skill, like a penalty shot for instance, is necessary. Some sports, such as gymnastics, totally rely on the ability to repeat closed skills consistently and to a high level of technical accuracy in order to succeed.

Coaches and teachers help develop skills by being able to offer constant guidance and instructions to the performer. There are several methods used to help learning and different skills are suited to one or more of them. In training it is important that the practices or drills are performed at speed and are similar to situations of the competition. This will allow the athlete or player to transfer skills readily to the competitive environment.

3 — Lifestyle choices

Diet

All of the information in section 3.1.2e Diet, pages 133 to 144 is applicable here.

Activity choices

There are many reasons for choosing different types of activity and taking part in sport. A person will choose a type of activity according to the benefits they want from physical exercise and what suits their personality. A person may choose exercise because they enjoy the activity, but other positive changes may result as well. Physical, mental and social well-being may improve, whether planned for or not. In some cases, people can gain employment in an area linked with their sporting interests. Owing to the wide range of rewards from exercise, most people can benefit whether the activity is strenuous or not. It is the health and fitness rewards that make exercising special in comparison with other leisure pursuits.

Enjoyment

A person voluntarily takes part in physical activity so they will choose one they enjoy. When enjoyment is the top priority any type of activity can be included. One activity that is enjoyable to one person may not be to another. There is a sport suitable for everyone and those who seek exercise can usually find a pursuit to satisfy them.

Company

Group activities provide the chance to meet with other like-minded people. Being a member of a club, regularly attending fitness classes or being part of a team will provide company with others.

Training with club mates and performing against other teams gives a person the opportunity to meet a large number of people. This can expand the variety of acquaintances a person has. Through these experiences a person can become more outgoing and confident in the company of others.

By being a member of a club, a person meets others with the same interests. After a club event there is usually a social drink and, by regularly attending such social events, friendships can form.

Maintain and improve fitness

The reason for taking part in an activity can be to maintain or improve fitness. Exercising can increase strength, stamina, mobility and flexibility, as well as help tone muscles and help posture. The more you exercise, the more your body is able to meet the demands of exercise. Activities for maintaining and improving fitness can include aerobics, running and swimming.

With regular exercise the muscles become toned. This is the tightening of the muscles in a state of readiness to work. Depending on the type of training programme, the shape and size of the muscles will begin to develop. Exercise at the correct level burns calories and, as long as the dietary intake remains the same, a person may lose weight with the extra activity.

257

Regular exercise increases the efficiency of the heart, circulatory system and lungs. This also leads to an improvement in a person's general health. A person who has good general health can suffer less from minor ailments and may recover from serious illness more quickly due to the condition of their body.

Relaxation

Particular activities provide the chance to relax. Walking and fishing are examples of activities that provide an opportunity for a person to reflect and be calm.

Excitement

Some activities are attractive because they are exciting to perform. Skiing, climbing, skateboarding and BMX track racing are all examples of sports that attract people because of the thrill and adrenalin rush they provide.

Factors affecting activity choices

When choosing a sport, very often the age, physical maturity and fitness levels of a person will have a bearing on the type of activity that is chosen. Someone may take part in an activity because there are people of the same age already involved, whereas other activities may have an age limit to join them. It is important to choose an activity which suits the fitness levels of the individual in order to minimize injury.

Age

As people become older, they often remain competitive by taking part in fewer contact sports. Invasion games demand the body to readily adapt to other players' actions and can involve physical contact. With age, the bones and joints can wear, making the body less able, flexible and stable to withstand such demands.

An older person may move towards more individual activities, which are physically less demanding but which can still be performed in a group situation if desired. Jogging, golf, swimming and badminton are examples of activities that still require the application of skill and fitness but with fewer dangers to the individual.

Physical maturity

For some activities it is essential to have reached physical maturity in order to be safe when participating. Weightlifting and plyometrics can put pre-adolescents physically at risk because:

- Bones are still developing and can be severely damaged by overloading.
- The musculoskeletal system has only had a little time to adapt to strength and power training, and may not be strong enough to cope with extreme stresses.
- At this stage, young people can have poorer body awareness and body control, resulting in technique loss, which can lead to dangerous loading of the body structures.

Overuse injuries can occur, especially on lower limbs, due to placing too many demands on a young body. These include Osgood-Schlatter's disease (patellar tendonitis) and Sever's disease (heel inflammation).

Although people develop at different rates due to age, body size, previous levels of physical activity and phases of growth, it is generally thought that a person should wait until their sixteenth year to lift major weights and train using plyometrics. At this stage, the joints of the body are strong enough and developed enough to withstand the stresses of lifting heavy weights.

Fitness levels

Sports need different levels of fitness. These levels are influenced by:

- Length of activity or competition
- Intensity of the activity on the cardiovascular and respiratory systems, bones and joints and the muscular strength required
- The time required for recovery due to the demands of the activity.

Some activities need high fitness levels to take part in and be safe. To reach a physical state capable of meeting the demands, takes a commitment in time and effort. These activities can include invasion games, canoeing, skiing, long-distance events and gymnastics.

Some activities can be undertaken with low levels of fitness as the demand on the body systems is light and little preparation is needed to take part. These activities can include those involving slower individual actions, often target based sports such as bowls, golf and snooker.

Summary

Everyone makes lifestyle choices. Deciding on what to eat and what activities to pursue has an effect on a person's life. Choosing a particular physical activity to regularly take part in can depend on several factors, including whether it suits the person's personality, age or physical maturity. Taking part in sporting activities can provide a source of company, relaxation, excitement and enjoyment for the participant.

Exam questions

Short answer question

1. State the positive reasons of testing for the performer and coach.

   (3 marks)

Longer answer questions

2. Name a recognized test that measures flexibility and a sporting action that needs good flexibility. Describe the test.

   (8 marks)

3. Name a recognized test that measures agility and a sporting action that needs good agility. Describe the test. Use the diagram below to help you.

   (8 marks)

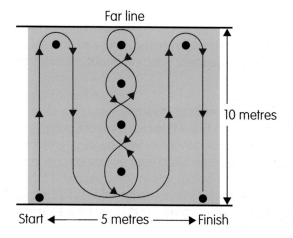

Far line

10 metres

Start ◄——— 5 metres ———► Finish

3.4.3 ～ Risk assessment and safe practice

What you will learn about in this topic:

1 — Safety issues and ways of applying them to sport
2 — First aid and emergency arrangements

1 — Safety issues and ways of applying them to sport

Safe condition of the environment (indoor and outdoor)

Checking equipment and facilities

All facilities and equipment should be regularly checked for their condition and suitability for use. Checks can be made on equipment in different ways: visual – seeing that there is need for repair; tactile – to feel the rough edges or stability of the item; service checks – made by recognized firms specializing in such maintenance. Such maintenance and upkeep is the duty of the owners or custodians of the equipment. If the equipment is in a private club then the owners employ staff to maintain standards. In publicly run facilities the upkeep of the equipment is the responsibility of the local council.

Before a match the officials are responsible for the playing area and should check the field of play, whilst organizers of events follow guidelines to ensure the safety of the performers and spectators.

Reducing the risk of injury in specific activities

There are certain safety requirements a club must fulfil. These are to do with the safety of the sports area and the safety of the spectators. People watching the event should be managed properly and be able to watch the match without intimidation from other supporters. The St John Ambulance Brigade attends large venues to deal with any first aid requirements.

There are strict guidelines to do with venue exits, making sure the spectators are able to leave the venue safely. The players should also be able to play their game without fear of the crowd invading the pitch. In top-class events, stewards and police play a part in ensuring the players' safety.

In 1989, in Hillsborough, during the semi-final of the football FA Cup, over 90 Liverpool fans were killed due to overcrowding. Following this disaster the Home Office set up an inquiry under Lord Justice Taylor. Recommendations were made for crowd control and safety at sports events. As a result:

- All top division football stadiums should be all-seaters, making it easier to manage spectators who buy a ticket for a specific seat.
- It is recommended that rival fans be segregated to stop violence.
- CCTV is used at games to spot trouble quickly.
- Alcohol cannot be brought into the ground. If a person is suspected of being drunk they can be refused entry. Alcohol can be sold and drunk in designated areas so that consumption can be monitored.

Clubs are also responsible for the state of the playing surface. The ground should have the correct netting and corner flags. The surface should be level and safe, not slippery, and free from litter, sharp or protruding objects, and so on. The playing surface condition may change due to the weather, so pre-stated guidelines help officials make the most appropriate decision.

Potential safety hazards.

Task 1

Study the illustration above. Record the hazards and the injury each one could cause in your workbook.

Lifting, carrying and placing equipment safely

Correct techniques must be used to lift, carry and lower equipment safely. In gymnastics there are many specialized pieces of equipment. Sessions on how to set up and put equipment away are integral to gymnastic lessons. Each piece of equipment needs clear tuition on its movement. For example, when carrying a bench:

- Two to a bench, one at each end
- Face the way you are to travel
- Have a firm grip
- Bend knees to grasp sides of the bench

- Lift together
- Walk to the placement area
- Bend knees to place the bench down carefully.

Trampolining

Setting out and putting away a trampoline should follow strict guidelines and always be supervised. The weight, size and tension of the trampoline are potentially dangerous. The trampoline should be securely locked when not in use so that it cannot be used without qualified supervision.

Moving and setting out a trampoline requires well-trained teamwork. Each person should know their role and be able to carry it out at the correct time, at the correct pace and in the correct way. An awareness and understanding of the energy and resistance the springs contain should help to reinforce how important everyone's role is.

It can take a team of six people to set out a trampoline safely. In general, the procedure is as follows:

- Move to the site and align squarely to the space and on a level surface.
- Open the legs of the trampoline.
- Lift leg at one end of the trampoline.
- Remove the wheels and store them safely.
- Lower leg.
- Lever over the ends.
- Engage the braces.
- Check the braces and safety cushions are in place.
- Arrange the mats around the trampoline.

A note of caution: Remember to keep elbows out of the way whilst the end of the trampoline levers over.

Carrying javelins
There is an obvious potential danger when working with javelins. Total understanding and discipline is required by all, in order to keep the activity safe. The procedure needs to be structured and clear as follows:

- Take a javelin out of the store bottom point first. Bring to vertical, hold at the grip, all wait to go together.
- Carry vertically to the throwing area. All javelins to be in one place sticking vertically into the ground.
- Follow the throwing procedure – throw from the same line and, often, all throw at once.
- All walk to retrieve the javelins together, approaching them from the side.
- Lift the javelins from back end to the vertical and carry at the grip, walking back to the throw line.
- Securely stick the javelin in the ground and wait for instructions.

Correct technique when performing

Some skills or activities are more technically demanding than others. Coaching each phase and building up skills and experience is vital in the more technically demanding events.

The pole vault event is the most technically demanding of all the athletic events, requiring methodical coaching so that the athlete understands all aspects of the action. The whole vault includes the following phases: approach – run-up and carry – transfer – take-off – flight phase – hang and push press – swing and extension – turn and clearance – landing. The poles are rated and should match the performer's body weight. The performer needs training in using the pole in the correct way, including which way the pole should be held (soft side) and the grip.

Active challenge

Choose a sporting activity that requires good technique to perform safely, especially on landing.

Research your choice and prepare a mini presentation to deliver to a small group in class.

Appropriate clothing and footwear

Wearing the correct clothing and protective equipment not only identifies the team, but gives the necessary defence for the body to avoid injury.

Protective clothing
Some activities have more protective clothing than others due to the nature of the action and equipment involved. In football, the action mainly takes place at ground level, therefore the lower leg needs protecting. Shin pads are essential for protecting the tibia as well as padding around the ankle as they are also prone to dangerous contact.

Specialized equipment should always be worn properly. Loose straps and poorly fitting helmets can be a danger. Cricket players need to fasten the chin straps on their helmets and make sure the straps on their pads are secure, are out of the way and allow free movement when running.

In activities such as cricket and hockey where there is high-speed movement of a hard missile-like ball, extra protection is required. In cricket the batsman and wicket keeper regularly wear the most protective equipment on the field, in the same way the hockey goalkeeper wears the most protection during a hockey match.

Without proper protection, hockey goalkeepers and cricketers would be in danger of serious injury.

Task 2

Study the photographs of the hockey and cricket players above. Make a list of all the protective equipment required for safe play in these sports.

Use the Internet to help you.

Summary

Assessing the risks of an activity and taking appropriate action can help to reduce the dangers of participation. Checking the space to be used for hazards, using the correct techniques when performing and wearing suitable clothing and protective wear if necessary all help to make an activity safe.

The importance of warming-up and down to prevent injury

A warm-up and warm-down are essential in order to prevent injury. Each warm-up should be specific to the activity and focus on the muscles and joints to be used in the event.

Athletic warm-up example
The following is a brief overview of the order an athletic warm-up should take:

Aerobic phase (five to ten minutes) – jogging or sidestepping to increase body temperature.

Flexibility phase (five to ten minutes) – static stretches to reduce muscle stiffness.

The lying hip abductor is an example of a static stretch: lying on the floor, one leg reaches over to the floor on the opposite side.

Hip bends are an example of a static stretch: one leg crosses over the other and the body twists around.

Stretch phase (five to ten minutes) – dynamic (moving) stretches to reduce muscle stiffness. Flexing, relaxing, lifting, lowering and rotating parts of the body make up the dynamic stretches phase of the warm-up.

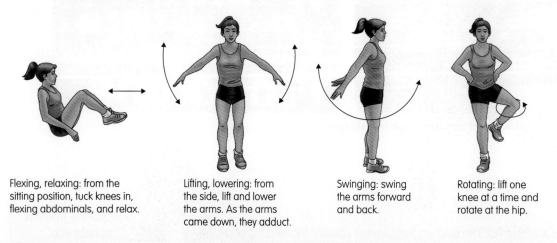

Flexing, relaxing: from the sitting position, tuck knees in, flexing abdominals, and relax.

Lifting, lowering: from the side, lift and lower the arms. As the arms came down, they adduct.

Swinging: swing the arms forward and back.

Rotating: lift one knee at a time and rotate at the hip.

Skill phase (10 to 15 minutes) – specific drills for the sport, focusing on the upper body, the lower body and techniques, for example:

* Holding the shot in both hands in front of the body, lifting the shot up and out.
* Pushing the shot out like a basketball chest pass.
* Pushing the shot from the put position (when the shot is in contact with the neck) using only the wrist (to warm-up the wrist).

Increased intensity phase (two minutes) – working on technique with greater intensity, imitating the action used in the event at speed:

- Lighter weighted shot substitutes can be used.
- Practise full speed glide action without the shot.

A note of caution: Different teachers and coaches use different types of stretches. Before designing your programme check which type your teacher would prefer you to use.

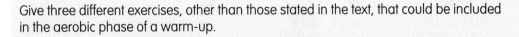

Task 3

Give three different exercises, other than those stated in the text, that could be included in the aerobic phase of a warm-up.

Football warm-up example
Psychologically, the warm-up for football will focus the mind of the performer and will help them prepare mentally for the game. In brief, this is the order a warm-up should take:

Aerobic phase (five to ten minutes) – jogging or sidestepping to increase body temperature.

Flexibility phase (five to ten minutes) – static stretches to reduce muscle stiffness. Include work on hips, knees, ankles, back, shoulders and neck joints.

Side leg stretches.

Sitting leg stretches.

Stretch phase (five to ten minutes) – dynamic (moving) stretches to reduce muscle stiffness. Includes work on hamstrings, quadriceps, gastrocnemius and deltoids.

  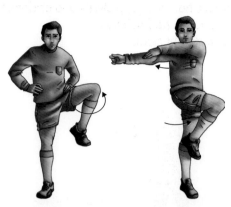

Leg stretches: gently raise and lower, stretching at the groin.

Groin stretches: knees lift and lower, stretching at the groin.

Hip rotation: standing on one leg, lift the knee and make large circles.

Waist twists: on one leg – twist arms to the right – lift right leg and cross it to the opposite side.

Skill phase (10 to 15 minutes) – specific drills for the sport such as passing, give and go, or jumping to head the ball.

Increased intensity phase (two minutes) – working on technique with greater intensity, imitating the action used in the event at speed. This phase can include shooting, sprinting and changing direction.

A note of caution: Different teachers and coaches use different types of stretches. Before designing your programme check which type your teacher would prefer you to use.

Active challenge

With a partner, agree on three examples of dynamic stretches that would exercise the arms and waist. Decide which muscles and joints would be used and say what sport they could link with.

Netball warm-up example
A netball warm-up should include the following phases:

Aerobic phase (five to ten minutes):

1. Jog freely around one court – on the whistle, change direction.
2. Jog freely around two courts – jump into the air when a line is reached.
3. Jog freely around one court – on the whistle, jump, land, step and stop.
4. Divide into four teams, each with a different coloured bib. On command, a colour is called out and that team tags the others. If tagged, they continue by hopping or skipping whilst the game continues until the next whistle change and a new tag team is chosen.

Flexibility phase (five to ten minutes) – static stretches to reduce muscle stiffness. This phase ensures the muscles around the joint are prepared for full extension.

Stretch phase (five to ten minutes) – dynamic (moving) stretches to reduce muscle stiffness.

Areas for special attention are the muscles of:

- the lower body – gastrocnemius, hamstrings, gluteals and abdominals
- the torso – latissimus dorsi, pectorals and deltoids
- upper body – biceps, triceps and trapezium.

Shoulder stretch: arm reaches across the chest whilst the other arm applies pressure at the elbow to work the shoulder.

Torso twists: arms out in front and they swing round the back of the body.

Hamstring stretches: with one leg straight out, the body leans forward so the hands can reach comfortably as far as possible down leg.

Skill phase (10 to 15 minutes) – specific drills for the sport. The muscles are gradually exercised closer to the manner needed in the game by incorporating the skills needed for play.

A note of caution: Different teachers and coaches use different types of stretches. Before designing your programme check which type your teacher would prefer you to use.

This is an example of a passing drill:

Phase 1

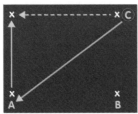

C has the ball, throws ball to empty corner

A Runs to empty corner to receive

C Runs to space **A** has left

Phase 2

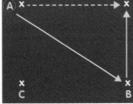

A Has the ball, throws ball to empty corner

B Runs to empty corner to receive

C Runs to space **B** has left

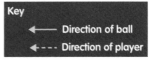

Key

⟵ Direction of ball

⟵--- Direction of player

Phase 3

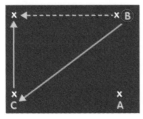

B Has the ball, throws ball to empty corner

C Runs to empty corner to receive

B Runs to space **C** has left

Phase 4

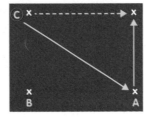

C Has the ball, throws ball to empty corner

A Runs to empty corner to receive

C Runs to space **A** has left

This is an example of a shooting drill for pressure training for the shooter:

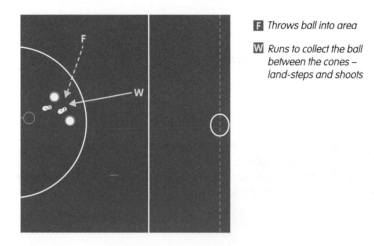

F Throws ball into area

W Runs to collect the ball
between the cones –
land-steps and shoots

Key

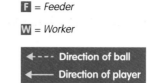

F = Feeder

W = Worker

←--- Direction of ball
←— Direction of player

Increased intensity phases (two minutes) – the increased intensity phases should be similar to the game, involving sprints and modified games, such as a four against four mini game using one third of the court and the circle.

Task 4

Using the ideas above, choose a different sport and devise a warm-up you would do for that sport.

Appropriate warming-down routines

The aim of a warm-down is to reduce the stresses on the body in a gradual way and to prevent discomfort after the exercise session. The phases of a warm-down include a gentle aerobic work phase and a stretches phase. The aerobic work gradually becomes less intensive and the stretches are held for over ten seconds.

Aerobic exercise phase (five to ten minutes) – jogging or walking to gradually decrease the body's temperature, remove waste from the body and gradually reduce the stress on the muscles and body systems.

Static stretches help the performer's body recover after a training session or competition.

Stretch phase (five to ten minutes) – static stretching concentrating on the muscles used in the event to decrease body temperature, allow the muscles to relax, prevent muscle soreness (Delayed Onset Muscle Soreness – DOMS), reduces the chance of dizziness and fainting as it stops blood pooling and gradually reduces the levels of adrenalin in the blood, and stretches and lengthens the muscles to impro

Task 5

Select an activity and state the muscles most necessary to stretch in a warm-down.

Summary

Warming-up gradually prepares the body for increased intensity and strain, reducing the likelihood of injury. A good routine will exercise the body parts needed in the game or competition. Not only should the heart, lungs, temperature, muscles and joints get a gradual start from a warm-up, but it can also focus the mind to prepare for immediate competition too. A warm-down routine gradually reduces the exercise intensity to stave off aching and dizziness.

Awareness of the risks involved in an activity and how to minimize them

Using the correct specialized equipment is important for safety. Having equipment that is too big or too heavy for an individual could lead to risk of injury. The equipment should suit the size, age and experience of the user.

Invasion, striking and racket games

The size of the equipment should relate to the age and experience of the performer. Using full-size footballs for under elevens, for example, will not match the strength and skill of the players. There are many modified games which resemble the full game but have been adapted for a younger age group. These games have lighter equipment, smaller playing areas, smaller team numbers and simpler rules. These games include mini tennis, tag rugby and non-stop cricket.

Gymnastics

Whether training or competing, the landing areas should be safe and stable. Competition landing areas are 120–200mm thick and have safety mats around them to a depth of 22–60mm. The landing after a vault, for instance, needs to be technically correct for a good overall mark and also for the safety of the performer. A two-footed landing on the toes, cushioning the force of landing, reduces the risk of a jarring injury to the back. The safety requirements for landing areas are set out by the governing body, the Federation International of Gymnastics (FIG).

The supports for the asymmetric bars and fixings are specialized and fitted by professionals. This ensures they can withstand the forces put on them by gymnasts during practice and competition.

Short-handed rackets are used for younger players.

A teacher should check equipment in school before a lesson starts. The correct technique should be taught for lifting and lowering vaulting boxes so back injuries are avoided.

Each piece of equipment must be set out so that it does not interfere with any other piece.

A gym safely set out for a gymnastic training session.

Dance
The surface the dance is performed on should always be safe and non-slippery. It should be smooth with no splinters. Costumes worn to add to the drama of the performance should be fitted to each performer securely and allow free movement during the event.

Athletics
All surfaces to run on, throw from and jump off should be flat and free from obstacles and protruding objects.

Throwing events, such as the discus and hammer, require netting or a cage around the throwing area. These should be maintained regularly to prevent equipment escaping through gaps in the fencing. The throwing area should be clearly marked and marshalled. As the competition begins, warnings should be sounded to alert other judges, marshals and competitors that the throw is about to commence.

In jumping events, guidelines for the size, depth and composition of the landing areas are regulated by the governing body. Mats should have a continuous covering over them to keep them together. Throughout the high jump and pole vault competition a check should be kept on the correct placement of the landing area in relation to the bar.

Some equipment is dangerous, the javelin being an obvious example, therefore, storage should be secure and safe. There are special carry cages and trolleys for transporting awkward equipment. In schools, how to move and use such equipment, especially javelins and shot-putt, should be reinforced in every lesson.

In the winter, the standard and condition of facilities may drop. For example, maintenance of throwing cages may not be scheduled out of season. Landing areas may not be kept and dug over properly. For athletes training for throwing events, especially shot and discus, wet weather makes the equipment slippery and hard to control.

The throwing cage protects people at the event from a miss-throw. Robert Harting prepares to throw.

Equipment, such as javelins, need to be stored correctly for safety reasons. Carolina Kluft safely selects a javelin.

Swimming

All safety information and equipment should be clearly on display at the poolside. Any change of depth to the pool should be clearly marked on the pool edge and visible on the wall too. The surface around the pool should be non-slip and clean to prevent injury and infection.

Although it may be seen as unglamorous, the swimming cap is a safety aid in a variety of ways. It keeps hair out of the eyes, giving a clear view of the direction for the swimmer and it keeps hair out of the swimmer's mouth, allowing clear, unhindered breathing. Keeping the hair in a cap also helps prevent loose hair entering and blocking the swimming pool filters.

NO running
NO fighting
NO bombing
NO young children unsupervised

Safety information is displayed on signs at the poolside.

Although a verruca can be painful, a person can still swim. However, they must take care when changing so they do not infect the floor and should wear a verruca sock when swimming to prevent it spreading. Gels are also an effective way of treating verrucas as they are easy to apply and are waterproof.

Wearing goggles allows the swimmer to see underwater when their face is submerged. This allows turns to be made safely. Goggles also protect the eyes from the chemicals in the water.

Active challenge

With a partner, choose a sport and think of as many risks as possible related to that sport. Use examples from television, personal experience and incidents you know about.

Safety precautions laid down by governing bodies

The governing bodies of sport are responsible for all aspects of that sport, including making the participation safe for the performer. Most governing bodies set out safety considerations to be taken into account when performing. Setting out the risk assessment in this way prepares the performers and coaches for potential dangers they may encounter.

Active challenge

Choose a sport and research their safety policy and risk management strategies. Present your findings to a small group in a prepared speech.

Summary

Suitable equipment should be used, especially for young performers and all equipment should be checked and kept in good order. Safety rules and guidelines should be followed with regard to water sports, landing areas and the use and storage of specialized equipment, particularly athletics equipment such as javelins.

2 — First aid and emergency arrangements

First aid and emergency arrangements may be necessary following an injury. Various types of injury may come about as a result of the nature or intensity of an activity. There are minor and major risks of injury involved with most sports. There is less risk of injury in sports where teams stay on their side of a net, such as volleyball and badminton, but the risks increase in contact sports where players invade the territory of the other team. The nature of the sport may present safety problems: the weather may play a part in increasing the risk or technical problems may occur.

Expert training cannot always prevent injury.

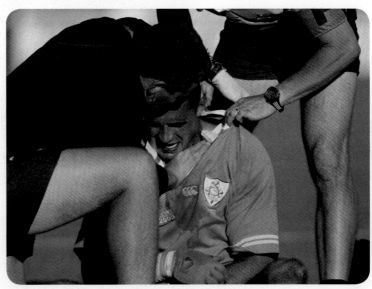

The nature of the game can make injuries more likely.

Injuries can occur in any sport due to overstretching the tissues. Such injuries include sprains (ligament injuries) and strains (muscle or tendon injuries). Torn cartilage can occur after trauma to the knee when the pads of connective tissue that act as shock absorbers and enhance stability (menisci) tear. Where there is greater contact with the opposition then impact injuries can occur through tackling for instance. The following pages contain the procedures for dealing with a series of injuries such as RICE. However, only trained and qualified first aid and medical personnel should deal with serious injuries.

Strain (for example, a pulled hamstring muscle) – a joint and muscle injury

How it happens – overstretching of the muscles or moving them too quickly

When it happens – twist or wrench of the muscle

Where it happens – muscles of the body

How to avoid – warm-up thoroughly; although it is difficult to avoid when an activity requires the performer to contract and relax a muscle quickly

What to do – use RICE (see page 275)

What happens – sharp pain, swelling, bruising, muscle may spasm

Effects on the body – muscle may be weakened as a result

Sprain (for example, a ligament injury) – a joint and muscle injury

How it happens – ankle or wrist joint is twisted suddenly

When it happens – changing direction or landing badly

Where it happens – at the ankle or wrist joint

How to avoid – improve the strength of the area, although sometimes it is difficult to avoid

What to do – use RICE (see page 275). If more severe it can look like a fracture or dislocation so treat as such and have an X-ray

What happens – can be a snapping or popping sound, feeling of ankle giving way, swelling and bruising may occur

Effects on the body – tears ligaments at a joint and is extremely painful

Dislocation

A **dislocation** is a hard tissue injury and occurs when the joint is moved outside of its designed range. A forceful blow can move the joint out of position and all major joints are vulnerable. When it happens the joint looks deformed, it may be very painful and the person will have no control over the movement in that area. In these cases the person should be made comfortable, the joint immobilized and medical help found quickly. Do not attempt to put the joint back into place. Strength training exercises for the muscles and tissues around the joints will help prevent this happening.

Cut – a soft tissue injury

How it happens – studs impact, collision with a sharp, abrasive object or surface

When it happens – during a tackle

Where it happens – on the surface of the skin

Effects on the body – bleeding and soreness

How to avoid – difficult to avoid as another player may be responsible for the impact, can wear protective clothing, equipment can be checked for sharp surfaces, players should be checked for jewellery and long fingernails

What to do – clean and dress with a plaster, or bandage if it is a bad cut, if worse, go to the hospital

Bruising – a soft tissue injury

How it happens – impact with equipment, ground or player

When it happens – during a tackle, missing a landing or interception

Where it happens – muscles of the body

How to avoid – difficult to avoid as other factors and opposition may be out of the players control. Can avoid collisions and wear protective clothing

What to do – put ice on the injured area to reduce swelling

Effects on the body – blood vessels damaged beneath the surface leading to bruising which change colour on the skin from blue and purple to green and yellow

The principles of RICE

Use the RICE procedure to treat soft tissue injuries. Each initial stands for part of the treatment: rest, ice, compression, elevate.

Rest the injured part.  Rest prevents further injury.	Apply **ice** to the injured part to stop swelling and help pain.  Ice – applied for ten-minute periods stops swelling, pain and the flow of blood to the area.
Compression – put a bandage around the injured area for support and to stop swelling.  The bandage should be just tight enough to reduce internal bleeding and swelling.	**Elevate** – lift the injured part to restrict the blood flow to the area and reduce swelling and painful throbbing. 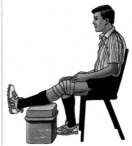 Raising the injured area above the level of the heart lowers internal bleeding and stops swelling and throbbing. In some instances raising an injured part slightly is enough to reduce any pressure on it.

Task 6

Write out the following paragraphs in your workbook, filling in the gaps as you go.

1. Strains and sprains are examples of _____. Strains are to do with _____ and sprains are to do with _____ and _____. Each occurs when rigorous over _____ and twisting take place. _____ too far to reach a ball in tennis or _____ at speed in basketball can cause these problems.

2. Both injuries are treated using the RICE procedure. The initials stand for _____, ice, _____ and elevation. These are the _____ and the _____. The reason for resting the injured part is so that no further _____ is done. By putting ice on the injury it _____ the _____. _____ the part also stops the swelling as does elevating the injured part.

3. Tennis and golf elbow affect the _____ attaching the muscle to the bone at the elbow. This can be caused by playing the sport _____ and by using the _____ equipment. Again, RICE is the treatment for this injury.

Fractures – hard tissue injuries

Fractures occur when an excessive impact or force is put on the bone. This can happen with a blow or a twist. When a bone is fractured, the limb becomes immobile and there is extreme pain. The area is tender and there may be swelling, leading to bruising. The fractured area immediately looks deformed. Fractures are difficult to avoid as they are a result of spur-of-the-moment accidents. Keeping to the rules of the game and not tackling recklessly reduces the risk of fractures.

Compound or open fracture
In a compound or open fracture the broken end of a bone comes through the skin. This causes complications as there is a risk of infection from germs entering where the skin is damaged.

Simple or closed fracture
In a simple or closed fracture the break of the bone is under the skin.

In rugby, because of the upper body impact of tackling and falling on an outstretched hand, a fracture of the clavicle is a common injury. When this happens the casualty may automatically cradle the arm on the injured side under the elbow. They may also lean their head to the injured side too.

The impact of two legs meeting with force in a football tackle can cause a fracture. The tibia and fibula (lower leg bones) are the most common leg bones to fracture. If both are broken, the limb will rotate and have an angle at the point of the fracture. If the tibia (shin bone) is broken then there is a possibility that the fracture will be open.

Medical help should be sent for immediately and the casualty should be made comfortable and kept warm without moving the injured part.

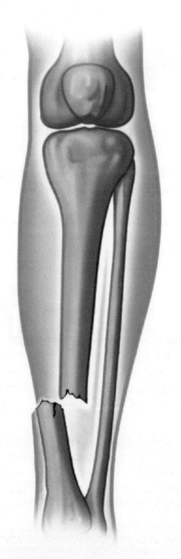

A compound or open fracture of the tibia.

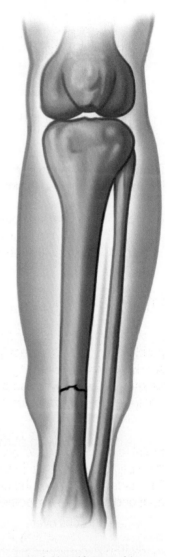

A simple closed fracture of the tibia.

Concussion

Concussion can result from a blow to the head and cause temporary unconsciousness or incapacity – the effects of which may only become evident some time after the incident. Temporary loss of consciousness can occur from a direct blow to the head caused by the impact or blockage of the windpipe. Any blow to the head should be treated as serious. Medical advice is always necessary.

How it happens – a blow to the head due to fainting, stroke or shock

When it happens – impact with another player, raising the pulse too high, blocking or compressing the windpipe

Where it happens – affects the whole body

How to avoid – wear protective equipment, especially head gear and take care in the sport

What to do – send for medical help and place the injured athlete in the recovery position

Effects on the body – a temporary loss of mental functioning

The purpose of the recovery position is to make the unconscious casualty comfortable, keep them from further injury, make sure they are able to breathe clearly and are safe from choking.

- The chin is lifted to keep airway clear, hand supports the head when turning and laying down.
- The arm and leg are bent to make position stable.
- The chest is flat on ground, so breathing is easier.

Hypothermia

Hypothermia is an extreme environmental injury. The cold weather can cause a major problem if a team is not equipped to deal with it. Its effects are obvious in adventurous sports, like mountaineering and sailing, but problems can occur even in regular team game situations. The answer is to prepare for possible changes in the weather and adapt plans to suit the situation. It is better to prevent the problem happening than have to deal with it.

How it happens – a rapid drop in the inner core temperature of the body (lungs, heart and brain) to below 35°C. The loss of heat from the body is related to the size of the individual and the type of environment they are in. Generally, the bigger a person is, the slower the heat loss. The colder and windier the air is the greater the heat loss. Therefore, children will tend to lose heat and suffer from hypothermia quicker.

When it happens – activity in a cold, wet and windy environment when the energy required is more than the energy available.

Where it happens – any cold environment, hostile mountain areas, sea, river or lake.

How to avoid – when the weather is colder, put on extra layers of warm clothes. Be aware of the wind chill factor which often causes hypothermia. Always take the proper equipment for the activity and know the safety procedures. Keep an eye on all members of the party. Long-distance swimmers can use grease to keep the cold out.

What to do – If the individual is unresponsive, send for help and take them to a sheltered spot and keep their body from the wet ground. If the casualty is responsive try to make them more mobile, but stopping inactivity will have to be matched by energy intake. Immediate action is necessary to heat the core of the body: replace wet clothes with warm, dry ones; cover the head; provide a sugary, warm drink; give quick energy food like chocolate. Check their pulse and breathing regularly. If available, put the casualty into a warm bath, but not more than 40°C, to warm the body gradually.

Effects on the body – shivering, pale complexion, dry complexion, pulse rate could be slower than normal, shallow breathing, behaviour may be irrational, be in a state of confusion, a lack of energy leading to unconsciousness.

Hypothermia starts as shivering.

The sufferer may become abusive.

As more heat is lost, the casualty loses consciousness.

Key terms

RICE – rest, ice, compression, elevation, a procedure for the treatment of minor injuries

Dislocation – disturbance of the arrangement of bones so that they move out of their usual joint arrangement

Compound or open fracture – break of the bone that pierces the skin, causing a risk of infection

Simple or closed fracture – break of the bone where the skin is not broken

Concussion – injury to the brain, caused by a blow to the head, may cause a person to temporarily lose consciousness

Hypothermia – condition of the body when its core temperature falls below 35°C

Summary

There are many injuries that are caused by sport: some may occur in training and some in the game itself. In general, soft tissue injuries such as minor cuts and bruises happen frequently and, if treated early with basic first aid, clear up quickly. If left they can become more serious. Injuries to joints and muscles are more complicated and can require specialized medical treatment in order for the performer to gradually return to fitness.

Head injuries should always be treated seriously, however minor they seem at the time. Blows to the head may have no immediate effects but could, after time, cause concussion.

Players or performers are sometimes not aware of an injury or condition that is gradually affecting their bodies, like the cold for instance. Knowledge and experience of the event and the effects of the environment are crucial to the well-being of the performer, and preventative measures can be taken to counter the dangers.

Exam questions

Short answer questions

1. Choose a sport where lifting and carrying an object is necessary and say how a person can ensure the action is safe.

   (3 marks)

2. Describe the cause and effect of a muscle strain.

   (3 marks)

3. What considerations should a player make towards equipment?

   (2 marks)

Longer answer questions

4. What hazards may be present when using a public facility?

   (4 marks)

5. Wearing safety equipment is important in sports where there is physical contact and danger from impact by the ball. Choose an activity using such protective equipment stating the name of the equipment and the injury it can prevent.

   (4 marks)

6. Warm-ups are essential for preparing the body for action. For a team game of your choice say what you would include in your warm-up.

   (6 marks)

7. What safety considerations must be in place when working with javelins?

   (6 marks)

8. What are the safety considerations and the procedure when setting out a trampoline?

   (8 marks)

9. What is a strain injury, how does it occur and what is the treatment?

   (6 marks)

10. Study the illustration. What has happened to the person lying down, what is the name of the procedure being carried out and how should it be performed?

   (5 marks)

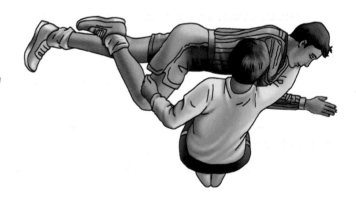

Key process C: Evaluating and improving

What you will learn about in this topic:

1 — Organizing and managing the environment
2 — Designing original and effective plans for improvement
3 — Critically analysing and judging performances
4 — Making informed decisions on how to improve the performance
5 — Developing and implementing action plans for further improvement
6 — Role requirements

Analysis of performance forms part of your Active Participant unit, which is necessary for all courses. There are three key processes, two based on personal performance in an activity and Key process C: Evaluating and improving, which is addressed here.

Analysis of performance presents the link between the theory and the practical work. Any activity available for practical assessment can be analysed. Often, choosing a sport you already have an in-depth knowledge of could be a good option, although choosing a sport that has simple, straightforward skills and tactics may suit you better.

The following coaching model is useful when breaking down analysis and linking performance to feedback.

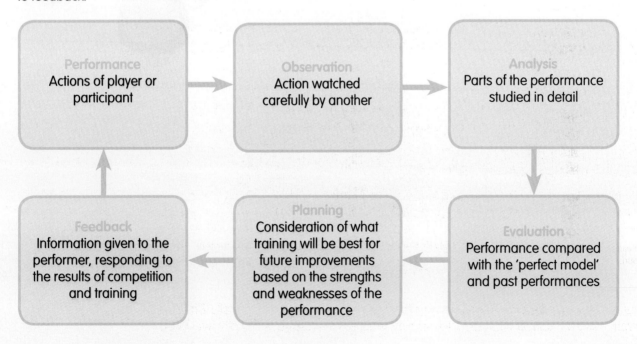

Performance
Actions of player or participant

Observation
Action watched carefully by another

Analysis
Parts of the performance studied in detail

Feedback
Information given to the performer, responding to the results of competition and training

Planning
Consideration of what training will be best for future improvements based on the strengths and weaknesses of the performance

Evaluation
Performance compared with the 'perfect model' and past performances

1 — Organizing and managing the environment

When evaluating a performance several things should be considered, including the practical side of observing action and safety matters:

- Positioning of observer (to the side or above of the playing area)
- Observers in relation to the type of action
- Players protected from recording equipment
- Recording equipment protected from play
- Sports equipment safely stored
- Playing conditions are safe.

2 — Designing original and effective plans for improvement

It is important to understand the progressions necessary to improve performance. Using different practices and drills can help develop skills. Progressions in tennis may include:

- A build-up of intensity to play strokes – from hand feed to racket feed to rally for example
- A player needing to increase mobility may play hand and throw tennis (played like tennis but the ball is not struck with a racket but thrown underarm to a space in a court, the opposition catches the ball and throws it underarm back into a space until the ball is missed).

Strategies

A strategy is a pre-planned scheme to outplay the opposition and makes the most of a person's strengths and exploits the opposition's weaknesses.

The following is a tennis example of how to develop strategies, tactics and practices to make the most of a person's strengths and expose the opposition's weaknesses.

Baseline play will show power, control and accuracy, and serve-and-volley will show speed at the net and fine touch.

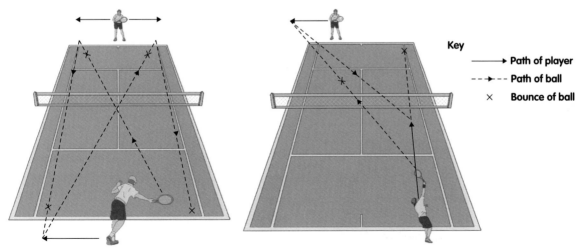

Key

→ Path of player

--→-- Path of ball

× Bounce of ball

Attacking baseline play – plays the ball deep, side to side of the court.

Net play – serve and volley – move from back to front of court – almost always attacking. When receiving, will chip the ball over the net and charge forward to gain control of the net again ('chip and charge').

The strategies used may depend on both the surface and the shots played in the rally. Baseline play can work better on slower surfaces such as clay, whereas serve-and-volley play works on the quicker surfaces of hard courts. Good players will mix up the shots they play and bring the element of surprise into operation to beat the opponent.

Active challenge

Using a sport of your choice, state strategies that would or could be applied to the activity.

Tactics

Tactics are short-term or immediate actions to out play the opposition. For a tennis singles player the tactics will come about by the amount and type of spin applied to the shot and the speed and depth at which the ball is hit. In doubles there are other additions to tactical play:

Doubles serving tactics:

• Who should serve first? • Where should they serve from? • Where should the serve be placed?

Doubles returning serve tactics:

• Where should you stand? • Where should your partner stand? • Where should the return be placed?

Doubles poaching tactics – interception played, often at the net:

• Committing only to a certain space to poach a shot.
• The player will cross the width of the court to play the shot.

Active challenge

Using a sport of your choice, state tactics that would or could be applied to the activity.

Practices

Practices often involve continued situations that may occur in a game situation repeated in a controlled environment. This helps a performer to prepare for any eventuality in the game. In tennis this may include ground stroke drills, volleying, returning serve, and so on.

Key

⟶ Path of player
--▸-- Path of ball
× Bounce of ball

Ground strokes for baseline play. Hand feed to player on forehand.

Hand feed to player on backhand.

Hand feed to play alternately on forehand and backhand.

The pressure can then be further increased by:

- Racket feeding
- Moment prior to feed, calling direction of feed to prepare the player to move either side.

Active challenge

Using a sport of your choice, state a basic, an intermediate and an advanced practice that would or could be applied to the activity.

3 — Critically analysing and judging performances

To be successful in this area, a full evaluation of strengths and limitations of performance should be made against a perfect model. Complete feedback should be provided on all aspects of the evaluation in order to recognize strengths and areas for improvement.

In order to realize whether a sporting action is good or not, an understanding of how the action should look in its perfect state should be appreciated. This is the 'perfect model' you will mark any performance against. There are several ways you can observe the perfect model:

- World-class sports coverage (on television or DVD).
- Training DVDs or coaching manuals.
- Action photos from magazines and books of top players.

When developing an understanding of the perfect model it is useful to view recordings of the best performers. This allows replays and pauses in the action to be made, giving time for you to appreciate the performance in question.

Use technical language in your analysis

Evaluate strengths

Use correct English and grammar when writing and recording your analysis

Evaluate performance

Evaluate limitations

Provide feedback on limitations

Provide feedback on strengths

When looking at a performance, the shape of the body in action will indicate how close it is to the perfect model. Some areas to look for are the head position, where the centre of gravity is, a balanced body position and how the weight is distributed.

Rafael Nadal serves in the French Open Tennis Championships.

A young girl practises her tennis serve.

Task 1

Study the two photos above and compare the differences in the following:
- head position
- centre of gravity
- balance of the body
- weight distribution.

Look back at pages 246 and 247 to compare the characteristics of a skilful and unskilled performance.

Task 2

1 – Give six examples where you have witnessed skilled performances.

2 – Develop four of these examples into sentences.

Understand the variables that may affect performance

The success of a performance can be influenced by a range of factors. When evaluating performance certain considerations should be taken into account:

Always have the perfect model in mind

Factors affecting the perfect model

Reaction and comments made appropriately

Rules
May be complex and competition strong so mistakes might be made.

Skills may be good but broken in performance.

Fitness
The performer may drop in standard due to lack of fitness.

Experience
Player may be relatively new to the game.

Weather
May make surface slippery.

Standard of game
A player's own skills may be fair but those of the other players may be poor.

Degree of difficulty of skill
The skill being performed may be complex and difficult to complete.

Open skills
Skills performed with many variables. May be affected by the actions of others in the environment.

Closed skills
Basic skills performed in isolation with no variables. Should not be influenced by the people and conditions around the performer.

Comment on good aspects of performance.

Comment on poor aspects of performance.

Have knowledge of how the bad points can be improved.

Suggest ways to improve.

Make allowances for difficult circumstances.

4 — Making informed decisions on how to improve the performance

Knowledge of the fitness components and their application to different sports will help with your observations. You will know which components to look out for in your chosen activity.

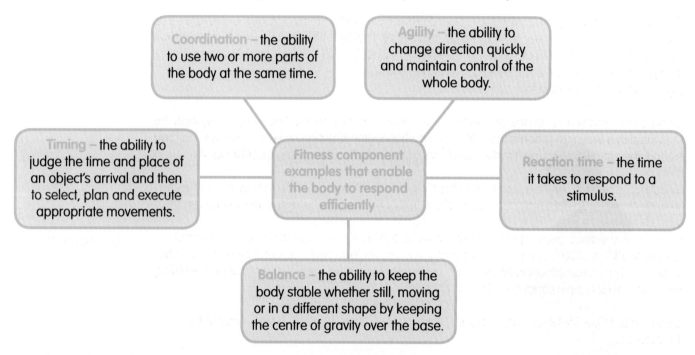

Coordination – the ability to use two or more parts of the body at the same time.

Agility – the ability to change direction quickly and maintain control of the whole body.

Timing – the ability to judge the time and place of an object's arrival and then to select, plan and execute appropriate movements.

Fitness component examples that enable the body to respond efficiently

Reaction time – the time it takes to respond to a stimulus.

Balance – the ability to keep the body stable whether still, moving or in a different shape by keeping the centre of gravity over the base.

Characteristics of a skilful performance

There are a number of skill types that can be identified in a performance:

- Basic skills can be simple or closed skills, such as a set shot in basketball.
- Intermediate skills can be skills performed in sequence with other skills, such as dribble to a position to play a set shot.
- Advanced skills can be performing linked skills with the opposition, such as dribble past a defender or making a set shot, avoiding a block from another defender.

Active challenge

Using a sport of your choice, state a basic, an intermediate and an advanced skill.

Making informed decisions on how to improve the quality of the performance requires close scrutiny. Consulting different evidence may be necessary:

- Compare original test results with new test results.
- Analyse performance data.
- Watch DVDs of personal performance.
- Study coaching manuals.
- Watch training videos.
- Study skill posters.
- Watch live coverage of the activity to compare performances.

5 — Developing and implementing action plans for further improvement

To develop and implement action plans for further improvement, you need to first decide on the area to improve.

Goal setting is important for improving performance. By setting out staged and achievable goals a coach or teacher can keep the performer motivated. Having knowledge of the phases shows the way forward and keeps the athlete focused on the task, reduces the possibility of boredom and gives a better chance to improve fitness and skills. Reaching a stage and moving on will signpost the athlete's physical progress.

Goals can mentally prepare the performer for an activity or competition. Each stage may train the individual in a way that grooms them for a more challenging situation so when it arrives they can handle the conditions, taking it in their stride, without it affecting their level of performance.

Reaching goals indicate the progress of training. It shows how the performance is developing in relation to the structured time settings and points out the need for changes to the training.

Knowing the stages gives an element of control to the performer. As each stage is reached and passed the athlete can see the progress and, rather than worry about their ability, can be confident that development is on track. For example, athletes gain much confidence in training when they reach a personal best time or distance.

Goals need to be SMARTER. When planning goals, the following seven points need to be focused on.

S – specific – these goals should be specific to the sport, such as time or distance for an athlete.

M – measurable – results can be measured and so set against recognized norms.

A – agreed or achieved – both the performer and coach must agree on the way forward so both are working together and are on the same wavelength. They should agree on the specific goal in accord with the targets to help with motivation.

R – realistic – the goals should be realistic to the level of skill and fitness of the performer.

T – time-phased – a timetable of training set out can give a target for a certain level of performance to be attained. The plan would follow the goals set and would allow time for improvement to be made. The time would also relate to the amount of weekly training sessions to be undertaken.

E – exciting – the type of training or practice needs to keep the attention of the performer and motivate them to continue with the set tasks.

R – recorded – results and progress should be recorded in order to compare them with past and future results to show how the performer has moved on and where they should be aiming for in the next stage.

Task 3

1 – Choose a sport and apply SMARTER to your choice.

2 – In sentences, describe how each point would apply to that sport.

3 – List two main targets you have for a particular sport.

Personal training programme (PTP)

A personal training programme (PTP) is a series of exercises or practices put together for a particular person. The exercise sessions follow all the guidelines of the principles of training to make them safe and suitable for the performer. To be effective, the PTP should be performed regularly over a period of weeks. There will come a time when the programme is physically too easy to have an effect on the performer, which can happen around week five or six of the programme. At this stage, reviewing the programme is necessary. By applying the principles of training, the programme can be made more demanding.

Link the PTP with the effects of exercise

The following diagram shows how the PTP develops. It always starts with the individual and their needs and capabilities, moving on to the planning, performing and then to reviewing. The review of the programme is most important if progress is to continue to be made. Re-testing the individual will show how their body has adapted to the programme. Increasing the FID principle according to the results will ensure further progress.

What is the purpose of the PTP?

- General health
- Sport specific
- Rehabilitation
- Strength improvement
- Flexibility
- Muscular endurance.

Look at the individual and consider:

- Their training test results
- Their cardio results (resting heart rate)
- Their respiratory results (VO$_2$ max)
- Their body composition (how much of the body is fat, muscle and bone)
- Which exercises they prefer
- Whether they like training on their own or in a group.

Devising a PTP

Review programme by applying the FID principles of training:

- Increase how many times the individual trains
- Increase the intensity
- Increase the time spent exercising
- Vary the type of exercise.

Plan the programme, choosing from a variety of training methods:

- Circuit
- Fartlek
- Weights
- Altitude
- Continuous
- Aerobic and anaerobic
- Interval.

Necessary skills to analyse and improve performance

Many people can look at a sporting activity, but only the trained eye can see what the performer is really attempting to do. The observation and evaluation part of the course requires you to have these skills and make a judgement on quality, success and ways of improving a performance.

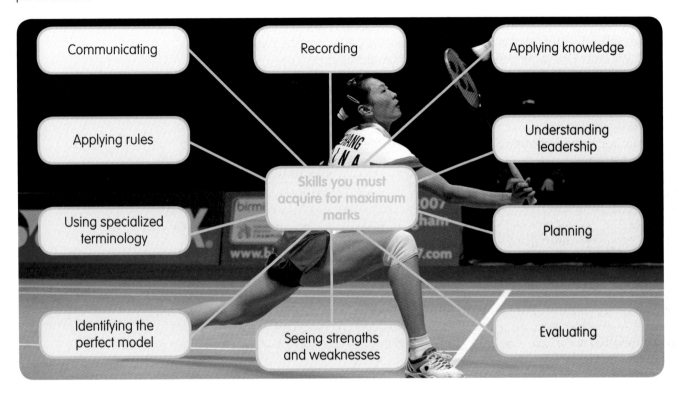

Communicating

Recording

Applying knowledge

Applying rules

Understanding leadership

Skills you must acquire for maximum marks

Using specialized terminology

Planning

Identifying the perfect model

Seeing strengths and weaknesses

Evaluating

Skills needed

The skills you will develop are similar to those needed by coaches who get the best out of their players.

Applying rules – show knowledge and application of the rules. Practice and experience in this area can be gained from officiating or judging a sport. Choose sports in which you feel confident, interested and have some experience of.

Using specialized terminology – each sport has its own language for describing skills, tactics and strategies. An ability to use this language shows an understanding of the sport.

Recording – making a record of the performance gives information (times, distances, circuit results, and so on), which can be analysed and acted upon; sometimes a training session is changed according to the results.

Evaluating – evaluating is the ability to watch a performer in action and work out how close their performance is to what is known as the 'perfect model'.

Identifying the perfect model – when analysing the performance, knowledge and understanding of what the best performance looks like is very important. Any performance can then be compared to this 'perfect model'.

Seeing strengths and weaknesses – each performance has positive and negative aspects and both must be recognized by the observer.

Communicating – being able to communicate an analysis of the action to the performer means improvement can be made. Even in weak performances it is important to comment on a good aspect in order to keep the performer motivated.

Planning – by working out the successes and failures of the performance, planned changes can be made to training, tactics and strategies so improvements can be made.

Applying knowledge – applying knowledge of training methods and principles is essential when linking them with strengths and weaknesses of the performer. The principles and methods will determine what goes into the training programme.

Understanding leadership – good leadership is the ability to get the best out of the performer. Examples of this include: leading through example, motivating, setting up achievable targets and rewarding progress.

Task 4

1 – For each of the skill areas listed, make a list of your own experiences.

2 – Re-list the skills, with the areas you need to work most on at the top, moving down to the ones you are most confident with at the bottom.

Observation

Observation needs to be planned in order to observe a performance meaningfully – an understanding of the perfect model is essential. Where the action is observed from is important too. Standing at different positions in relation to the action will give different views and so more than one viewpoint may be necessary for a full picture of an activity. Where to watch from may also vary according to the sport. A team game has lots of action so being near to the performer's positional area is good. A raised viewpoint is often useful. For smaller playing areas such as volleyball, badminton and tennis, court side is effective and if possible a raised position may give a better view.

The following spider diagram indicates possible places to view a large team game from.

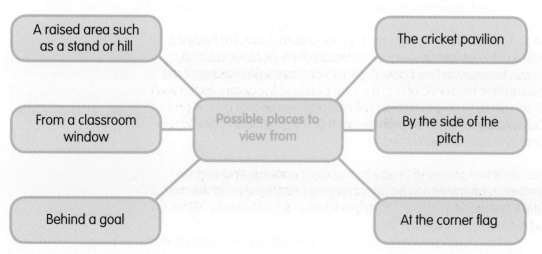

Equipment

Whatever method of analysis you use it will be useful to have a record of the performance you see. This will act as evidence and can be used to analyse the results of the performance with other data at a later date. Plan your observations well: record sheets, pencils and something to lean on are all basic and obvious requirements to do the job. Knowing that you have prepared the equipment you need in advance will allow you to concentrate on the process of observation. You may prefer to photograph or film the performance as well in which case greater planning is necessary in booking the equipment before the event.

Task 5

1 – For three sports, decide on the best viewing position for each. You can use diagrams in your answer if you wish.

2 – Say why you think some sports are best viewed at different positions, such as judo at ground level, but team games from a high position.

Gaining observational experience

There are different ways you can build up your observational skills. Using as many methods as you can will give you the broadest information base from which to work.

By watching an activity and then discussing the performance with others, you develop your knowledge, language and understanding of what you see.

Listen to the coaching points given by a teacher in class and then compare them with how a person performs the activity. This gives experience of linking the description of the correct action with a beginner's attempt.

There are many coaching manuals and books available for sporting activities. Reading them will give you the knowledge of what the perfect model should look like. These books break down the skills and illustrate or describe the parts of the action to concentrate on. This knowledge of the components of the correct skill can be watched for and compared with that of the observed performance. You can than decide on the strengths and weaknesses of the action you see.

Once you understand the skill you will appreciate how it can be broken down. For instance, in gymnastics, a judge will look for the following when marking a vault: flight on, flight off, elevation, shape of the body, distance carried, body alignment and controlled landing. It is these areas that the observer must be aware of in order to understand the action. As the vault only takes a short time to complete, filming the action will help you concentrate on one part of the action at a time. You can then build up your observation and appreciation of the whole action after several replays.

Your knowledge and experience of a game helps you know what to look for. Knowing the game well allows the observer to anticipate the action, prepare a mental picture of the best performance and compare it with what they see. This expectation of the action also allows the effectiveness of the build-up play to be observed too.

Ways to observe

There are various ways of watching top-class performers, each with positive and negative points for the observer. Some of these methods are readily available through watching television and reading newspapers and magazines, whereas some need seeking out through libraries and the Internet.

Study the progression of time lapsed photography

Watch the event live

Watch a recording of the game on video or DVD

How can I observe the best performers?

Study photographs of the performers

Watch specialized coaching productions on DVD or CD-ROM

Evaluating

There are a variety of areas that can be analysed when looking at performance. Some are more complex than others. The most straightforward ones range from individual, closed and basic skills to the complexities of the open, complex and advanced skills.

There are different skills required by different players on the pitch so the observer must be mindful of this in the analysis. An attacker may not need information on the number of tackles they make, but for a defender it would be an important part of the analysis. A strong team may often be on the attack, so their defence is only rarely involved. As a result, a defender may only make a few passes in the game, so for them, the percentage of successful passes rather than the actual number of successful passes made may say more about their personal play.

The skills required for good play are different for a defender and an attacker.

Individual basic skills

Individual intermediate skills

Individual advanced skills

Ability to perform and keep within the rules

Effectiveness of an individual in a competitive game

Tactics: defence, attack and adapting to the opponent's tactics

What can be analysed?

Technical correctness

Strategies

Fitness test results

Success in reaction to speed, height and distance

The fitness of the performers – is it having a bearing on results?

Different ways to record and evaluate

Keeping a record of a person's performance can be useful in several ways. Records taken at different times in the season are useful as they can show individual progress, the effectiveness of training and the strengths and weaknesses of performance.

The methods used to record performance vary and can include:

- Making notes on the performance – detailed notes are made by the observer based on the action of the performer.
- Check list for the performance – this lists the parts of the action the person needs to perform to complete the action and represents the perfect model. The observed performance can be compared to the components on the list and a simple 'tick off' system can be used.
- Individual's performance in the game – this records the actions of an individual in a game situation. The success or failure of the performer is recorded each time they are an active part of the game and can be indicated by a plus or minus response to stated criteria. In tennis, for example, there are many parts to the game important to record; such as the number of points won on first or second serve, or number of double-faults recorded.
- Team performance – this records the effectiveness of the team performance. It reflects the success of the chosen tactics and can include:

  – where successful shots come from
  – where on the pitch or court the attacks start
  – where the opposition attacks come from
  – how much possession the team has
  – how many corners the team earn.

Active challenge

With a partner, choose a basic skill you are confident in performing. Break down the skill listing, in order, into the different actions needed to complete it.

Task 6

Choose a sport and make a list of the parts of the game that can be recorded to give useful feedback to the coach. Make a record sheet of your list that could be used when observing the game.

Comments made on a performance can be based on subjective or objective evidence: each can comment about the same action but in a different way.

Subjective analysis is related to how the observer thinks the player is performing in comparison with the other players. Two people may have different opinions about a particular performance. The following statements are all subjective:

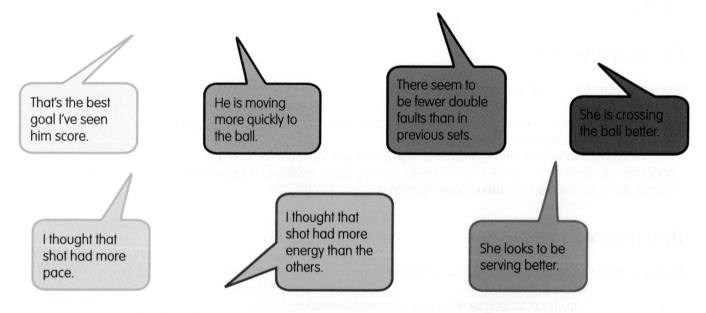

That's the best goal I've seen him score.

He is moving more quickly to the ball.

There seem to be fewer double faults than in previous sets.

She is crossing the ball better.

I thought that shot had more pace.

I thought that shot had more energy than the others.

She looks to be serving better.

Objective analysis is based on fact, not personal opinions. The aim is to have results and statistics to back up the observations. This is very helpful to the coach and performer as it explicitly identifies the strengths and weaknesses of the performer. Objective analysis provides:

- a statistical record of aspects of the performance
- records of heights jumped, distances thrown and speeds run
- comparisons between performer and the decided criteria (the perfect model).

Task 7

1 – For a sport of your choice give three examples of subjective comments.

2 – State why objective comments are more accurate than subjective ones.

3 – Give examples of how an individual can be seen to be successful in their sport.

6 — Role requirements

You may choose to be assessed in your chosen activities in different roles: organizer, leader or coach, choreographer, official or judge. Each of the roles requires a different set of skills, knowledge and approach to be successful. Your choice may be influenced by your personal experience in an activity or interest in the role.

The organizer

Assessment for this role will be on two key processes:

1. Key Process A – on written planning of the event, including the areas for performance, equipment, times of the event or competition, rules and judge or officials required for the event.
2. Key Process B – how well the plan is put into operation and of your ability in the role to run the event, including setting up timekeepers and collecting and collating scores and final results.

The leader or coach

Assessment for this role will be on two key processes:

1. Key Process A – ability to lead or coach a warm-up and suggest improvements in players' skills based on observations and analysis.
2. Key Process B – ability to observe, analyse and give feedback for improvements to a performance. Analysis should be made on skills, techniques and ability to lead or coach individuals or teams in a full performance situation.

The choreographer

Assessment for this role will be on two key processes:

1. Key Process A – ability to choreograph the core skills and techniques.
2. Key Process B – ability to choreograph the full performance.

The official

Assessment for this role will be on two key processes:

1. Key Process A – ability to explain the rules to performers, officiate or judge the core skills in a small-sided game and structured practices like dead ball situations and set plays.
2. Key Process B – ability to officiate or judge in the full activity or competition. How well you conduct and control yourself and the situation. Your understanding of the rules, regulations and composition of the activity and your ability to consistently identify infringements and communicate decisions.

Useful websites

The following are a selection of useful websites to help you increase your PE and sports-related knowledge.

The Assessment and Qualifications Alliance (AQA) – the largest of the examination boards, whose website contains information and support for all of the qualifications they offer: www.aqa.org.uk

BBC GCSE Bitesize: a BBC run website with useful information, revision tips and example questions: www.bbc.co.uk/schools/gcsebitesize/pe/

BBC Sport Academy: a BBC run website for up-to-date news on sport: www.bbc.co.uk/sportacademy

Brain MacSports Coach: information on coaching, sports, nutrition and more: www.brianmac.co.uk

British Bottled Water Producers: information about water and health: www.britishbottledwater.org

British Olympic Association: everything you need to know about the Olympics: www.britisholympicassociation.co.uk

Bupa: details about general health: www.bupa.co.uk

Interactive Resources for GCSE PE: GCSE PE questions answered: www.interactivepe.co.uk

International Paralympic Committee: everything you need to know about the Paralympics: www.paralympic.org

Leisure Connection: information about national sports centres: www.leisureconnection.co.uk

National Health Service (NHS): information about various health and body matters: www.nhs.uk

Peak Performance: all about sporting performance: www.pponline.co.uk

Rugby Fitness Training: tips on how to improve your rugby performance: www.rugbyfitnesstraining.com

Sport England: information on sport in England: www.sportengland.org

sports coach UK: the agency for development of the UK coaching system: www.sportscoachuk.org

Sports Injury Clinic: sports injuries and their treatments: www.sportsinjuryclinic.net

Sports Search: information on all sports for 11–17 year olds: www.sportssearch.org

Try My Sport: information on all types of sport and how to get involved: www.trymysport.co.uk

UK Sport: up-to-date information on UK sport: www.uksport.gov.uk

Women's Sport and Fitness Foundation (WSFF): about women in sport: www.wsf.org.uk

Youth Sport Trust: information on Top and Active Kids Programmes: www.youthsporttrust.org

Glossary

A

Abduction moving a limb or bone away from the body

Adduction moving a limb or bone towards the body

Advertising displaying a product, name or logo in public

Aerobic 'with oxygen'; when exercise is moderate and steady, the heart can supply all the oxygen the working muscles need

Agility the ability to change the position of the body quickly and to control the movement of the whole body easily

Altitude training training at a place situated between 1.8km and 3km above sea level

Amateur performer who competes for pleasure without monetary reward

Anaerobic 'without oxygen'; when exercising in short, fast bursts, the heart cannot supply blood and oxygen to the muscles as fast as the cells can use them, so energy is released without oxygen present

Antagonist a muscle whose action counteracts that of another muscle and so allowing movement

Apartheid official policy of racial segregation

Asymmetric bars a piece of gymnastic equipment used by females with bars at different heights

B

Balance the ability to keep the body stable whether still, moving or in a different shape by keeping the centre of gravity over the base

Balanced competition grouping based on size, age or experience for an even match

Balanced diet daily intake of food containing the right type and amounts of nutrients

Blood viscosity thickness of the blood

Body composition the proportion of body weight that is fat, muscle and bone, normally measured as a percentage

Brownfield sites underdeveloped, derelict, contaminated or vacant areas

C

Calcium an essential element for strong healthy bones; dairy products provide a good source of calcium

Capillaries blood vessels of hair-like thinness that connect the arteries with the veins

Carbohydrate loading building up carbohydrate levels in the body to use in endurance events

Cardiac output the amount of blood pumped by the heart in one minute

Cardiovascular relating to the heart and blood vessels

Cardiovascular endurance and stamina the ability of the heart to provide oxygen to muscles during physical activity for a prolonged period of time

Cardiovascular fitness the ability to exercise the entire body for long periods of time; this is dependent on the fitness of the heart, blood and blood vessels

Cartilage whitish, tough, flexible tissue found at the end of bones; more widespread in infants, as during growth it is replaced by bone

Circuit training a series of exercises completed in order and for a certain time limit

Circulatory system transports blood, using the heart, through all parts of the body

Closed skills basic skills unaffected by the sporting environment

Combination events an event where different activities make up the whole sport

Compound or open fracture break of the bone that pierces the skin, causing a risk of infection

Concussion injury to the brain, caused by blow to the head, may cause a person to temporarily lose consciousness

Continuous training aerobic exercising, at a moderate to high level, with no rests, lasting for a sustained period of time

Coordination the ability to perform complex moves using two or more body parts together

D

Dehydration extreme lack of water in the body, usually as a result of exercising in hot conditions or heavy sweating

Dilate open up or become wider

Dislocation disturbance of the arrangement of bones so that they move out of their usual joint arrangement

E

Ectomorph a somatotype, individuals with narrow shoulders and narrow hips, characterized by thinness

Element a part that contributes to the whole

Endomorph a somatotype, individuals with wide hips and narrow shoulders characterized by fatness

Endothelium internal space of the blood vessels

Endurance the ability to keep working over a period of time without tiring or losing skill

Energy drinks fluids containing carbohydrates

Ethnicity particular attribute or affiliation resulting from racial or cultural ties

Etiquette a code of polite behaviour

Exercise a form of physical activity done primarily to improve one's health and physical fitness

Extension increasing the angle at a joint

Extrinsic feedback external information gathered by the performer based on what is seen or heard at the time of the action

F

Fartlek training 'speed play', changing speed, distances and times of exercise, with rests in the same session

Fast twitch muscle fibres used in events requiring quick reactions and power; muscles contract rapidly providing strength and so tire quickly

Fatigue extreme tiredness and physical exhaustion

Fibrinogen a protein found in blood plasma that helps clotting

FID frequency, intensity, duration

FIT frequency, intensity, time

Fitness ability to meet the demands of the environment

Fixed practice repeating closed skills in the same conditions in training

Flexibility and suppleness joints' ability to move to their full range

Flexion decreasing the angle at a joint

Focusing blocking out other thoughts and concentrating on the performance only

Friction action of two surfaces rubbing together creating heat

G

Gender the sex of a person: male or female

Glycogen the form in which carbohydrates are stored in the muscle and liver

Goodwill supporting a performer or sport financially without any monetary return

Governing body a group responsible for rules, procedures and fixtures of a particular game or event

Guidance help and instruction given to complete a task

H

Haemoglobin found in red blood cells, transports oxygen to body tissue

Hardware devices and equipment that make up a computer system

Health a state of complete mental, physical and social well-being

Healthy, active lifestyle a lifestyle that contributes to physical, social and mental well-being, this includes regular physical activity

Heart rate the number of times the heart beats per minute

Hypothermia condition of the body when its core temperature falls below 35°C

I

Individual needs personal requirements for training

Infrastructure basic facilities and services for the functioning of a community or country for example, roads, schools and amenities

Infringement action in a game that breaks the rules

Insertion the point where a tendon attaches a muscle to bone where there is movement

Institute of Sports Sponsorship (ISS) promotes best practice in sponsorship, working closely with sports bodies, government and the media

Interval training mixing periods of hard exercise with rest periods

Intrinsic feedback internal information gathered by the performer at the time of the action about how they feel the performance is going

J

Joint the point where two or more bones meet

K

Knock-out tournament competitions where progress is dependant on winning each game played

L

Lactic acid produced in the muscle tissues during strenuous exercise, as a result of insufficient oxygen available

Ladder a competition where participants are allowed to challenge those ranked higher, in order to move up in rank

Leisure free time to do what a person chooses

Ligament tough, rounded, elastic fibre attaching bone to bone

Long bones those bones that are the longest in the body which make up the arms and legs

M

Main activity period of training, competition or performance when all-out effort is applied

Maximum heart rate calculated as 220 minus age

Mental of the mind

Mental rehearsal going through an activity in the mind

Mesomorph a somatotype, individuals with wide shoulders and narrow hips, characterized by muscularity

Minimum level of fitness the resulting fitness level over a period of weeks of three to five exercise sessions of 20 minutes, raising the heart rate to between 60 and 80 per cent of its maximum

Minority sport a sport with few participants or followers

Moderation balancing training and rest

Modified game a game with adapted rules, equipment and playing area based on a full game

Movement in motion, could be an action like running or swinging a racket at a ball

Muscle definition muscle shape

Muscle tone muscles in a state of very slight tension, ready and waiting to be used

Muscular endurance and stamina the muscles' ability to move weight over long periods of time without getting tired

N

National Healthy Schools Programme (NHSP) an initiative promoting the link between good health, behaviour and achievement

National Vocational Qualification (NVQ) qualifications based on competence and that test the candidate's ability to adapt learning to the workplace

O

Obese a term used to describe people who are very overfat

Open competition a competition inviting both professional and amateur performers to participate without restrictions

Open skills complex skills performed in constantly changing conditions

Optimum weight ideal weight for a person, giving them the best chance of success in an activity

Origin the point where the tendon attaches the muscle to a fixed bone

Overfat a person who has more body fat than is recommended for their gender and height

Overload exercising the body more than normal

Overuse injury this can be caused by using a part of the body too much or by too much repetitive training

Overweight having weight in excess of normal (not harmful unless accompanied by overfatness)

Oxygen debt the amount of oxygen consumed during recovery above that which would have been consumed in the same time at rest (this results in a shortfall in the oxygen available)

P

Part practice completing part of a complex action in training

Pastoral care following policies and procedures in order to look after the welfare of young people

Pay-per-view extra sporting events, bought individually by the viewer and available only via subscription

Performance how well a task is completed

Personal, Social and Health Education (PSHE) a subject providing learning opportunities for students to develop the knowledge and skills for use as a responsible member of society

Personal training programme (PTP) training designed specifically for one individual

PESSCL Physical Education, School Sport and Club Links, a strategy by the government, managed by the Youth Sport Trust (2003 to 2008) to increase sporting opportunities for 5 to 16 year olds

PESSYP Physical Education and Sport Strategy for Young People, the new name for PESSCL (from 2008)

Physical of the body

Physical Activity Policy an initiative for schools to promote physical activity

Posture the way the muscles hold the body when still or in motion

Power the ability to apply strength and speed in an action

Prime mover contracting muscle that causes movement

Principles of training ideas behind effects of training

Professional performer playing and training full-time for financial reward

Progression gradually increasing the stresses put on the body

Protect guard against threat

Q

Qualifying rounds a competition where a standard must be reached to allow the performer to go to the next stage of the competition

R

Reaction time the time between the presentation of a stimulus and the onset of a movement

Recovery rate the time it takes for the heart and metabolism to return to resting after exercise

Recreation time to relax and do something active

Regularity repeating exercise sessions in a week to bring about improved fitness

Resting heart rate number of heart beats per minute when the body is at rest

Reversibility when training stops, any gain to the body is lost

RICE rest, ice, compression, elevation, a procedure for the treatment of minor injuries

Rotation movement in a circular or part-circular fashion

Round robin a competition where all teams in a group play each other

S

Satellite television programmes available to those who purchase a receiver and pay a subscription

Shape form or outline

Simple or closed fracture break of the bone when the skin is not broken

Skeleton the arrangement of the 206 bones of the human body

Skin-fold calliper equipment used to measure a fold of skin with its underlying layer of fat

Slow twitch muscle fibres muscle fibres required in endurance events

Social to do with the community and society

Software programmes and applications that run on a computer

Somatotype classification of body type

Specificity matching training to the needs of the physical activity

Speed the fastest rate at which an individual is able to perform a movement or cover a distance in a period of time

Sponsorship backing performers financially in return for advertising a product

Strength the ability of muscles to apply force and overcome resistance

Stress a state of mental or emotional strain leading to anxiety and nervous tension

Stroke volume the amount of blood pumped out of the heart by each ventricle during one contraction

Synovial joints freely movable joints with ends covered in cartilage

Systematic training planning a programme for an individual as a result of the effect of previous training

T

Target zone the range within which an individual needs to work for aerobic training to take place (60 to 80 per cent of maximum heart rate)

Technique the way in which a skill is performed

Tendon strong, non-elastic tissue attaching bone to muscle

Terrestrial television programmes available to everyone with a television set and a television licence

Throwing cage a secured enclosure around a throwing area

Timing the ability to judge the time and place of an object's arrival and then select, plan and execute appropriate movements

Training a planned programme which uses scientific principles to improve performance, skill, game ability and motor and physical fitness

Training zone working above 80 per cent of the maximum heart rate (anaerobic threshold)

Trends current fad or fashion

U

UKCC UK Coaching Certificate

UK Sport a body responsible for managing and distributing public investment and proceeds from the National Lottery, aiming to lead UK sport to world-class success

V

Valves openings allowing blood flow in one direction, found in the heart and veins

Variable practice performing whole skills in changing conditions in training

Visualize create positive mental pictures of the successful attempt prior to actual execution

VO$_2$ max maximum amount of oxygen the body can take in

Voluntary muscles skeletal muscles, attached to the skeleton, worked consciously by the brain

Vulnerable being exposed to the possibility of being attacked or harmed, either physically or emotionally

W

Warm-down exercises after the main activity, which gradually bring the body systems back to near resting state

Warm-up exercises that gradually put stresses on the body systems in preparation for the main activity

Weight training progressively lifting heavier weights to improve strength or lifting weights more often to improve stamina

Whole practice repeating the complete action in training

Whole School Food Policy (WSFP) a government initiative showing the importance of eating the correct food and how it has a bearing on health and well-being

Index